Watercolor
FLOWERS

The Easy Way

Step-by-Step Tutorials for
50 Flowers, Wreaths, and Bouquets

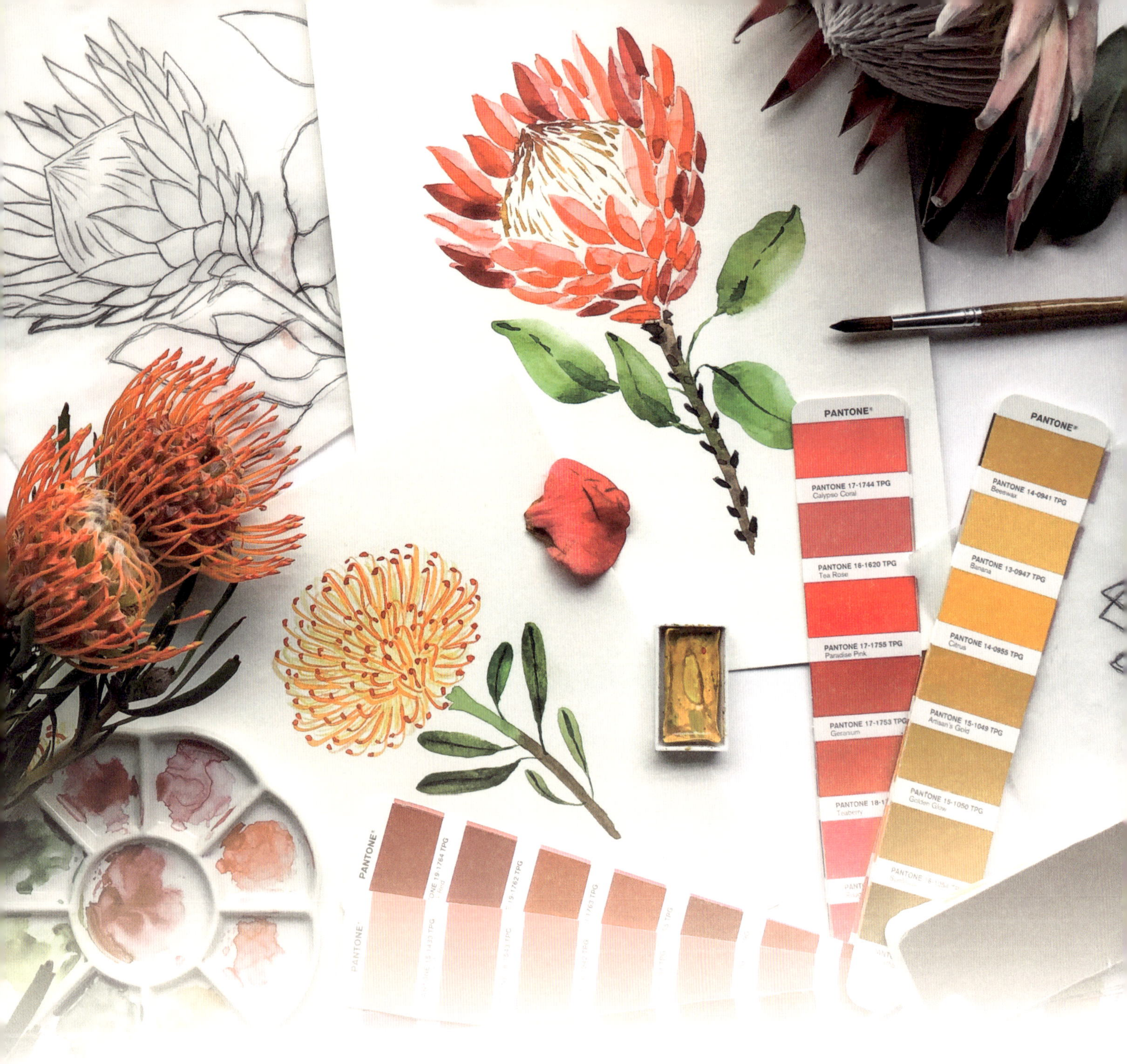

Watercolor the Easy Way Flowers © 2021 by Sara Berrenson and Better Day Books, Inc.

Illustrations by Sara Berrenson; book design by Michael Douglas

ISBN: 978-0-7643-6206-4
Printed in China
10 9 8 7 6 5 4

Copublished by Better Day Books, Inc., and Schiffer Publishing, Ltd.

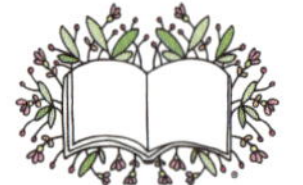

Better Day Books
P.O. Box 21462
York, PA 17402
Phone: 717-487-5523
Email: hello@betterdaybooks.com
www.betterdaybooks.com
@better_day_books

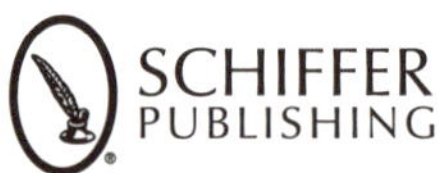

Schiffer Publishing
4880 Lower Valley Road
Atglen, PA 19310
Phone: 610-593-1777
Fax: 610-593-2002
Email: info@schifferbooks.com
www.schifferbooks.com

This title is available for promotional or commercial use, including special editions. Contact info@schifferbooks.com for more information.

Watercolor

FLOWERS

The Easy Way

Step-by-Step Tutorials for
50 Flowers, Wreaths, and Bouquets

SARA BERRENSON

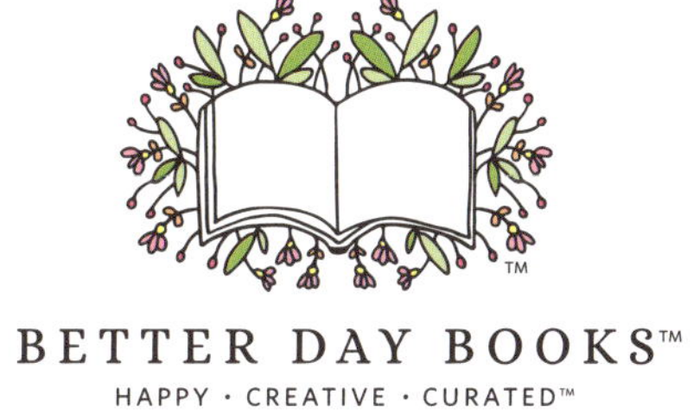

BETTER DAY BOOKS™
HAPPY · CREATIVE · CURATED™

Contents

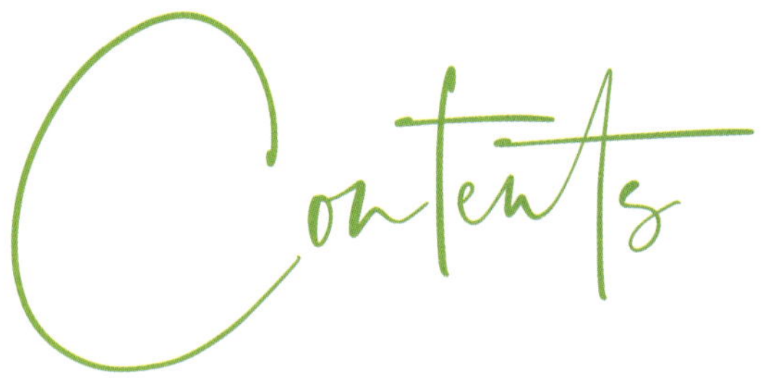

WATERCOLOR TUTORIALS | 26

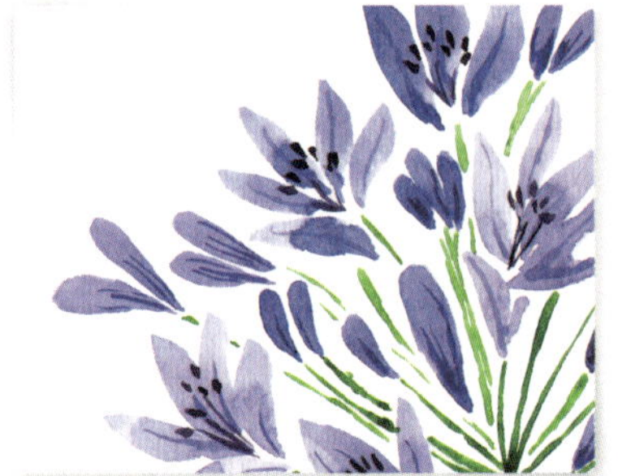

28 | Agapanthus

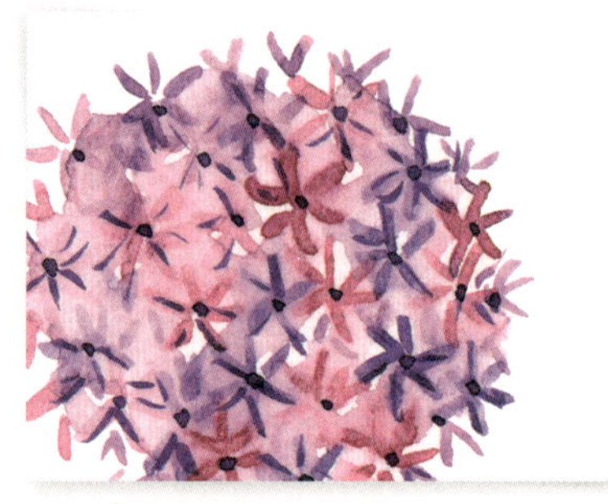

30 | Allium

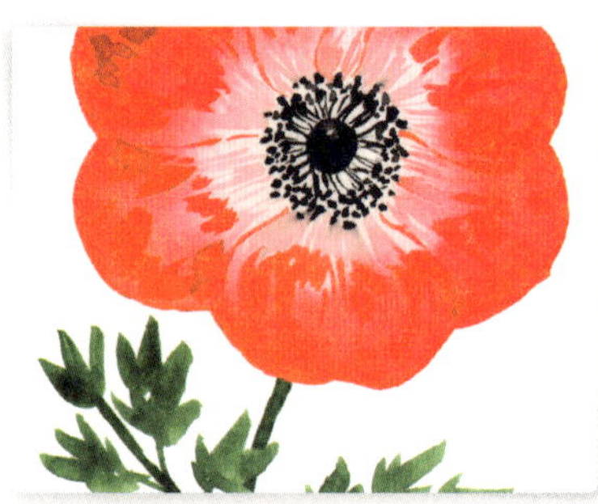

32 | Anemone

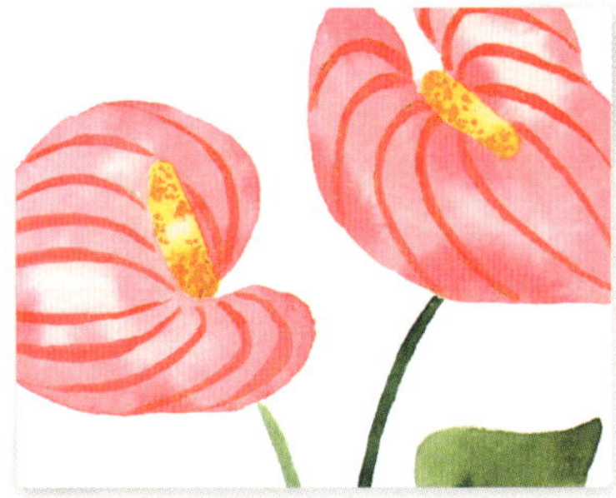

34 | Anthurium

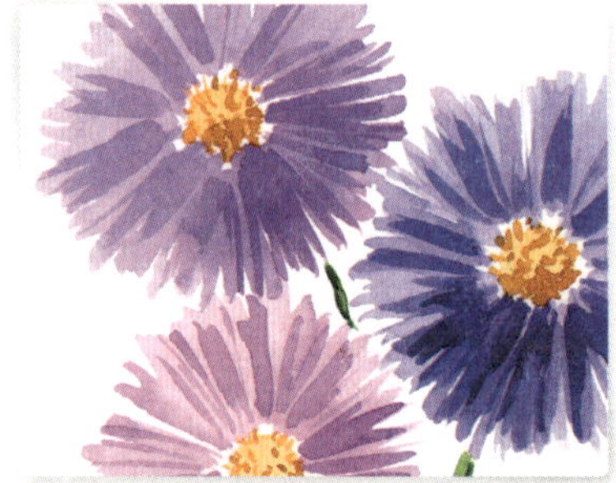

36 | Asters

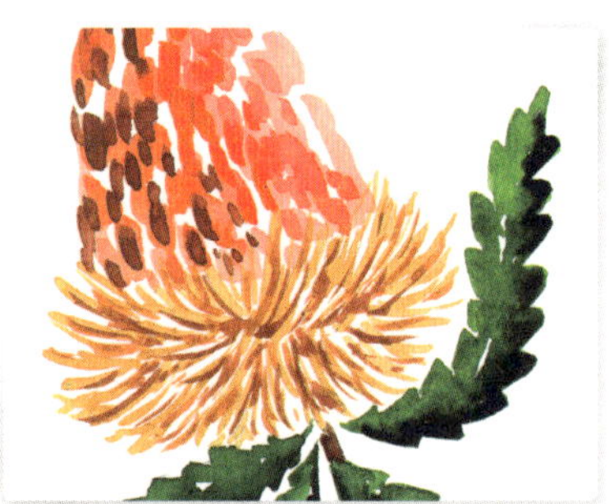

38 | Banksia

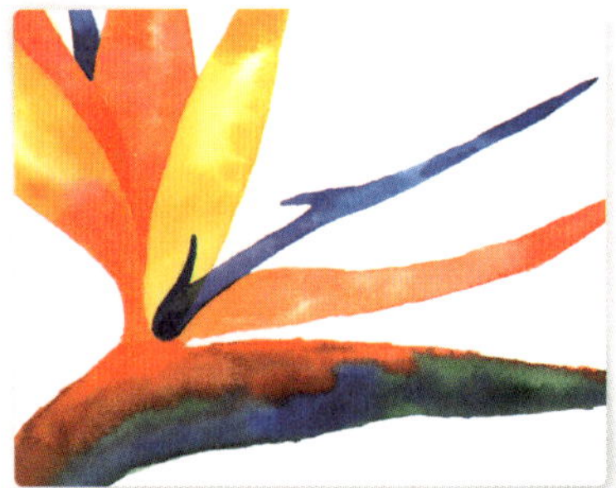

40 | Bird of Paradise

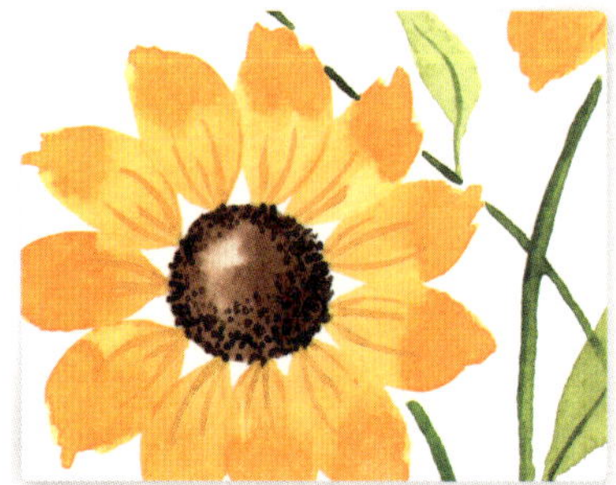

42 | Black-Eyed Susans

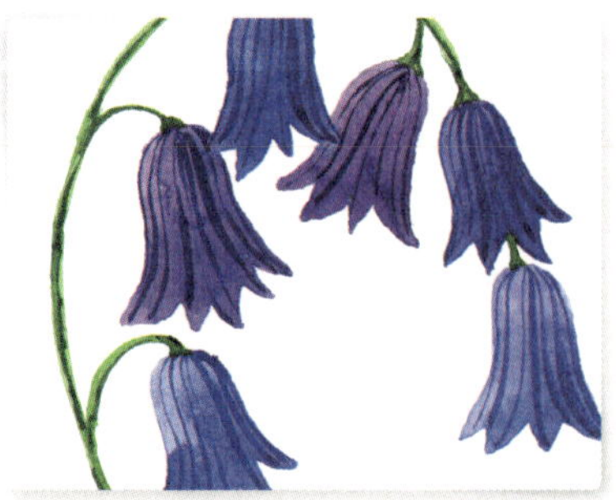

44 | Bluebells

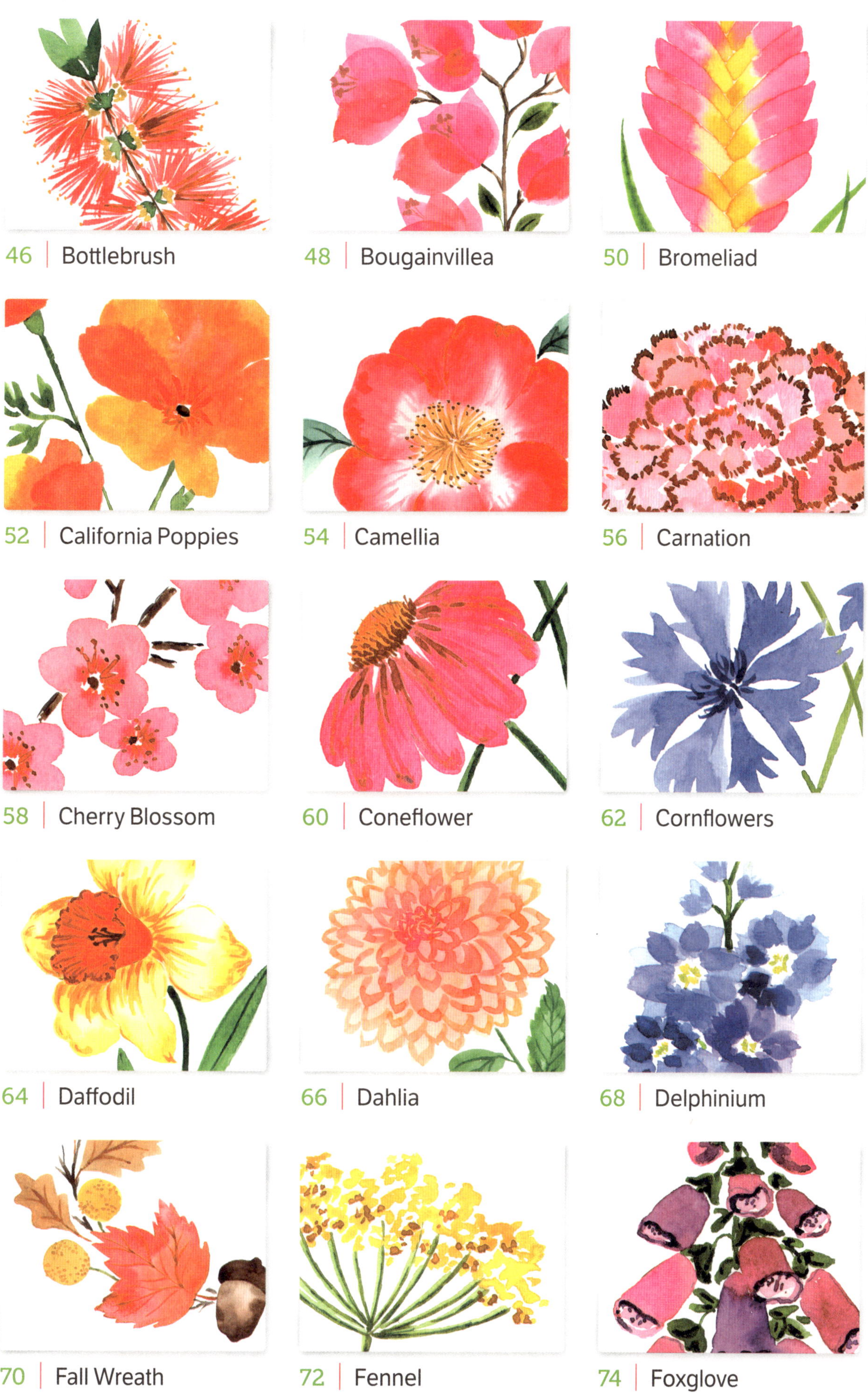

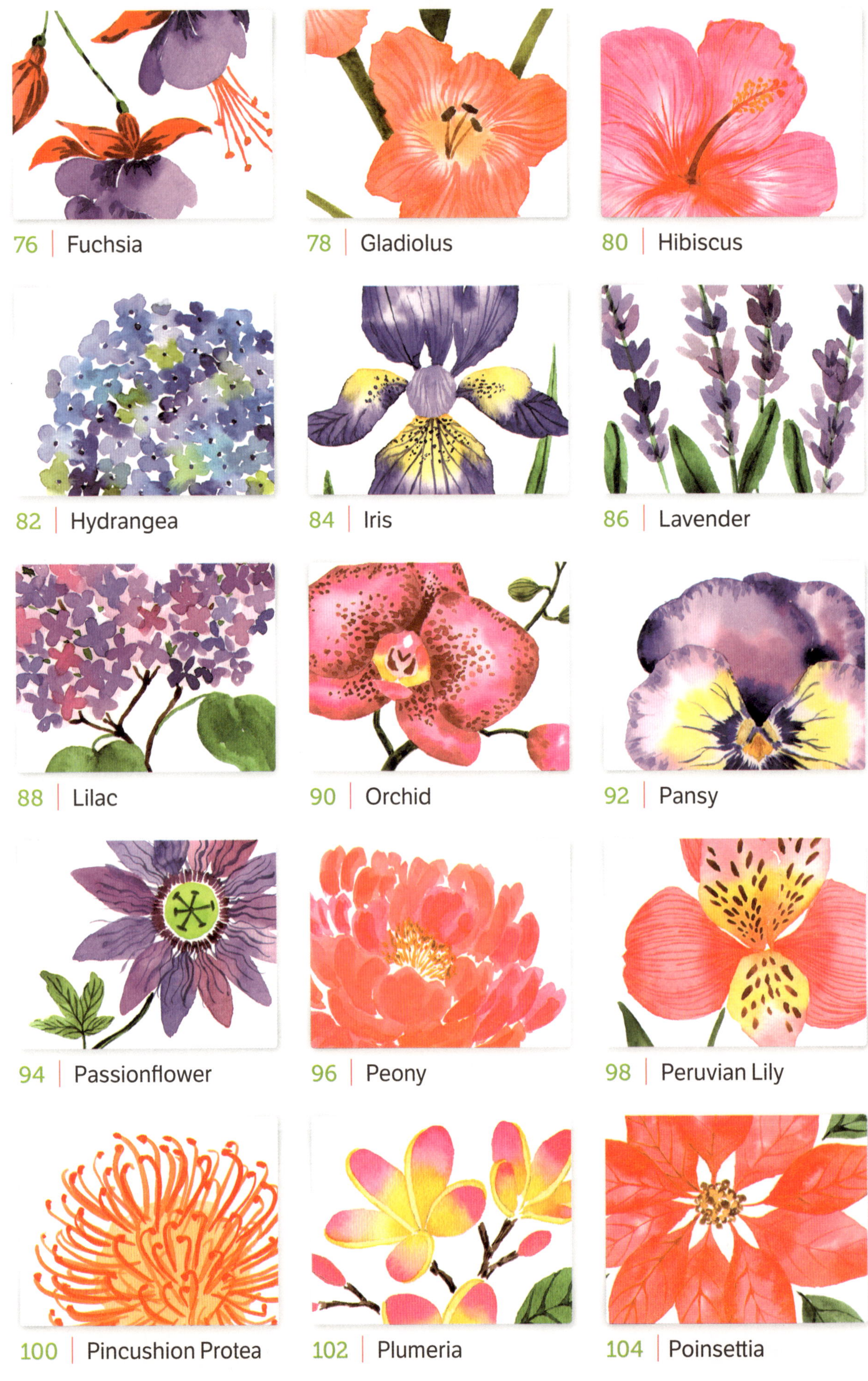

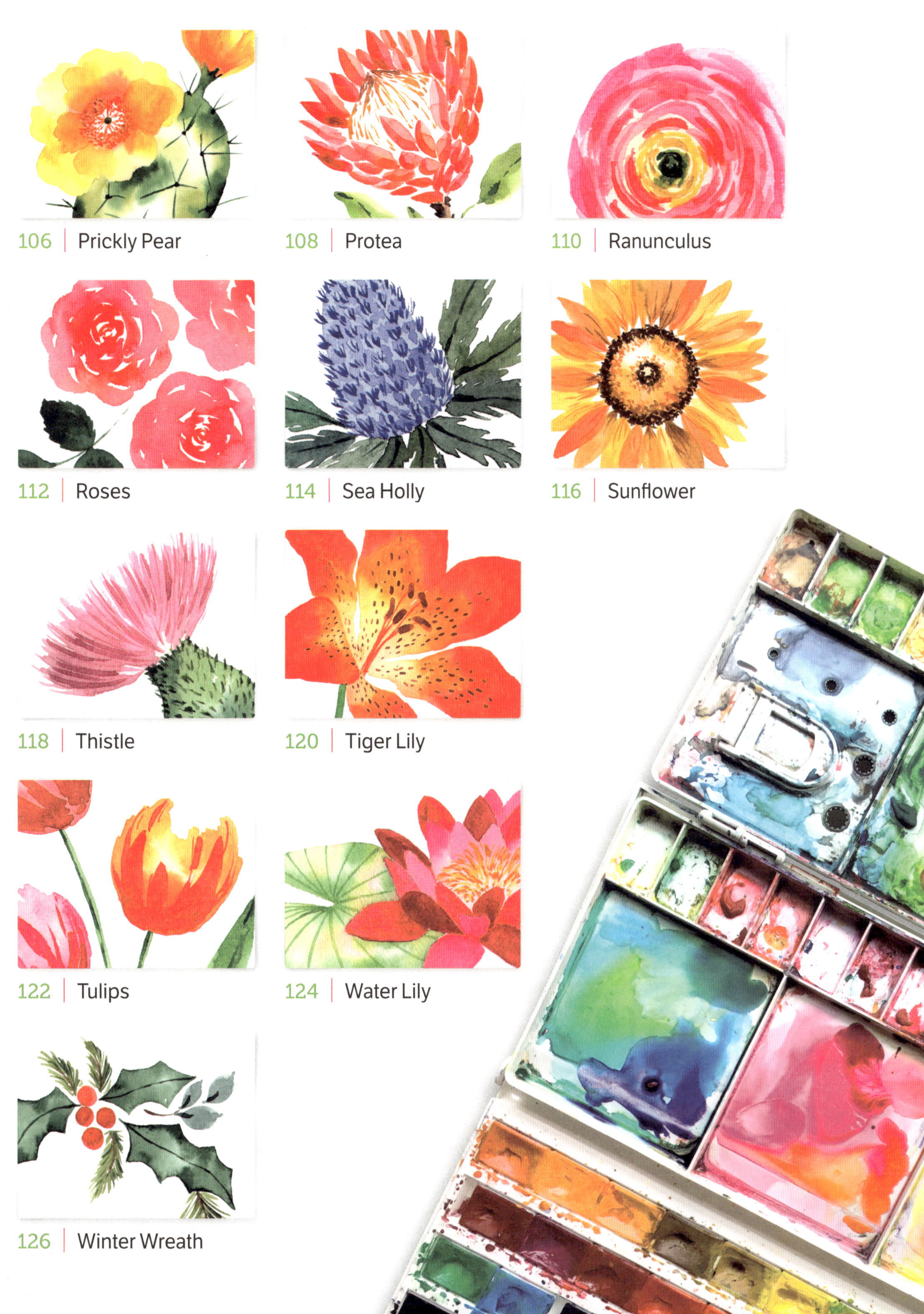

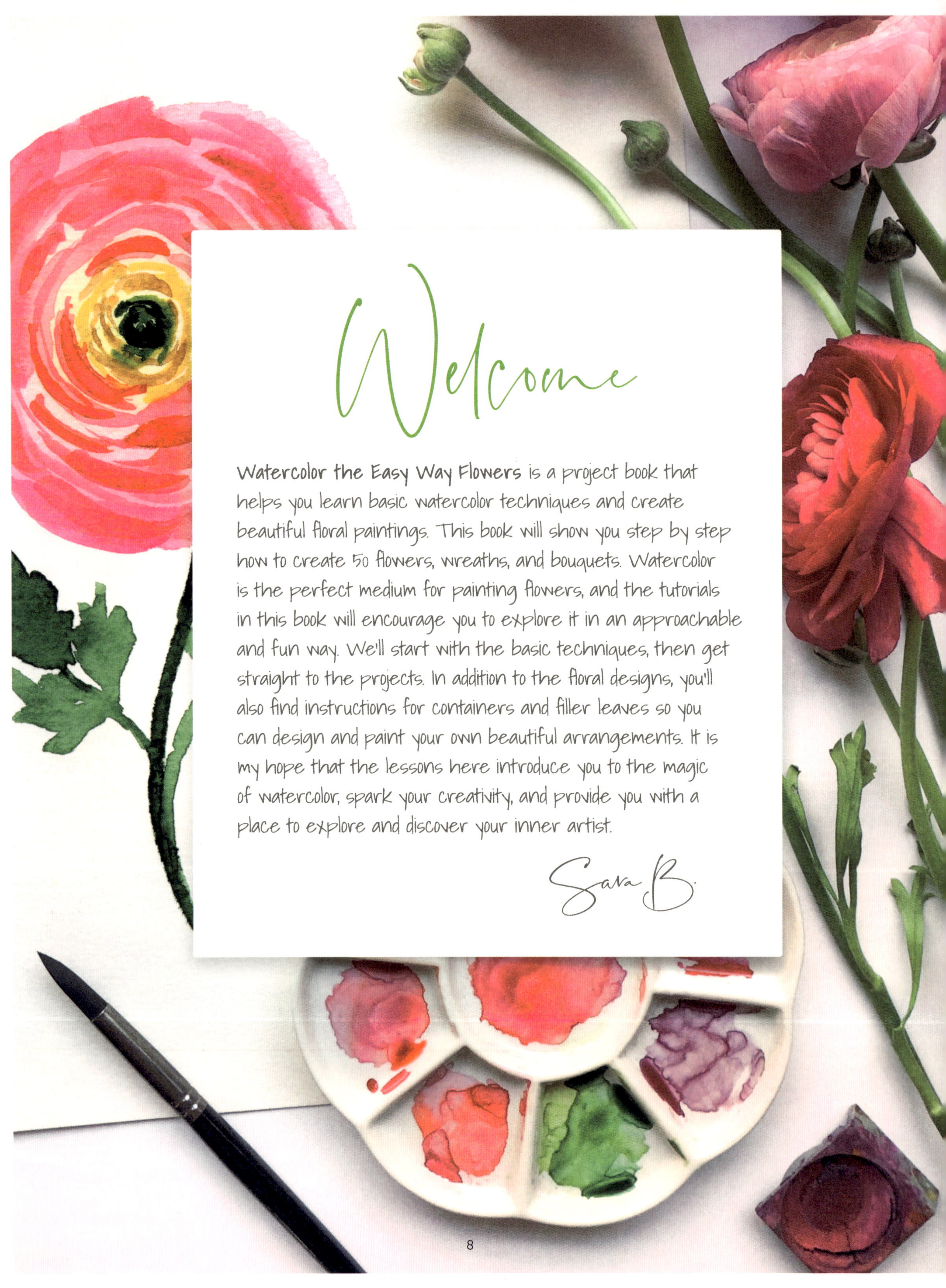

Welcome

Watercolor the Easy Way Flowers is a project book that helps you learn basic watercolor techniques and create beautiful floral paintings. This book will show you step by step how to create 50 flowers, wreaths, and bouquets. Watercolor is the perfect medium for painting flowers, and the tutorials in this book will encourage you to explore it in an approachable and fun way. We'll start with the basic techniques, then get straight to the projects. In addition to the floral designs, you'll also find instructions for containers and filler leaves so you can design and paint your own beautiful arrangements. It is my hope that the lessons here introduce you to the magic of watercolor, spark your creativity, and provide you with a place to explore and discover your inner artist.

Sara B.

Sara Berrenson is a painter and illustrator based in Santa Monica, California. She is inspired by color combinations, textures, and patterns found in nature. She has collaborated with brands like West Elm, Pottery Barn Kids, Trader Joe's, Mattel, and many others. On the weekends, you can find her at the flower mart looking for inspiration for her next watercolor, or at the flea market scouting out antique furniture and vintage fabric.

www.saraberrenson.com
saraberrenson

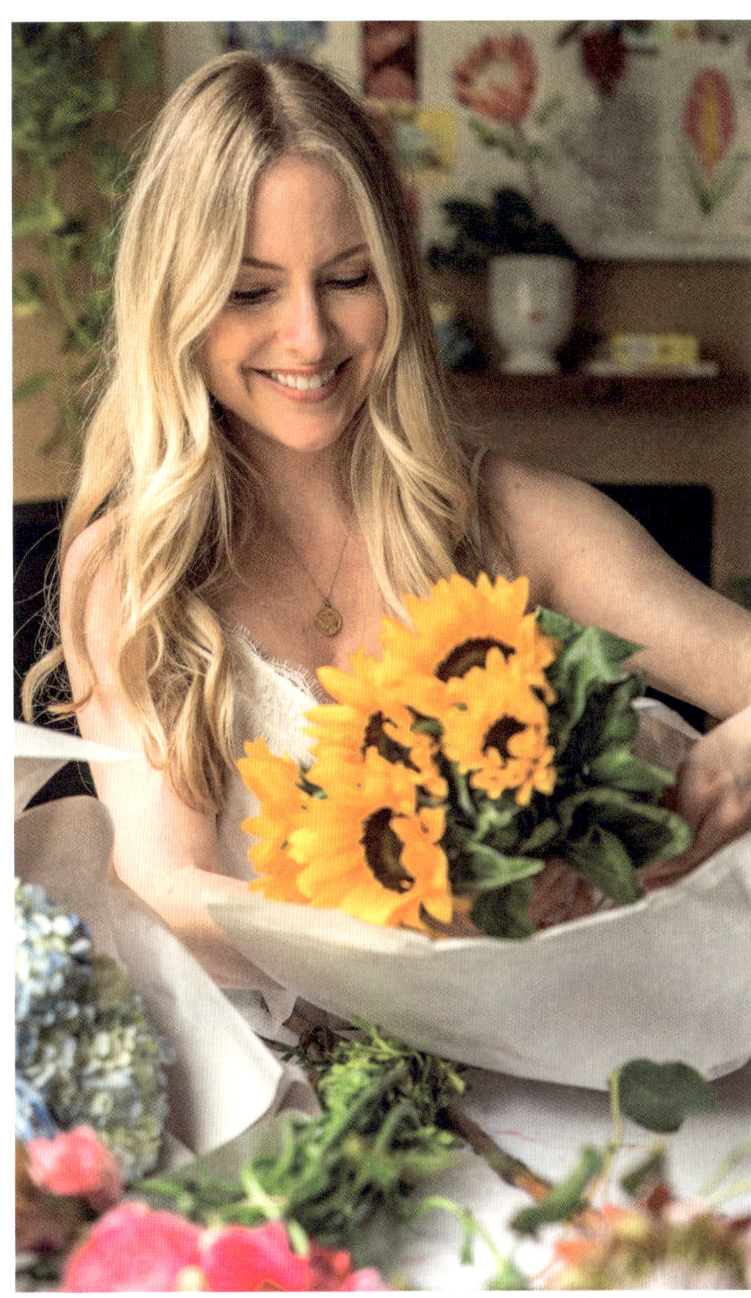

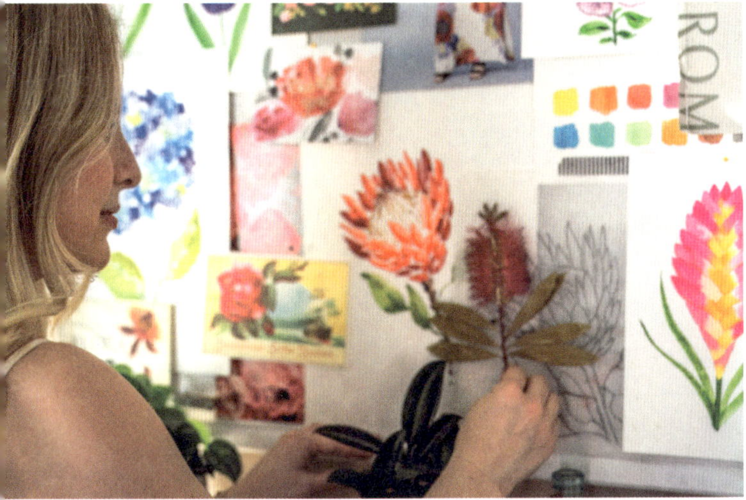

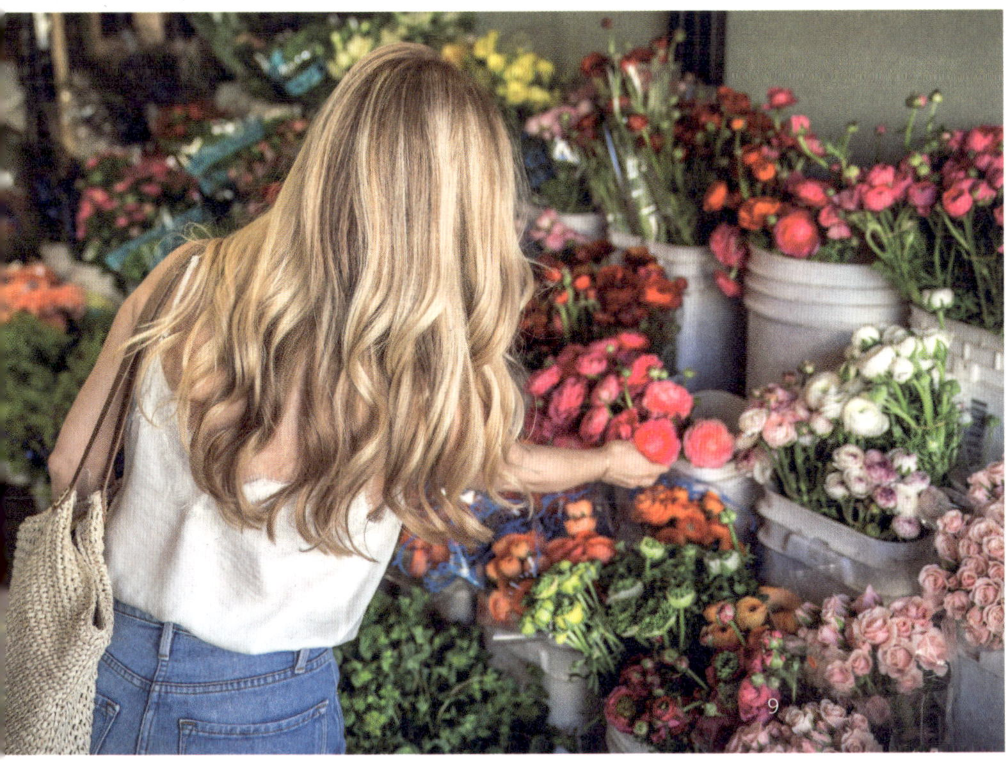

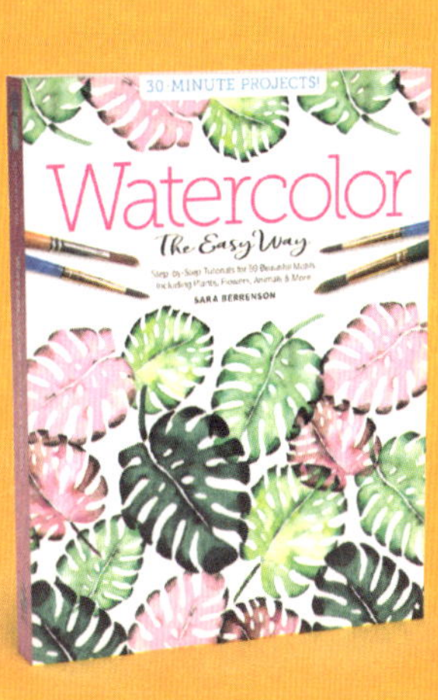

Also Available
For additional watercolor tutorials and designs, check out *Watercolor the Easy Way*.

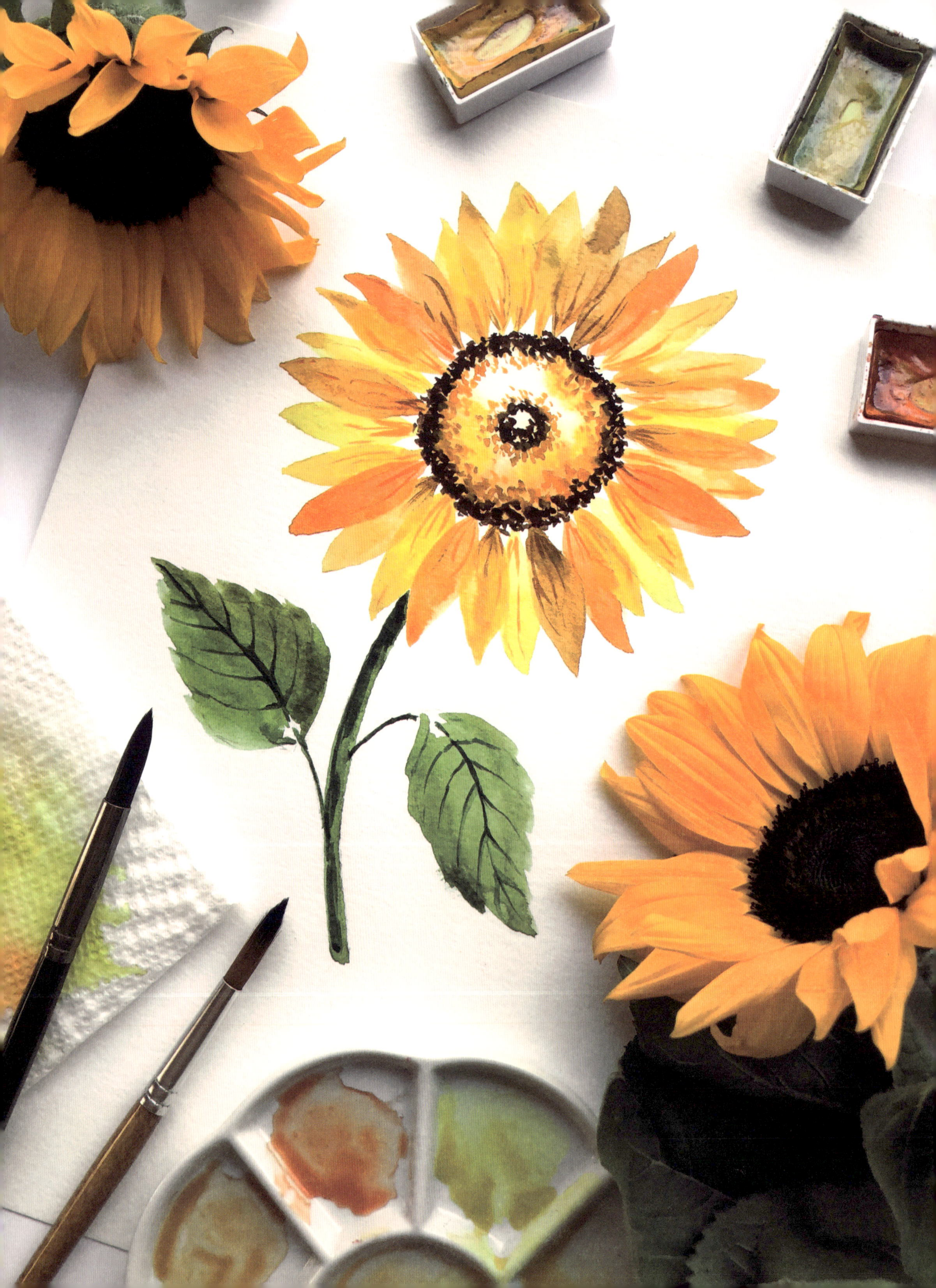

Getting Started

Watercolor Paint

Watercolor paint comes in student grade and professional grade. Professional-grade paints usually provide more intense color because they are highly pigmented. However, I use a variety of both grades and am always happy with the results!

Watercolor paint comes in tubes, pans, and bottles of liquid. I prefer pans because of their portability, but all options work well.

Brushes

For all of the projects in this book, I used round watercolor brushes in a variety of sizes. Brushes are numbered by size; the higher the number, the larger the brush. Larger brushes are good for broad areas of color, while smaller brushes add fine details. I would recommend using round brushes in sizes 4, 6, 8, and 10.

Paper

This book is printed on watercolor paper so you can paint right inside it! Otherwise, I recommend using cold-press watercolor paper, 140 lb.

Mixing Palette

Many watercolor pan sets come with a built-in mixing palette, but it is always nice to have additional space to mix colors. I use a plastic palette that folds open and closed and measures about 10" x 10" when open. It's portable and doesn't take up too much space when put away.

Clean Water

I usually use a standard mason jar for this. Make sure to replace your water when it starts to get too dirty so it doesn't muddy up your colors!

Paper Towels

Keep these next to your water jar to dab off excess water and paint from your brush.

**Tracing Paper and
Graphite Paper**

Each tutorial in this book has a sketch that you can trace and then transfer to your watercolor paper for painting.

Masking Fluid (Optional)

This brush-on liquid can be brushed onto paper to preserve the paper color or other previously painted areas. It repels both paint and water and peels away without marring the paper surface.

COLORS

I have provided color swatches for each tutorial so you can match them as best you can; however, it's totally okay if they don't match exactly. We will go over the basics of color theory and color mixing so you can learn how to create endless colors on your own.

For this book, I recommend starting out with some basic colors:

- Warm and cool versions of yellow, red, blue, and green
- Violet
- Rose
- 2 earth tones
- Black

I have also included 5 of my other favorite colors that I use often.

White is not included, because we use water to lighten colors.

I have given my recommendations, but feel free to include your favorite colors. If your paint color names are not all the same as the ones listed here, don't worry! There are slight variations in each brand, and art stores will carry substitutions for each of the colors.

I would suggest painting a swatch of each of your watercolors, and labeling it with the color name. This way you will have a reference to refer back to while using this book. I have shown the painted swatches for the color palette I used.

Basic Color Palette

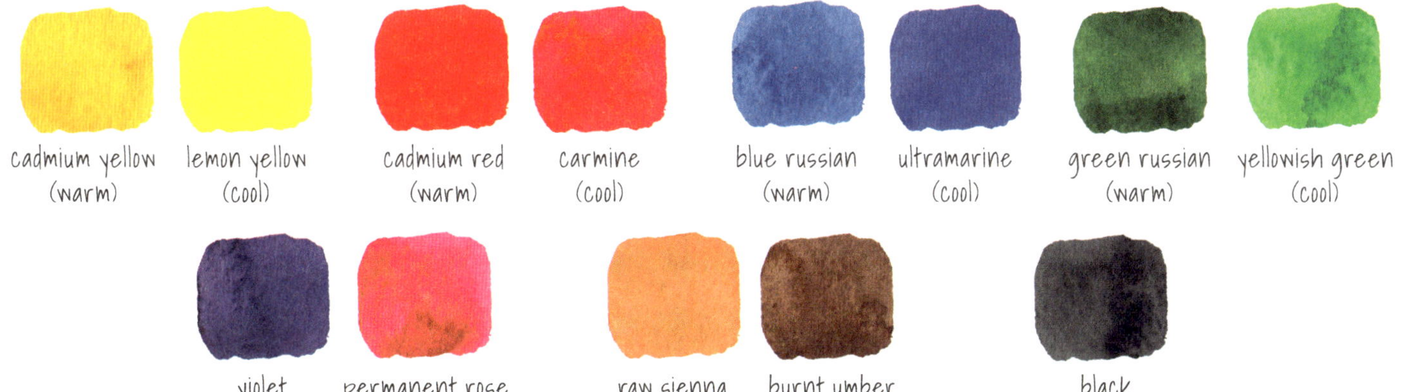

Additional Favorite Colors

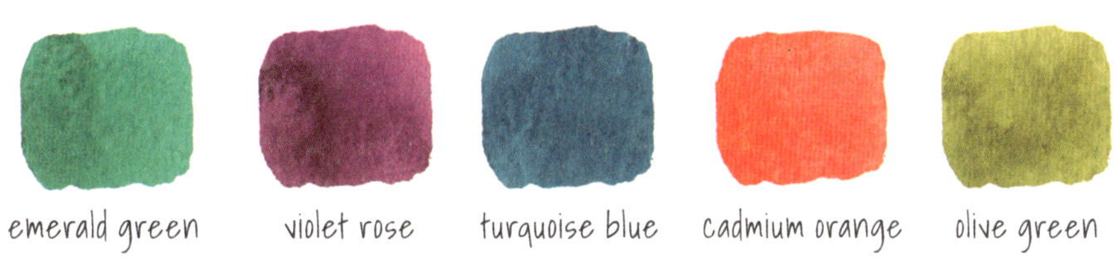

Creating a Paint Swatch

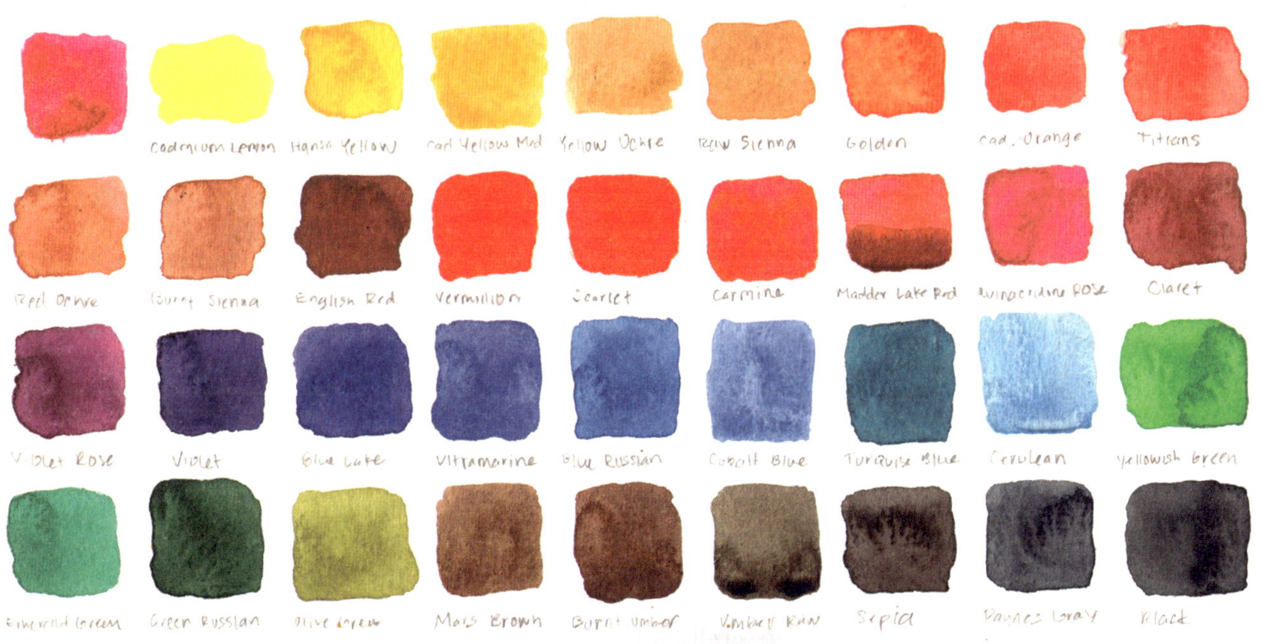

Before starting a new painting session, it's a good idea to create a swatch card. Simply paint a small stroke of each color from your palette and let it dry. Then, you have a color reference to refer back to while painting. Above are the actual paint swatches that I used to create this book (complete with abbreviations, scribbles, and misspellings!).

MIXING COLORS

Even though your watercolor palette may include many colors, it is always helpful to learn some color theory basics so that you can mix your own unique colors. Let's start with understanding the color wheel.

Primary colors: Red, yellow, and blue. These colors are the root colors from which all other colors can be mixed.

Secondary colors: Orange, green, and violet. By mixing 2 primary colors together, you get a secondary color.

Tertiary colors: Orange-yellow, red-orange, red-violet, violet-blue, blue-green, and yellow-green. By mixing 1 primary and 1 secondary color together, you get a tertiary color.

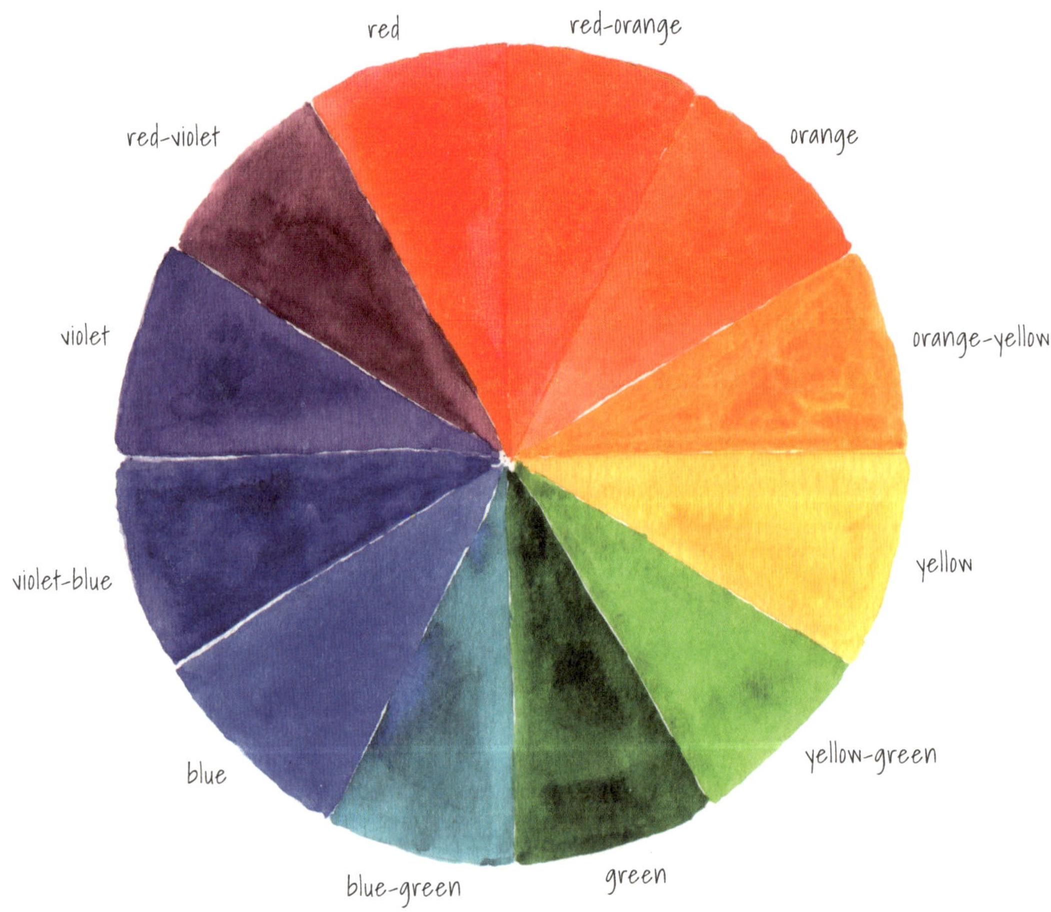

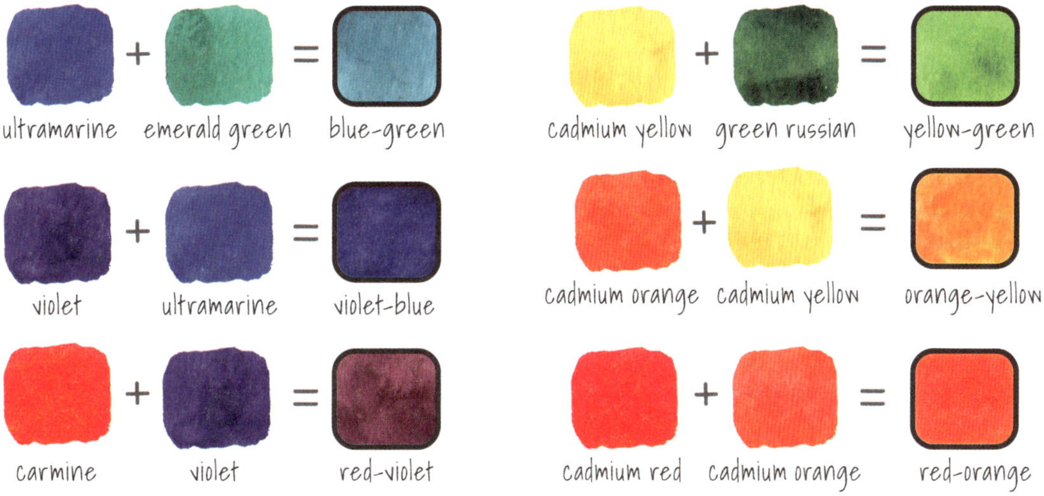

For this exercise I have listed out the exact paint colors that I use to achieve these combinations. Each color comes in a variety of shades, and each shade has either a warm or a cool undertone. In order to mix the most vibrant colors, a good rule of thumb is to mix cool colors with other cool colors, and warm colors with other warm colors. For example, a cool red and a cool blue will make a vibrant purple. However, if you mix a warm red with a cool blue, your purple will be a bit muddier and less vibrant.

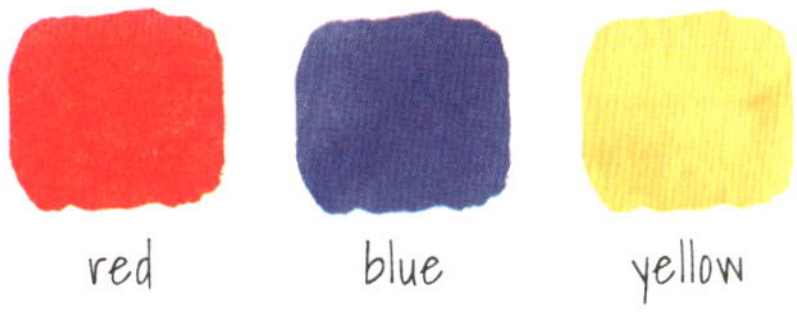

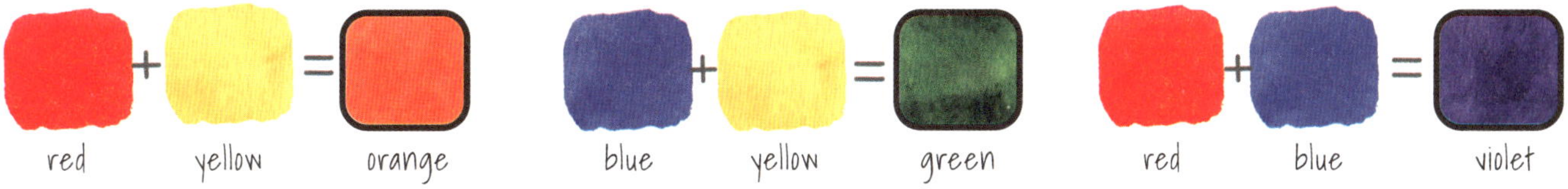

How to Darken Colors

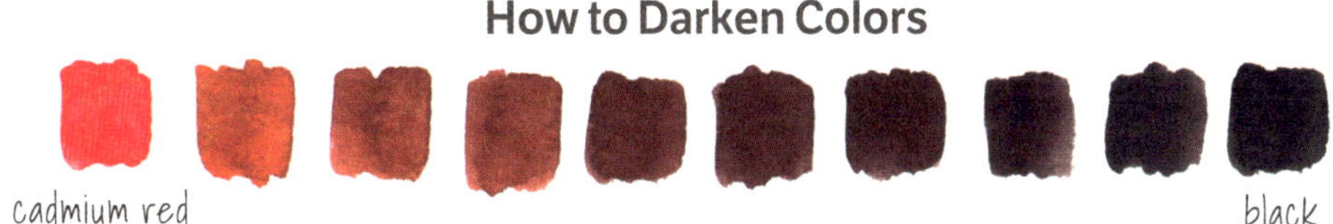

If you would like to darken a color, add a small amount of black to the mixture. Above, I started with the pure color cadmium red. I added a tiny bit of black to each swatch, until I end up with the darkest red.

I recommend you practice with your watercolors to create various color combinations. Have fun with it! The more you practice, the more you will get a feel for the colors and their broad possibilities.

Watercolor Basics

As the name implies, watercolor utilizes a combination of transparent color and water to work its magic. Depending on how much water and color are used, you can create a wide variety of effects.

I have experimented by painting a variety of circles. You can see that each time the edge of one circle touches another, the colors bleed into one another. When wet paint touches another area of wet paint, the two areas of paint will mix. I encourage you to play around with your paints to get a feel for watercolor and how it behaves. This circle exercise is a fun way to get started.

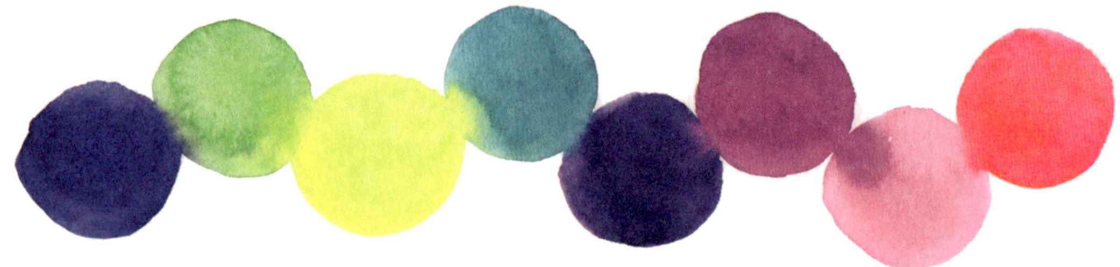

Brushstrokes

Lines

Brushes are numbered by size; the higher the number, the larger the brush. As you can see below, you can get a lot of line variation with each brush, depending on how hard you press down. To create a thin line, use the tip of your brush and press very lightly. To create very thick lines, apply a lot of pressure as you paint.

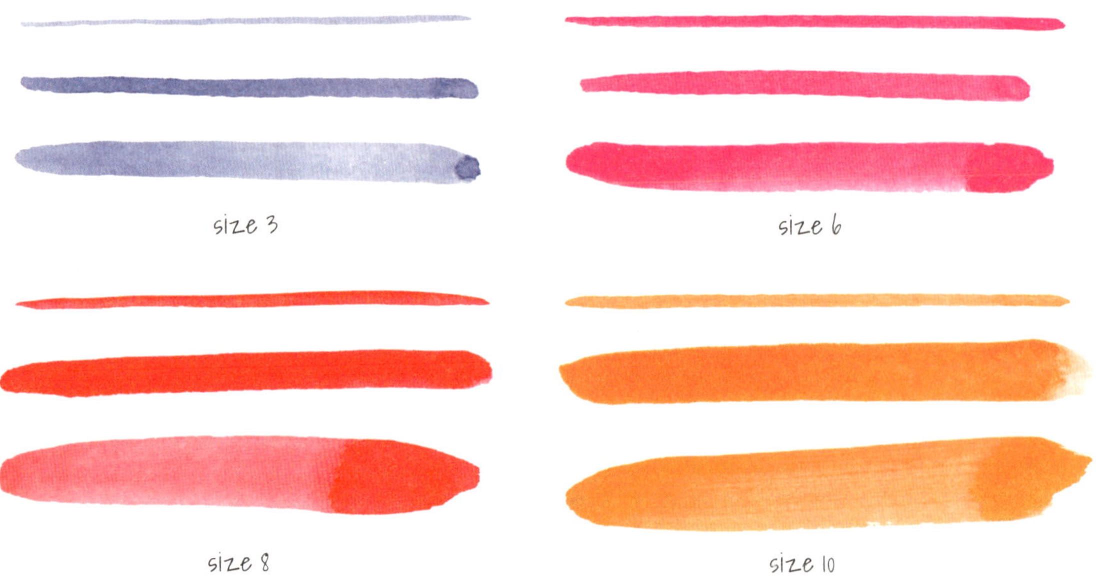

Strokes

You can achieve a lot of variety with your brush by experimenting with different marks.

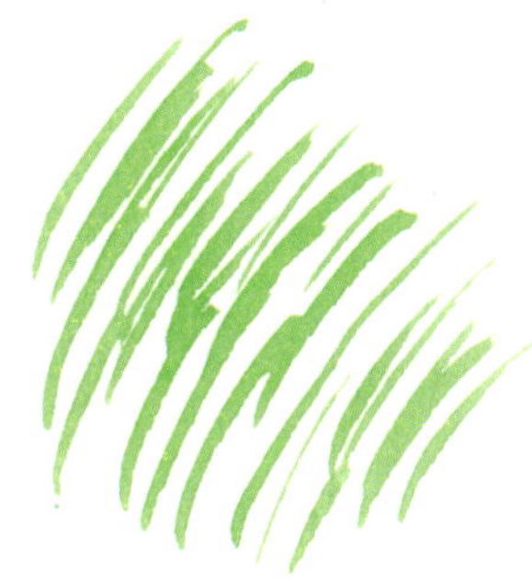

These strokes are good for feathery lines, such as the centers of flowers.

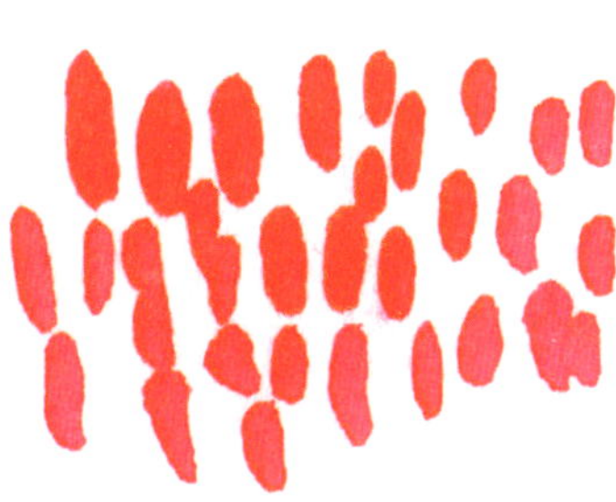

These strokes are good for adding detail to lily, orchid, and other flower petals.

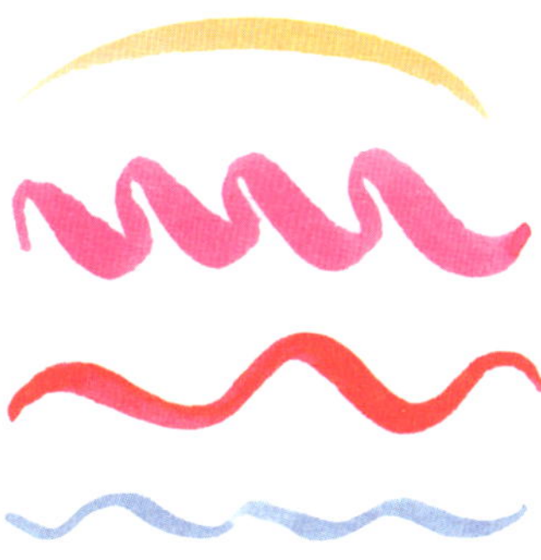

Play around with making curved lines and squiggles to get a feel for all the possibilities.

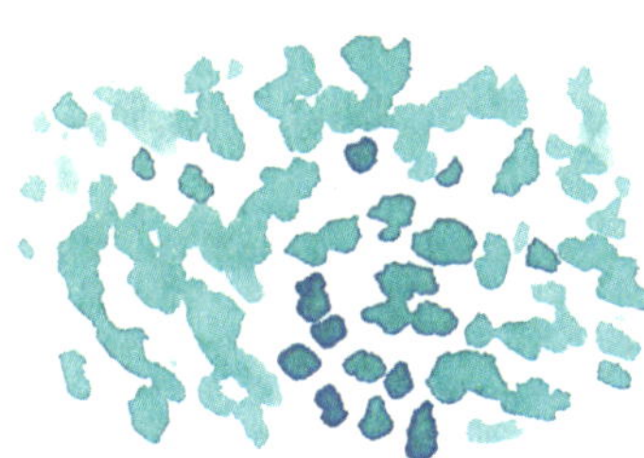

You can use these dots to add detail to the centers of leaves and petals.

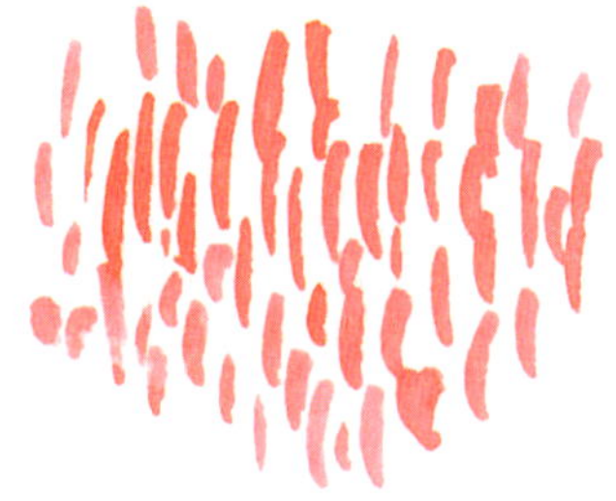

These short little strokes are good for creating fur.

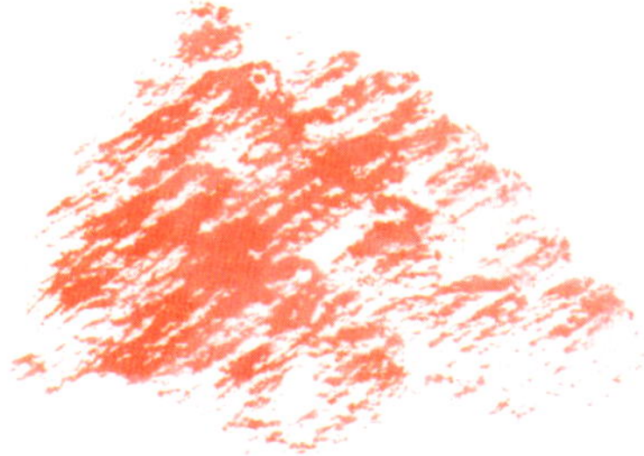

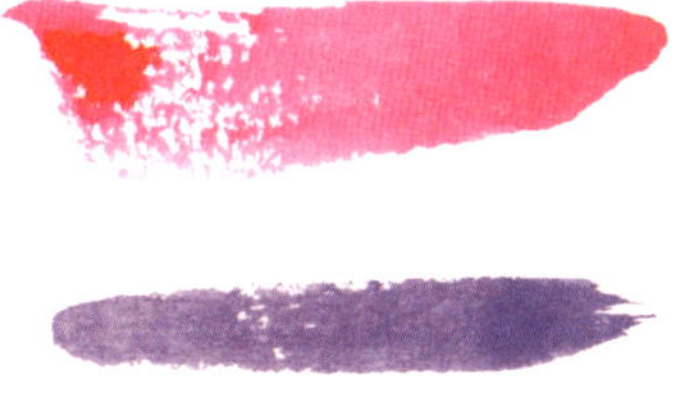

This technique is called dry brush. We barely use any water on the brush but a good amount of paint. It creates a nice effect for textures.

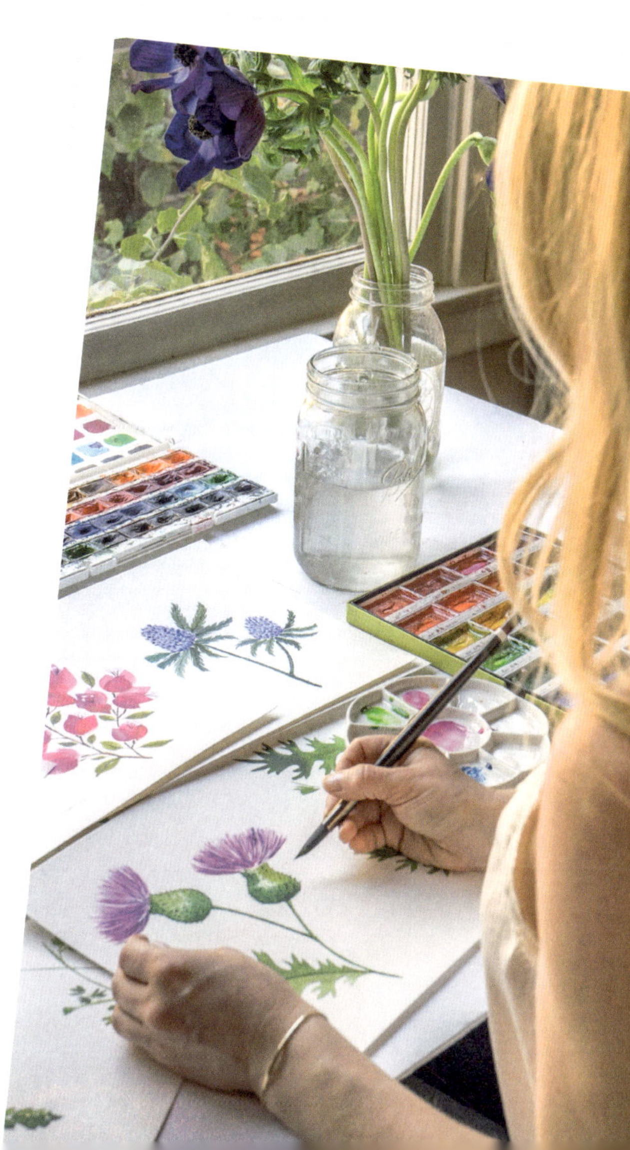

Wet on Dry

Wet on dry is simply applying paint to a dry surface, like dry paper or a layer of dried paint. Make sure your brush has enough water for the paint to flow smoothly. Use more water to produce a more transparent (or see-through), lighter color. Use less water to produce a more opaque, deeper, or darker color. Here, I've shown the color violet mixed with various amounts of water.

Layering. Watercolor is translucent, so you can use the wet-on-dry technique to paint layers on top of one another to create darker shades of color. When you add a layer of paint on top of another, the area where they overlap becomes darker.

Below is a layering progression. I painted a long stripe in violet. Then I built up the color by adding one layer at a time. The color darkens the more layers you apply.

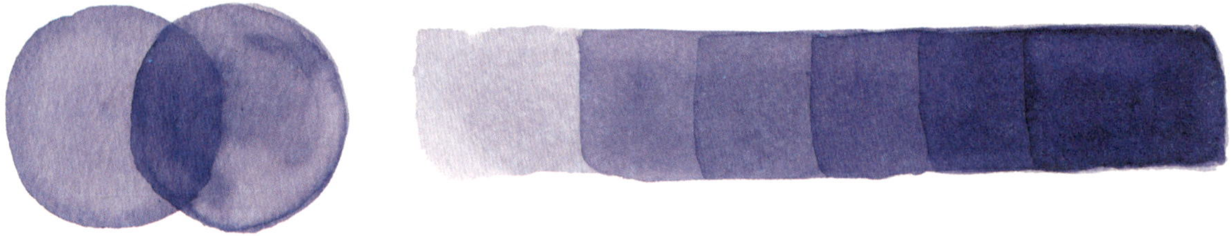

Adding details. You can also use the wet-on-dry technique to add details to your paintings.

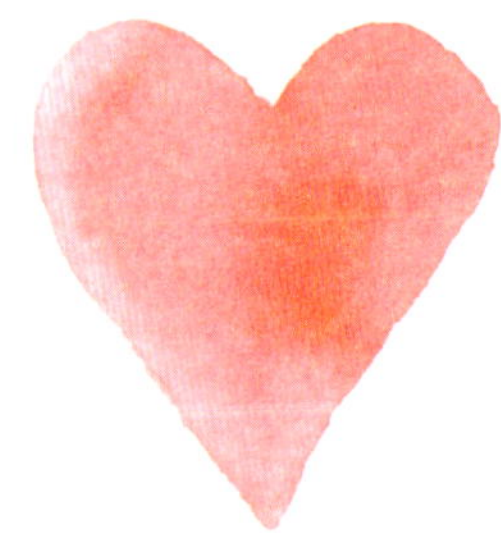

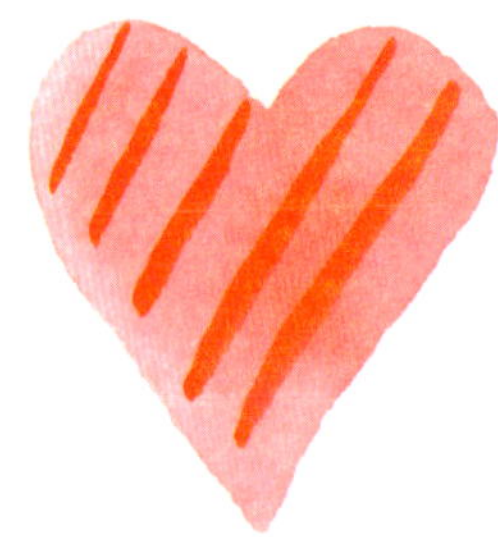

This heart is painted with a layer of red.

After it dried completely, I added stripes. You can see they are distinct and crisp.

Be sure to let the first layer of paint dry completely before moving on to the next, or your colors will bleed together.

Wet on Wet

Wet on wet is adding paint to a wet surface, like wet paper or a layer of wet paint. Because this technique is less controlled, the results are sometimes unpredictable, but that's part of the appeal!

Wet paper. Using a brush, wet the paper with a coat of water until it appears shiny and wet. If the paper really starts to buckle and warp, you may have used too much water. While the paper is still wet, add paint to your brush and touch it to the wet area so the color bleeds into the water. You can move the water and paint around with your brush to help control where the color flows.

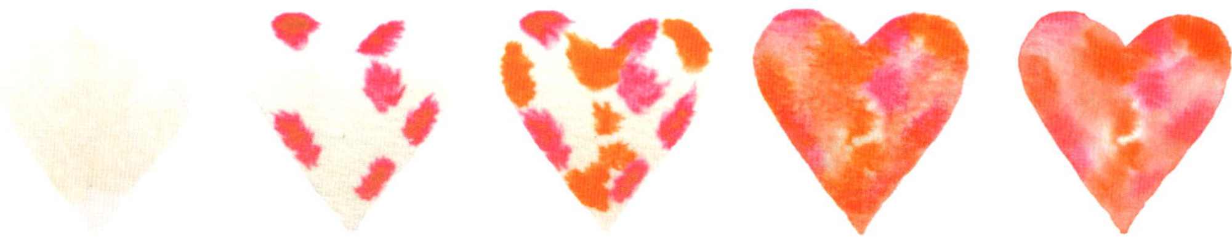

Wet paint. Apply a coat of paint to the paper. While it is still wet, add more paint to your brush and touch it to the wet area so the color bleeds into the first layer of paint.

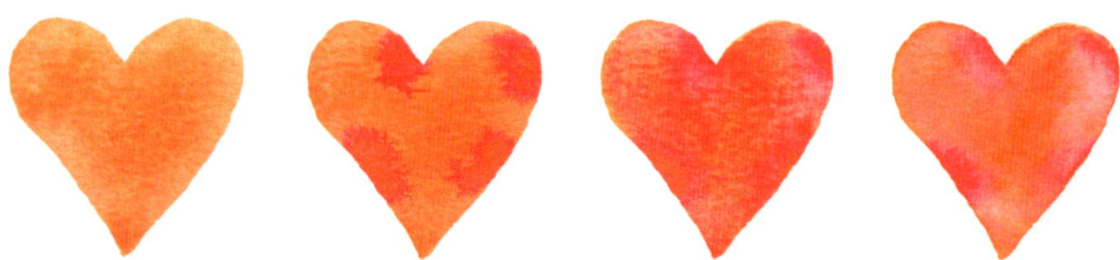

Lifting color. You can't erase watercolor, but you can remove some of the paint while it's still wet. Clean all the paint off your brush and dab it on a paper towel to remove excess moisture. Dip the dry brush into the paint you want to remove. The bristles will absorb some of the paint, lifting it off the paper.

Washes. A watercolor wash is when you apply paint evenly to an area of paper.

A flat wash has even color throughout. Load your brush with lots of water and paint. Paint up and down with a vertical motion as you make your way across the page. When the color becomes lighter, pick up more paint and continue where you left off.

A gradated wash goes from dark to light. Load your brush with lots of water and paint. Paint up and down, making your way across the page. The color will become lighter as the paint runs out, creating an ombré effect.

A variegated wash transitions from one color to another. Start painting your wash with one color. Next, load your brush with a different color. Place the brush directly next to the first color and continue painting. The colors will bleed into one another where they touch.

Loose Leaves

Loosely painted leaves are very fun to paint, and often they can be created using only one or two brushstrokes. By varying the pressure and angle of our brushstrokes, we can create many different shapes.

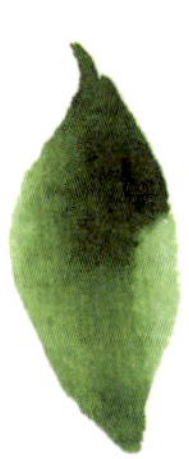

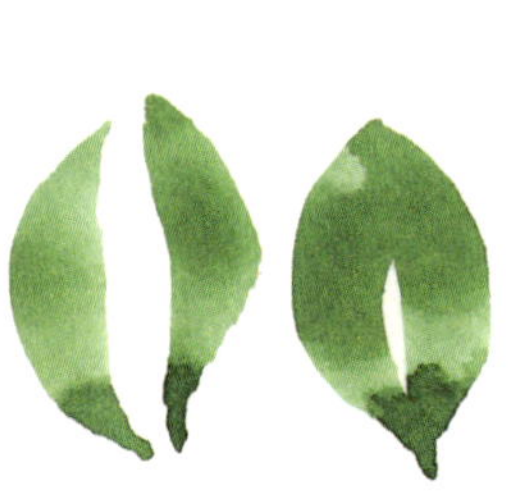

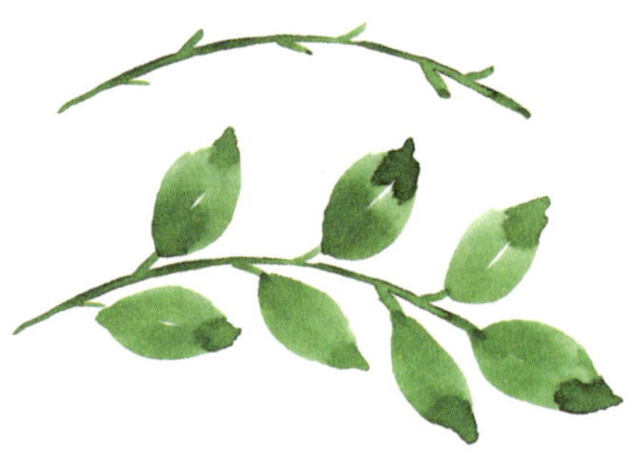

To create a leaf shape, touch the tip of your brush to the paper, press down, drag the brush along the paper, and then slowly lift up until only your brush tip touches the paper again. This will create a leaf shape that is thin at both ends, but wider in the middle.

To create a leaf with a line of white showing through the center, repeat this brushstroke, but this time give it a slight curve. Repeat this on the other side. The top and bottom of each stroke should be touching. You should get a leaf that looks like this.

If we add a stem, we can make sprigs of leaves very easily.

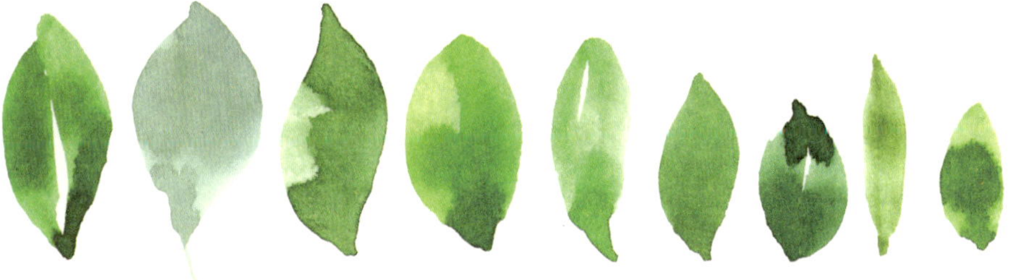

Try experimenting with your brushstrokes to create lots of different leaves!

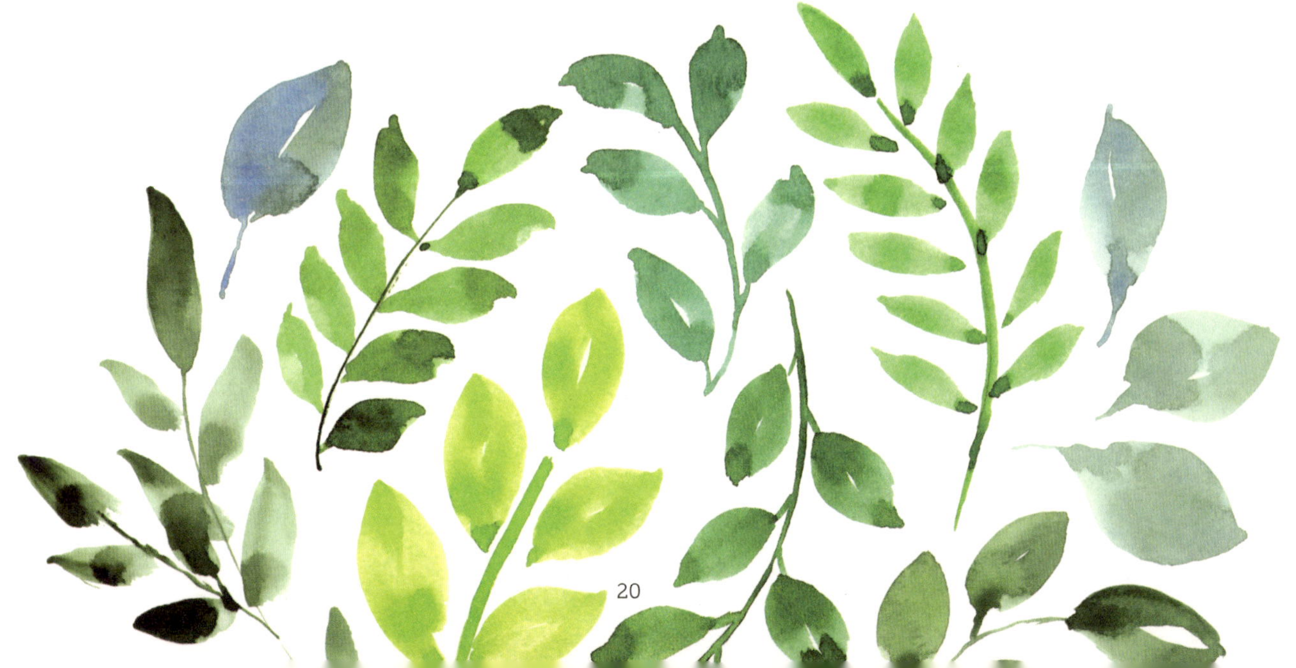

Loose Petals

For this petal, touch the tip of your brush to the paper, press down, drag the brush along the paper, and then slowly lift up until only your brush tip touches the paper again. This will create a petal shape that is thin at both ends, but fat in the middle.

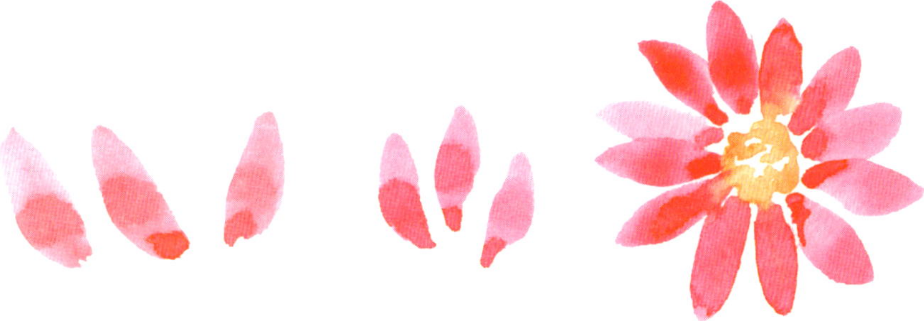

To create loose flowers, we can use the same technique as the leaves. With one brushstroke, we can create a petal. By varying the pressure and angle of the brushstroke, we can create different-shaped petals.

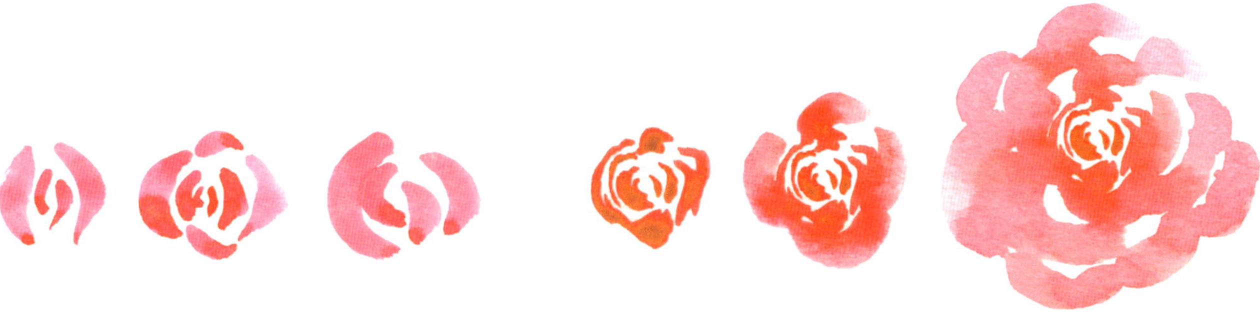

You can also create rose petals using this technique by slightly curving the brushstrokes as you go.

Start in the middle and work your way outward to create an entire rose.

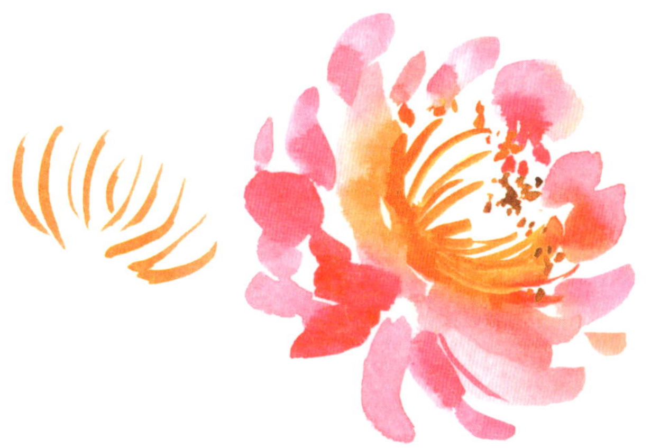

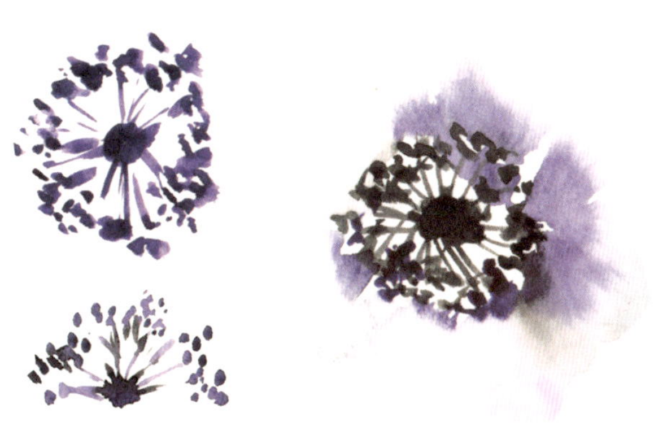

Very thin curved strokes make good centers for many flowers.

A combination of thin strokes and dots makes a nice center for various flowers, especially poppies.

Filler Leaves

Combine these leaf designs with the flower tutorials to paint your own beautiful bouquets.

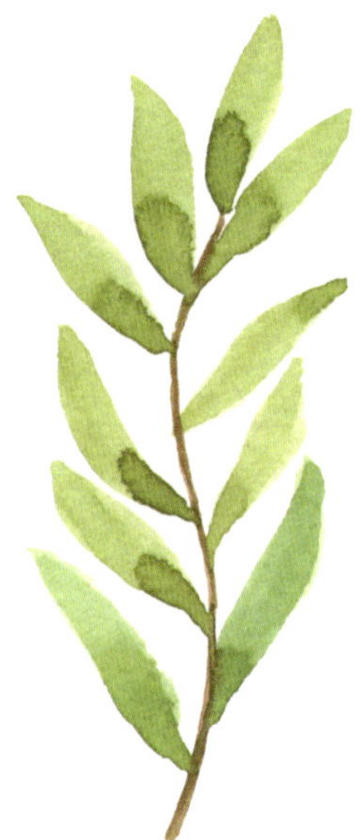

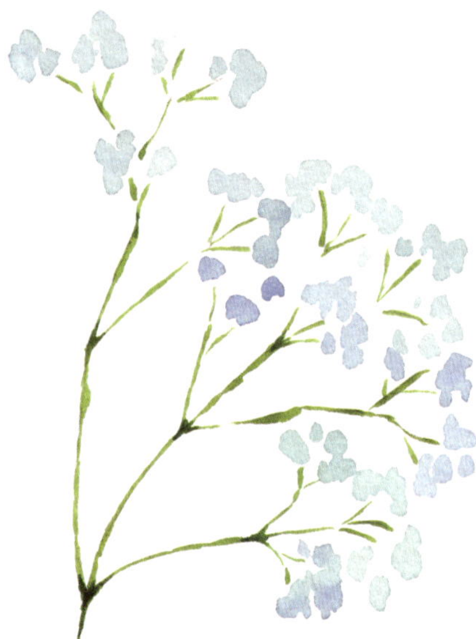

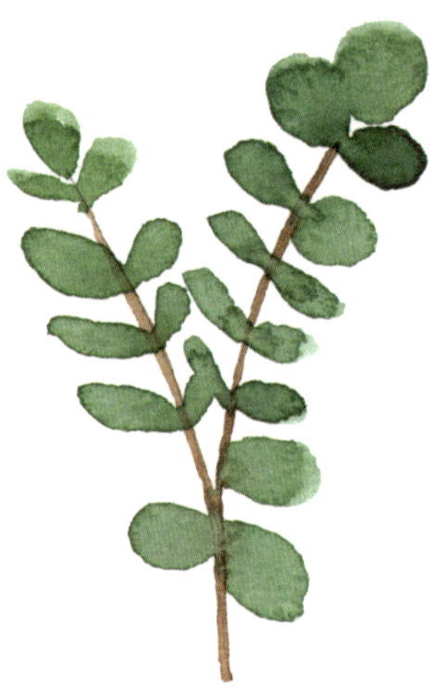

Olive Leaves

Paint the stem in brown. Using the Loose Leaves technique (page 20), paint the leaves in green.

Baby's Breath

Paint the branches in green. Next, using a light, watery shade of blue, paint loose clusters of dots for the flowers.

Baby Blue Eucalyptus

Paint the stems in brown. Next, paint the leaves in green. Make the leaf shapes circles or flattened circles.

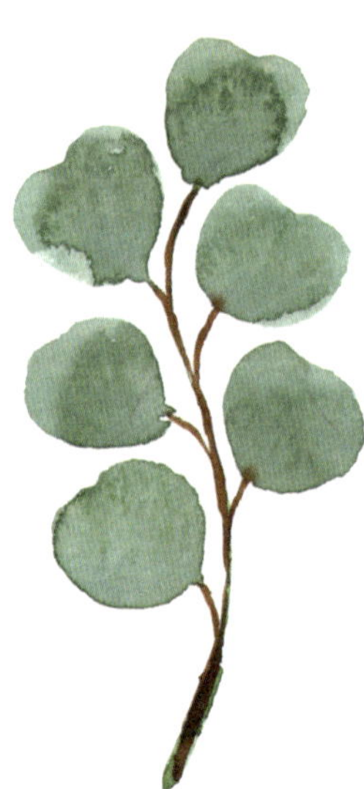

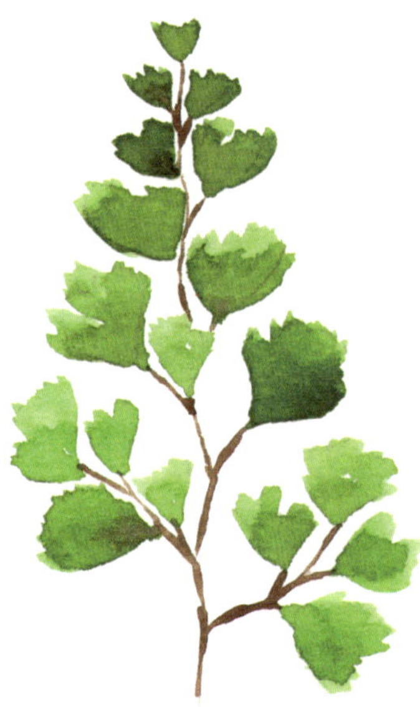

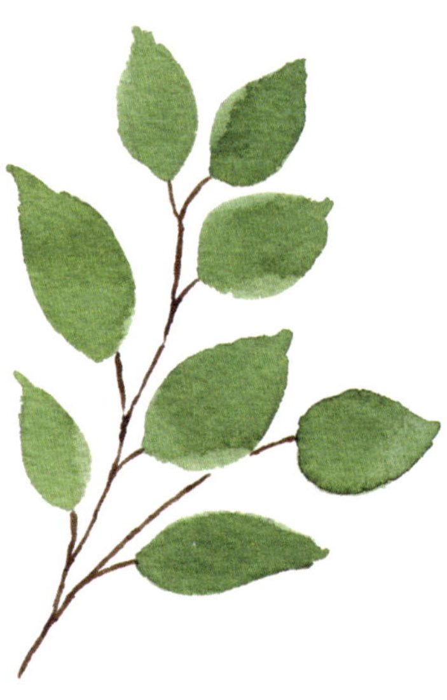

Silver Dollar Eucalyptus

Paint the stem in brown. Paint the leaves in light green. Make the leaf shape circular with a tiny indentation at the top, similar to a heart.

Maidenhair Fern

Paint the stems in brown. Paint the leaves in green. The leaves taper in at the base and flare out at the top with uneven edges.

Lemon Leaves

Paint the stem in brown. Using the Loose Leaves technique (page 20), paint the leaves in green.

Containers

These containers are perfect for painting floral arrangements. See how I put everything together on page 24.

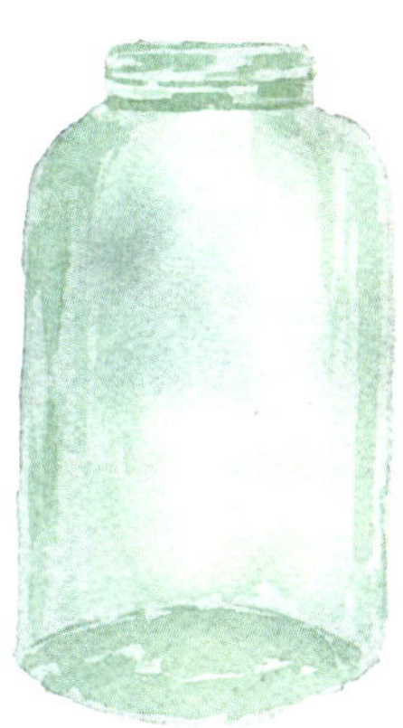

Mason Jar

Paint the jar shape with a coat of water. Drop in a light shade of blue, letting the color mix with the water. Once dry, paint some thin lines along the top of the jar and along the edges. Paint a circular shape toward the bottom to create the base.

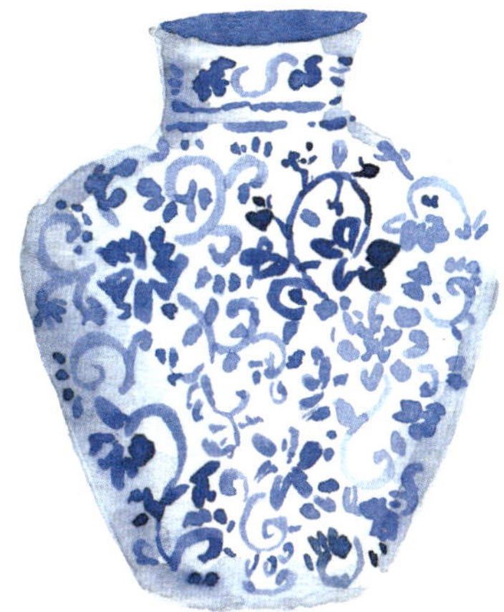

Chinoiserie Vase

Paint the vase shape with a coat of water. Drop in light blue along the edges to create depth. Once dry, paint swirly floral motifs in blue. This doesn't have to be exact—have fun with it! Finally, paint a circular shape at the top for the opening.

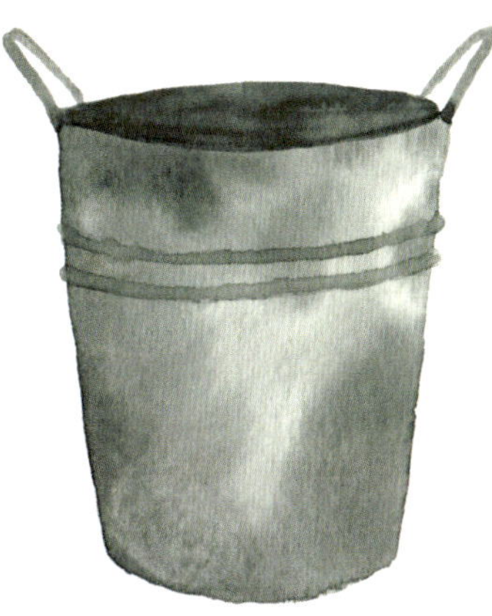

Metal Pail

Paint the pail shape with a coat of water. Drop in gray along the edges, letting it mix with the water. Once dry, paint two thin lines across the pail and two handles. Paint a circular shape at the top in dark gray to create the opening.

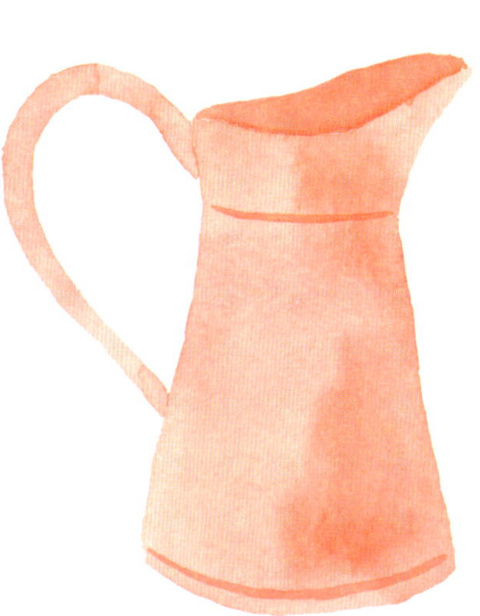

Pitcher

Paint the pitcher with a light shade of pink. Once dry, paint pink lines across the top and the base for detail. Paint a circular shape at the top for the opening.

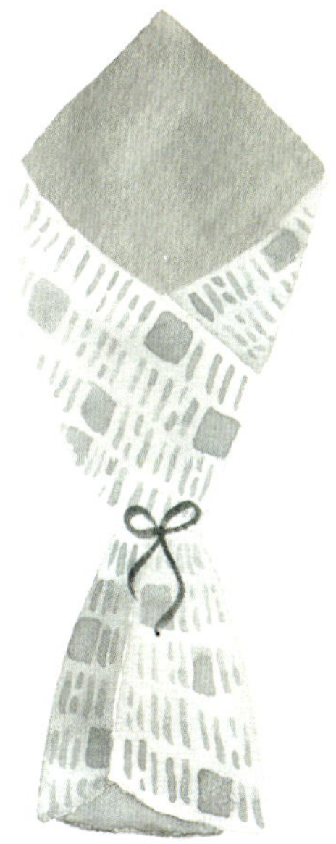

Newspaper

Paint the newspaper in a light gray. The front of the wrapped paper should be the lightest gray, while the paper behind will be a shade darker. Once dry, paint little lines and squares to resemble text and photos. Finally, paint on a ribbon to tie it together.

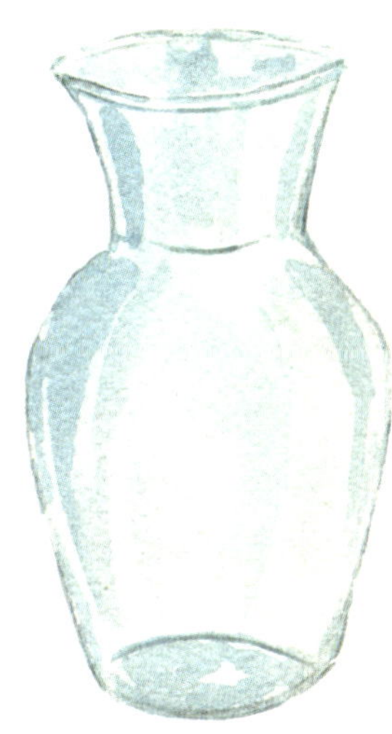

Glass Vase

Paint the vase shape with a coat of water. Drop in a very light blue, letting it blend with the water. Once dry, paint some thin lines along the edges of the vase. Paint a circular shape toward the bottom to create the base and toward the top to create the opening.

Putting It All Together

One of my favorite things to do is paint a variety of flowers in one painting. With the 50 unique flower tutorials in this book, you'll be able to paint your own bouquets and arrangements. Here are some tips to get started.

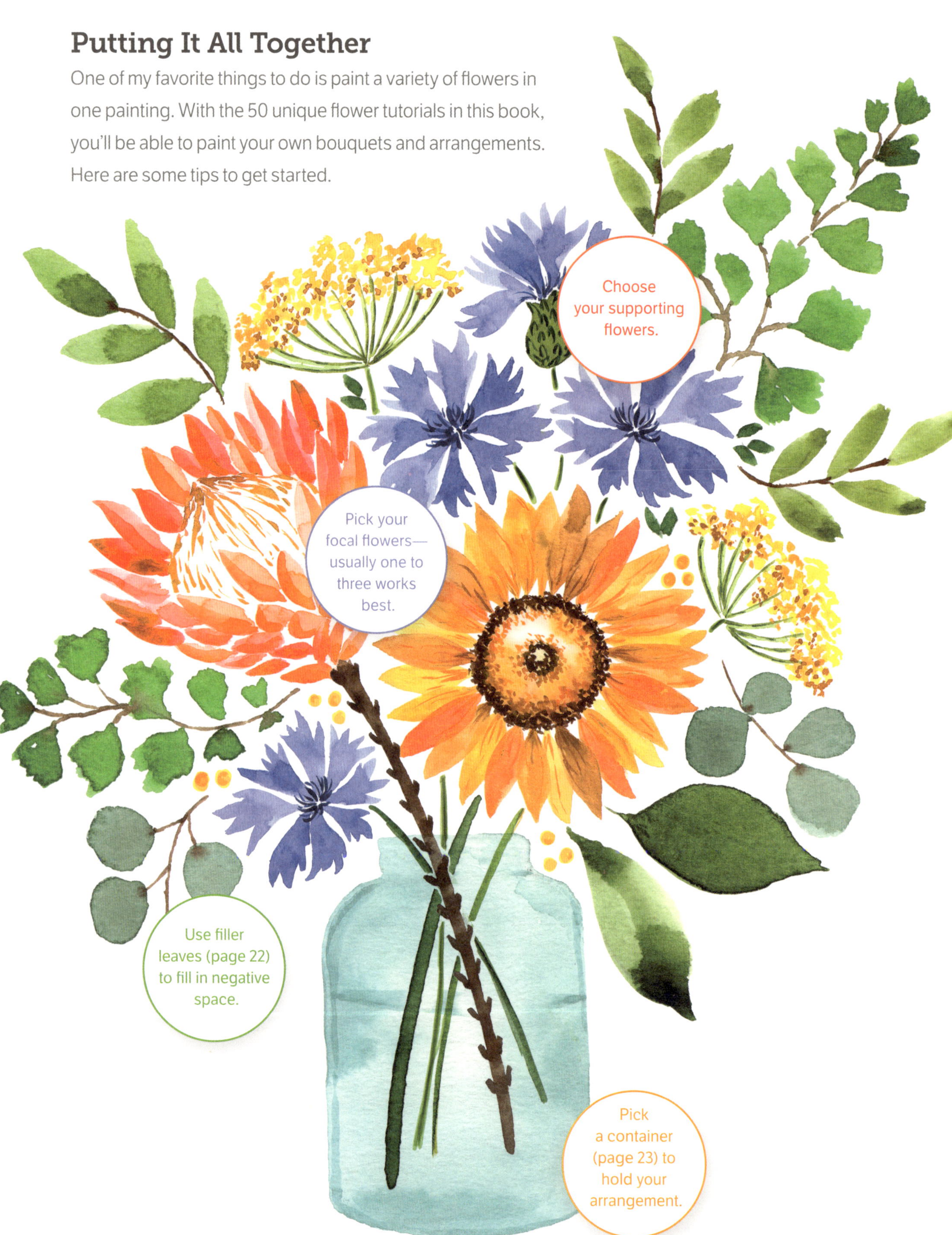

1. First, paint the container to hold the flowers. For this arrangement, I chose a mason jar.

2. Now, paint the tops of your chosen flowers. I chose a protea and a sunflower as the focal flowers, with cornflowers and fennel as the supporting flowers. When painting an arrangement, I paint the tops of the flowers only, without the stems and leaves. I find this keeps the arrangement from looking too cluttered early on.

3. Now add the stems. Because the mason jar is a clear container, I painted stems inside the jar.

4. Finally, add filler leaves. I chose olive leaves, maidenhair fern, silver dollar eucalyptus, and lemon leaves. I painted the leaves around the flowers to bulk up the arrangement and fill in any negative space. As a finishing touch, I painted tiny yellow dots to fill in some of the smaller gaps.

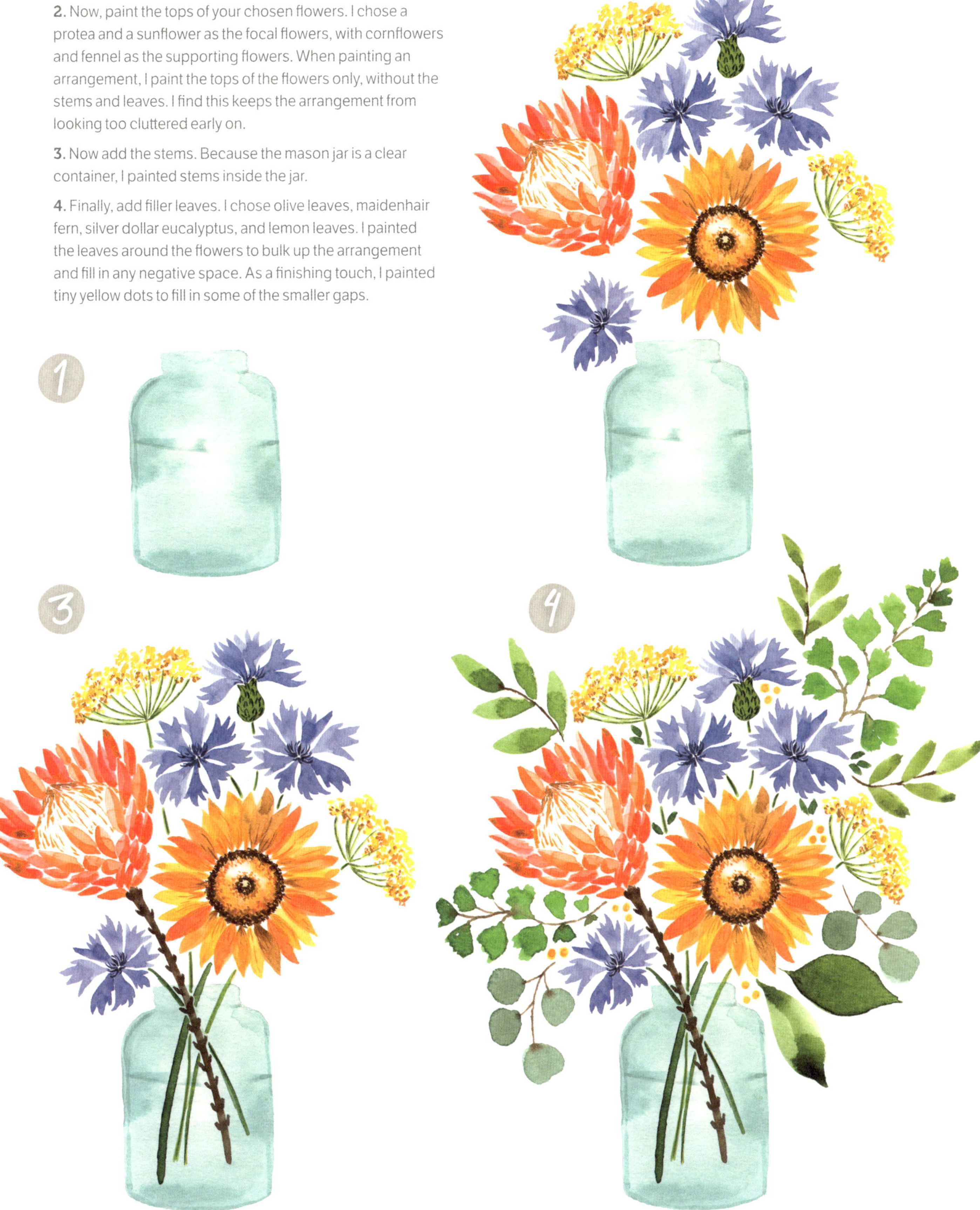

Watercolor TUTORIALS

Now that we have covered the basics,
it's time to start painting!

In this section you will find 50 flower tutorials that walk you step by step through the process of painting your own beautiful blooms. Each tutorial includes a hand-drawn pattern to guide your painting, brush recommendations, a suggested watercolor palette, and illustrated steps to demonstrate the painting process. Once you've mastered each flower, try combining them with the filler leaves and containers on pages 22 and 23 to create bouquets and arrangements. The ideas are endless.

Let's get started!

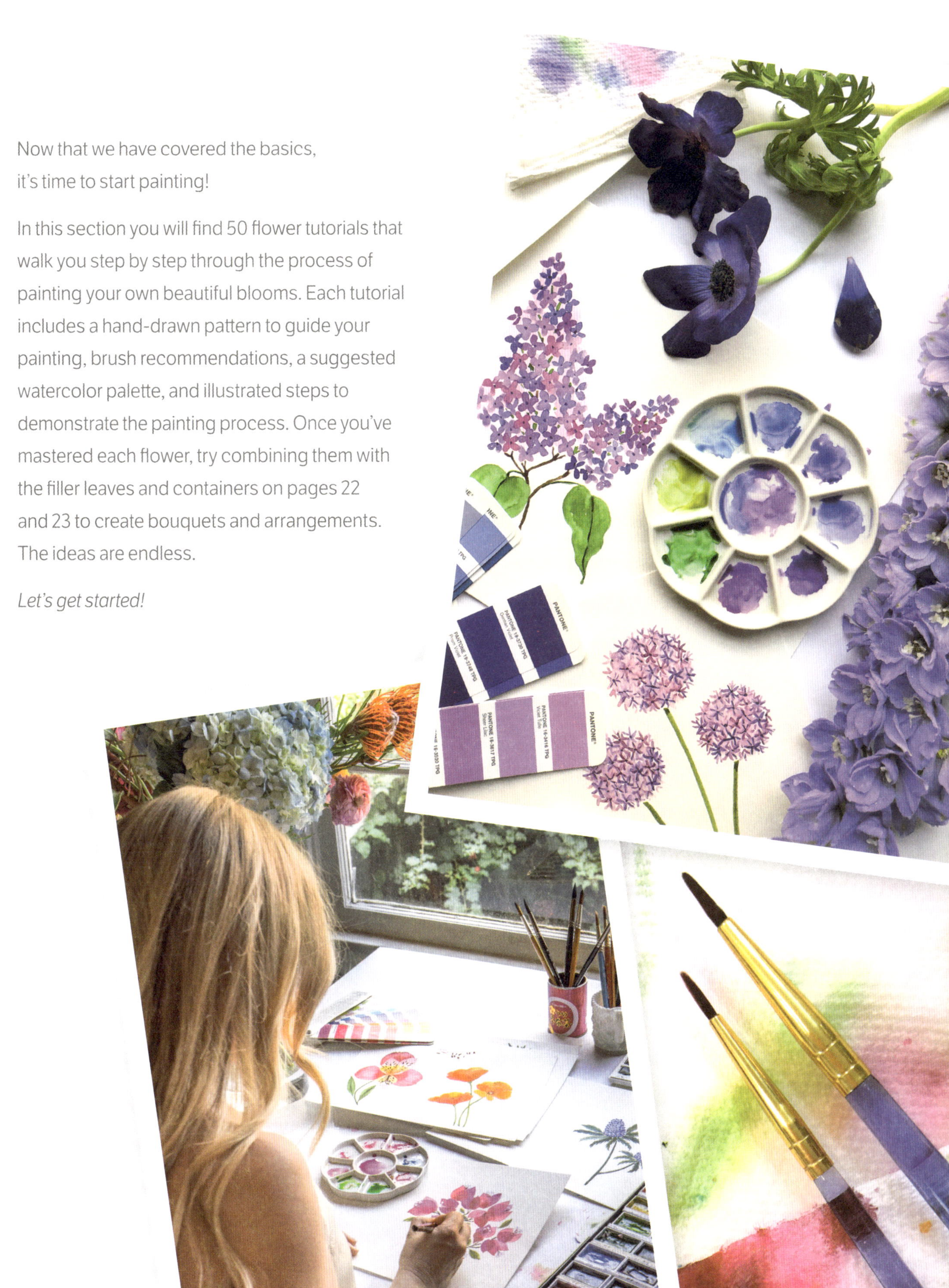

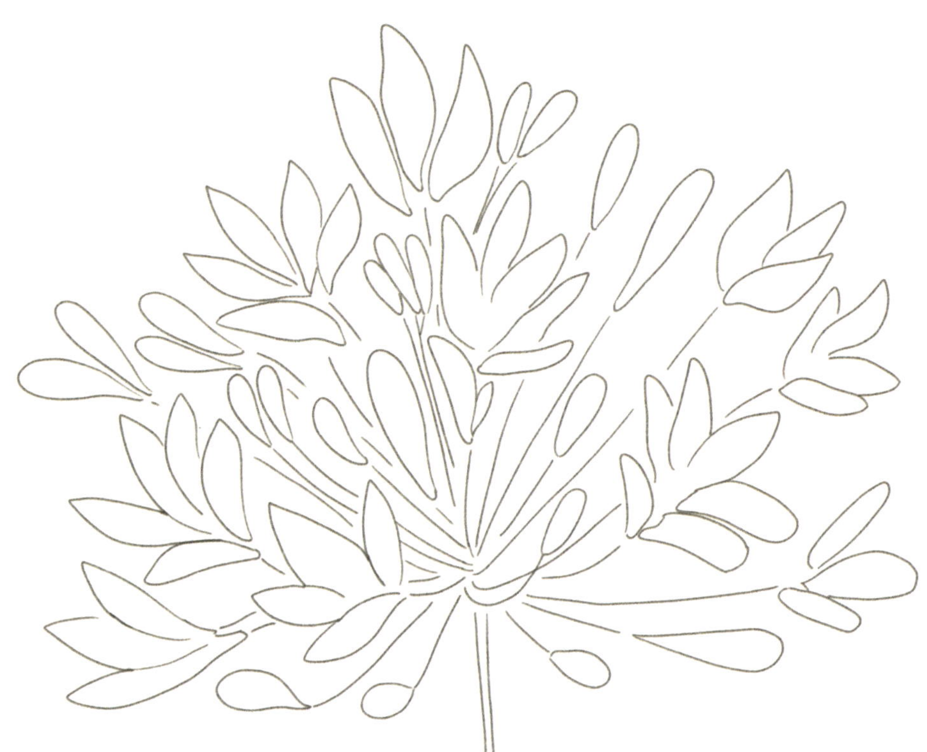

BRUSHES

- Medium brush (6)

COLOR PALETTE

 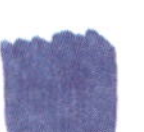 
  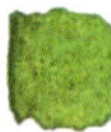

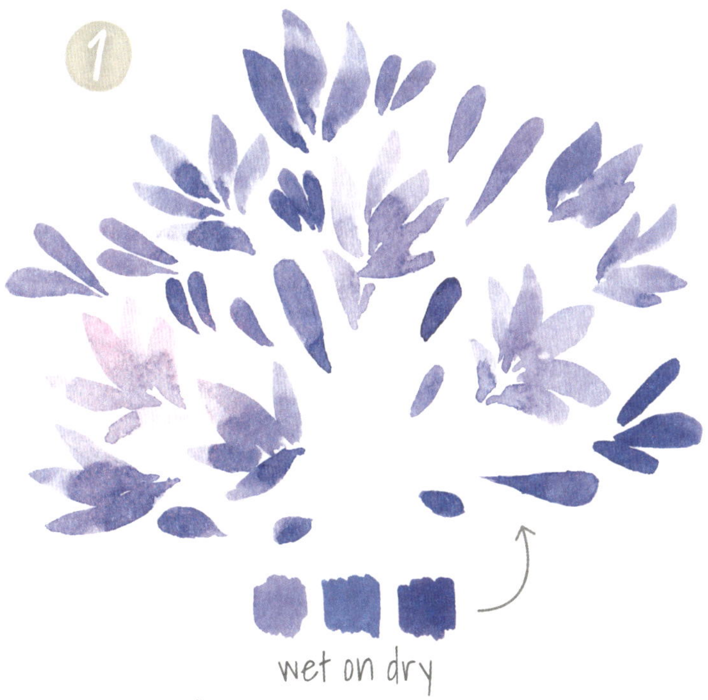

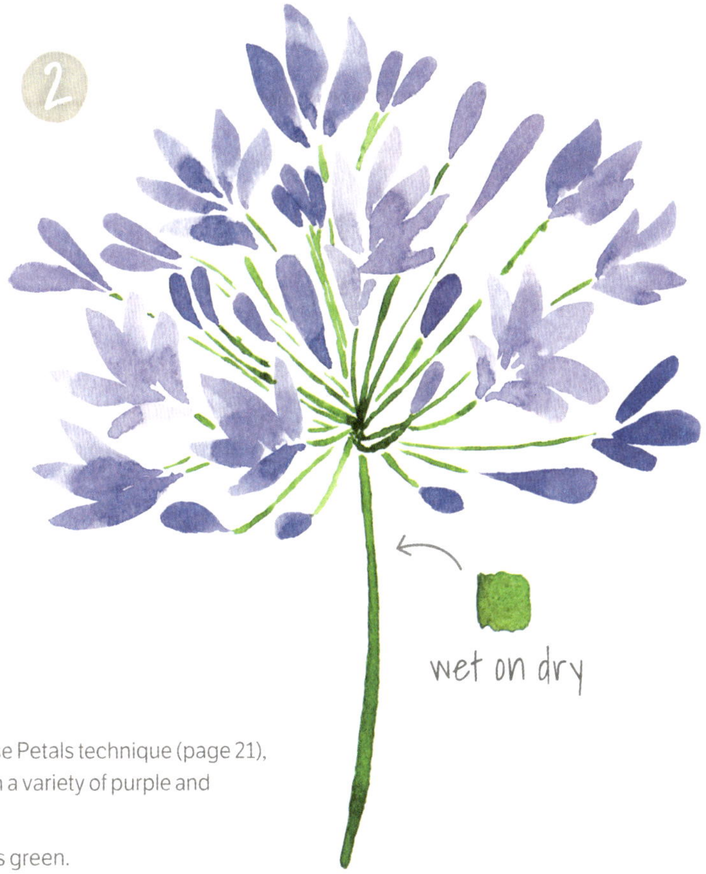

Agapanthus

1. Using the Loose Petals technique (page 21), paint the petals in a variety of purple and blue shades.

2. Paint the stems green.

3. Using darker shades of purple and blue, paint a thin line down the center of each petal for detail.

4. Using the darkest purple, paint thin lines with tiny dots on top for the stamens.

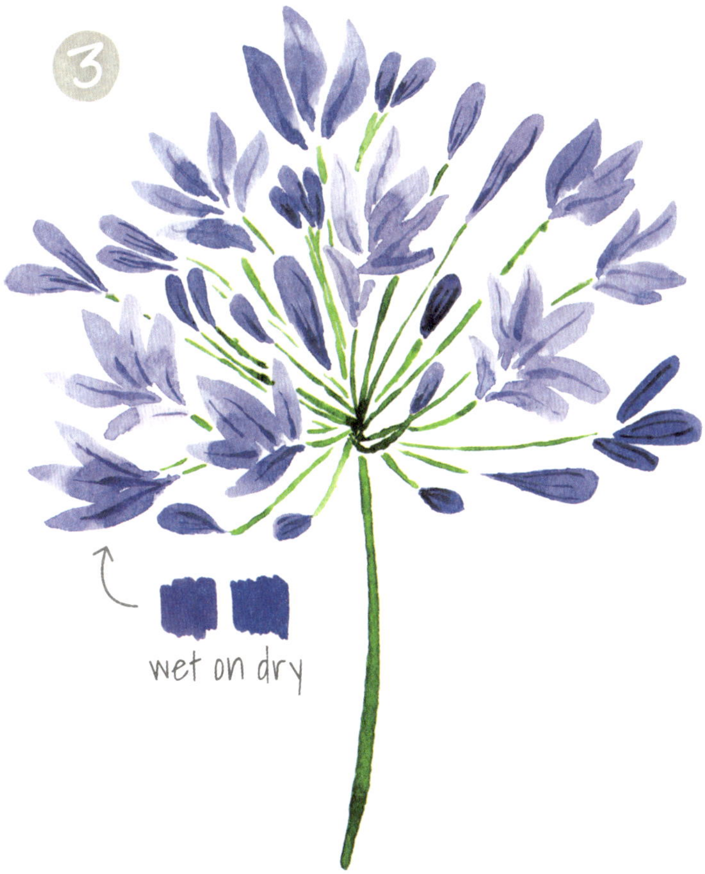

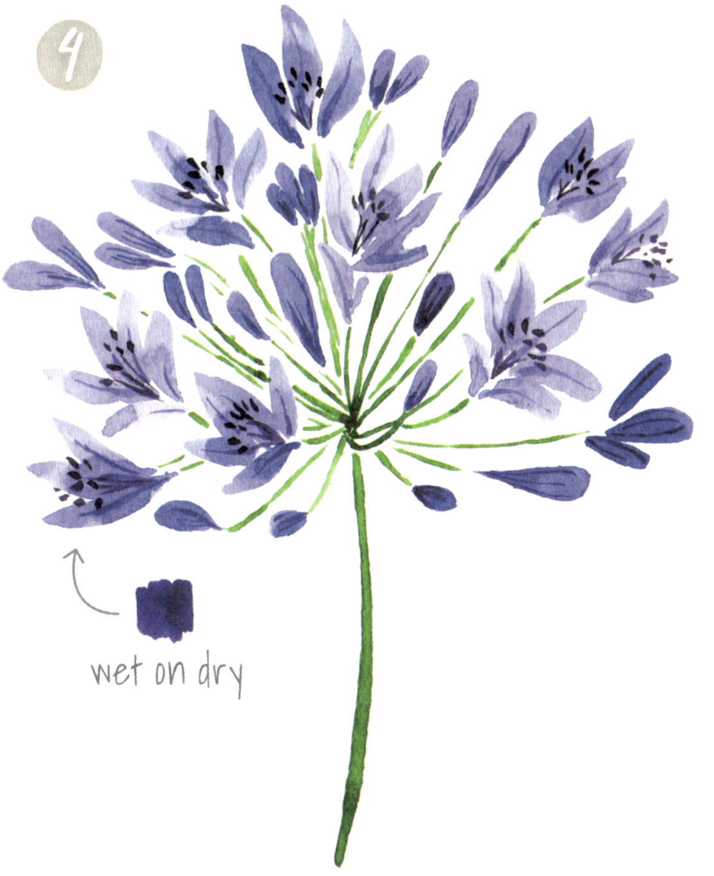

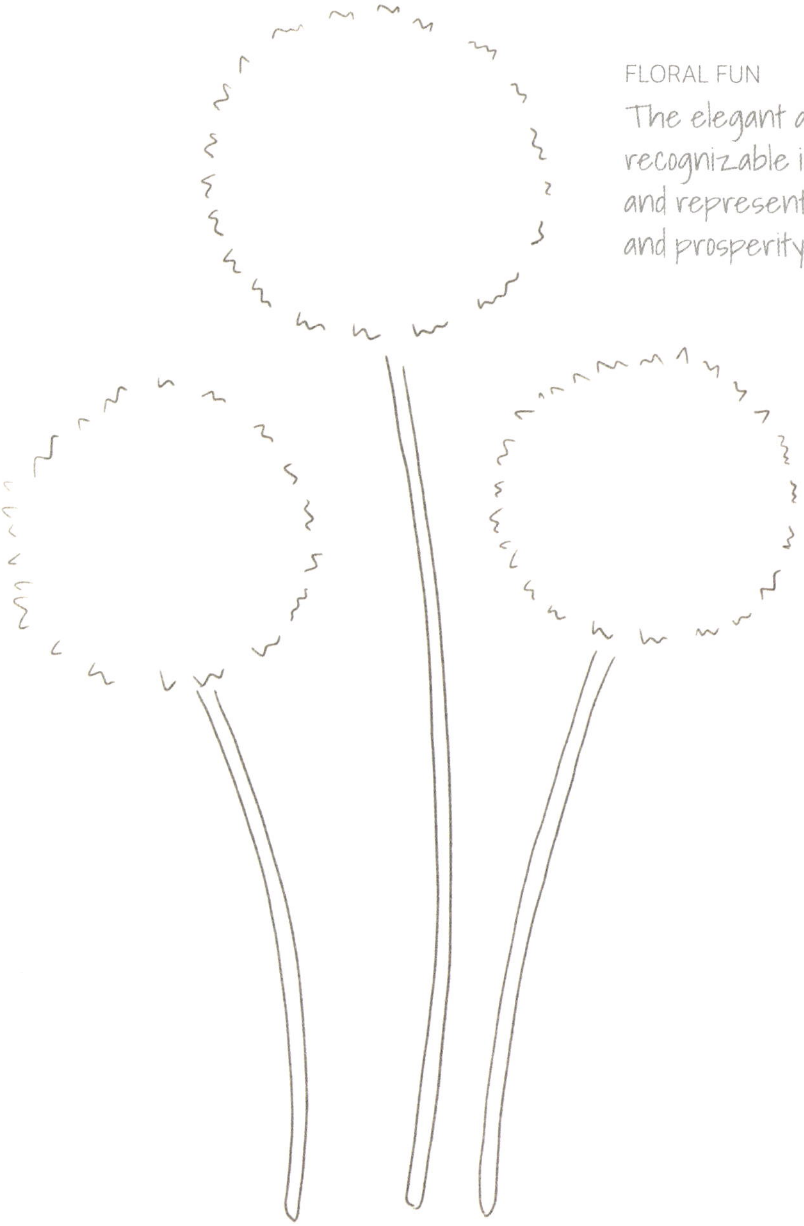

BRUSHES

- Large brush (8)

COLOR PALETTE

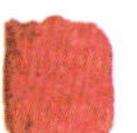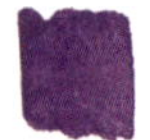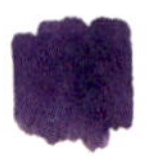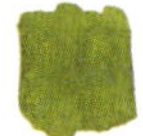

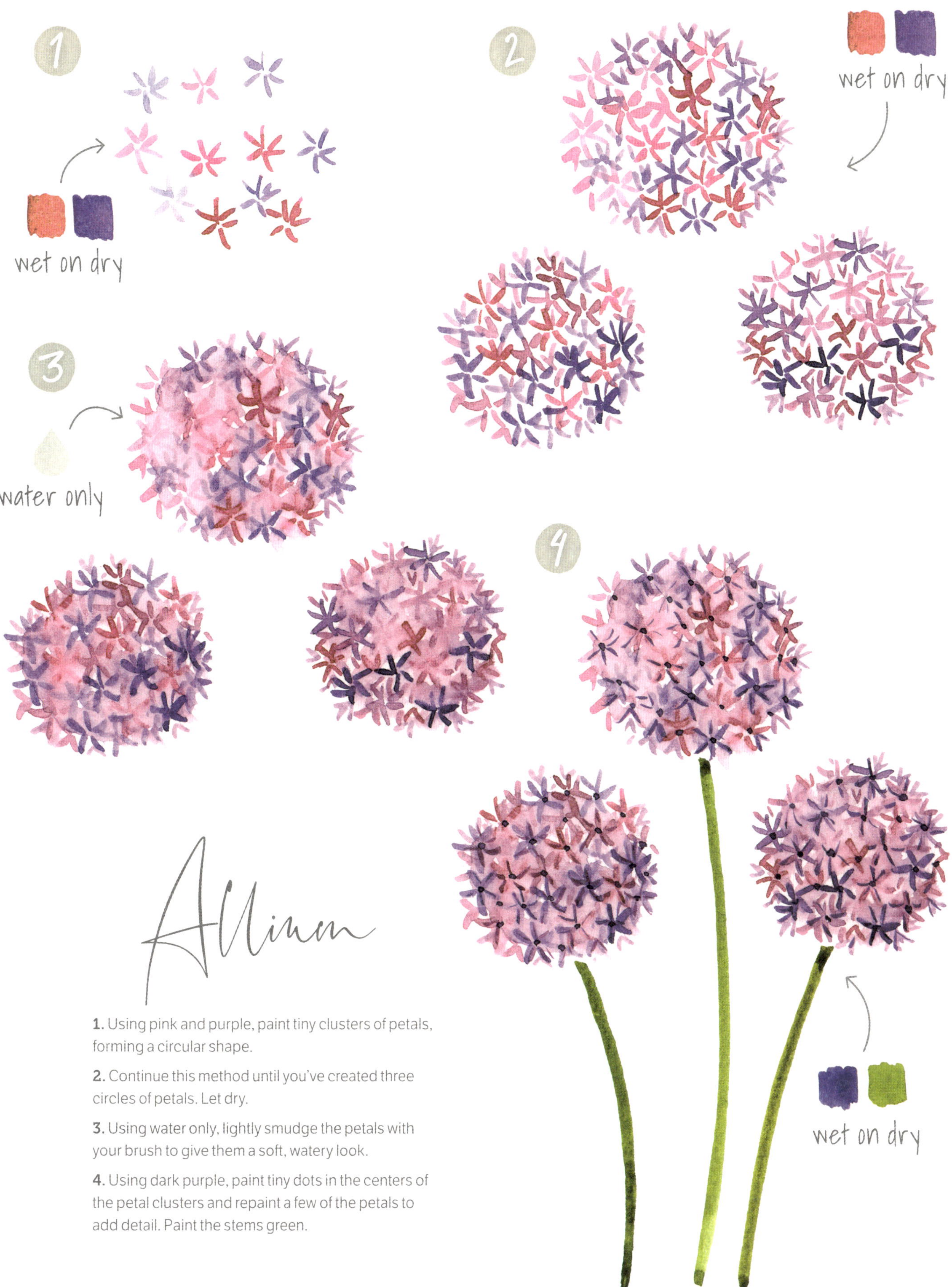

1. Using pink and purple, paint tiny clusters of petals, forming a circular shape.

2. Continue this method until you've created three circles of petals. Let dry.

3. Using water only, lightly smudge the petals with your brush to give them a soft, watery look.

4. Using dark purple, paint tiny dots in the centers of the petal clusters and repaint a few of the petals to add detail. Paint the stems green.

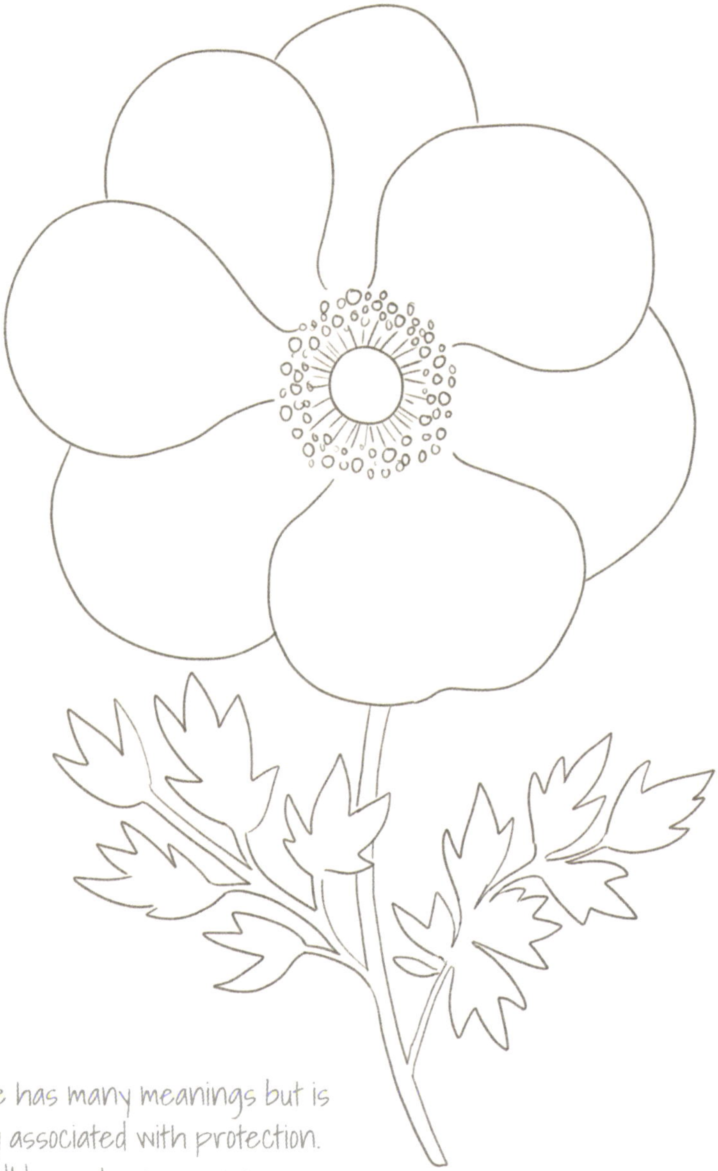

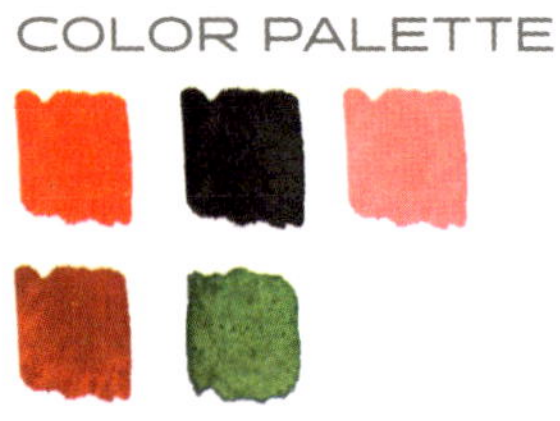

BRUSHES

- Medium/large brush (6, 10)

COLOR PALETTE

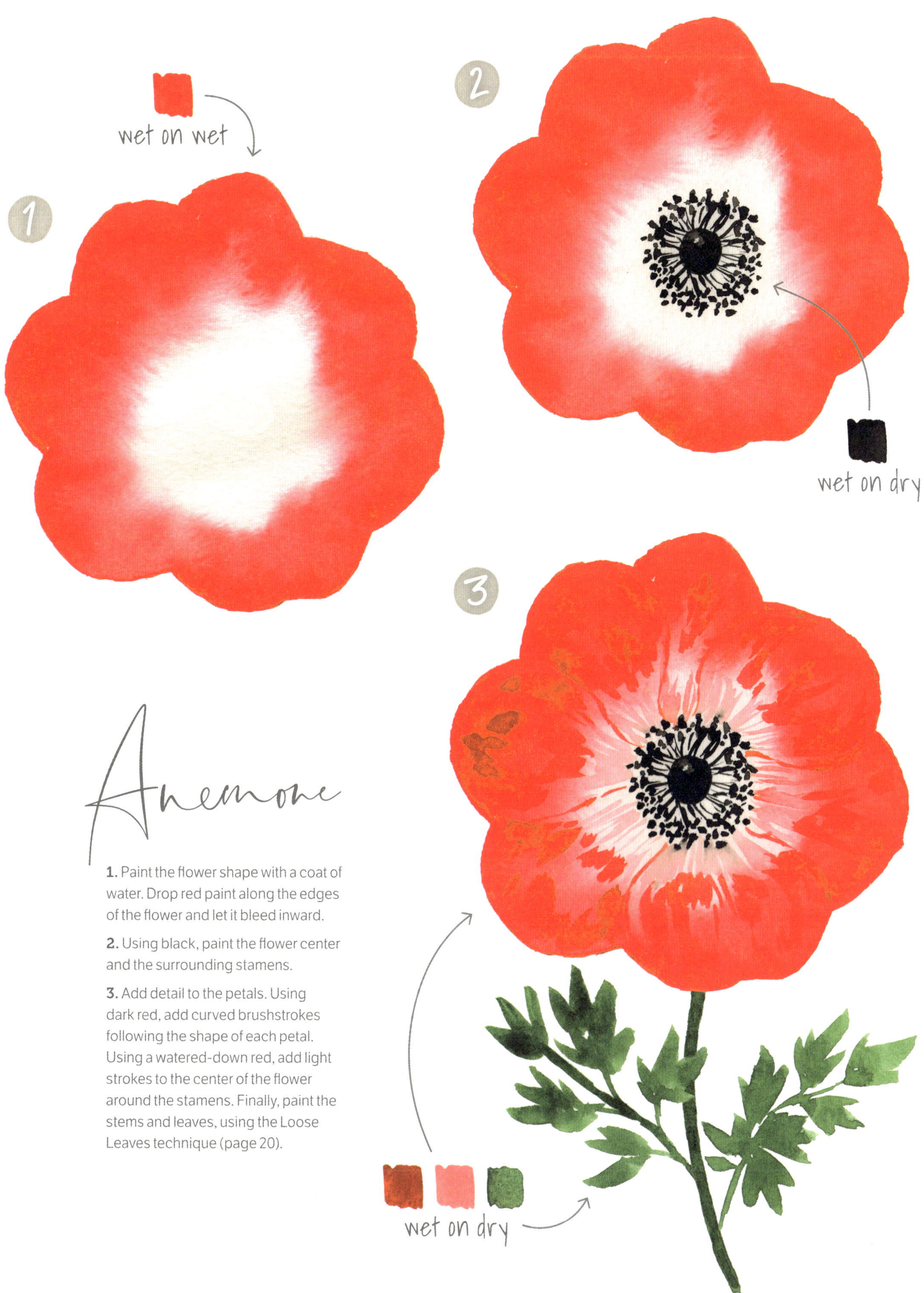

Anemone

1. Paint the flower shape with a coat of water. Drop red paint along the edges of the flower and let it bleed inward.

2. Using black, paint the flower center and the surrounding stamens.

3. Add detail to the petals. Using dark red, add curved brushstrokes following the shape of each petal. Using a watered-down red, add light strokes to the center of the flower around the stamens. Finally, paint the stems and leaves, using the Loose Leaves technique (page 20).

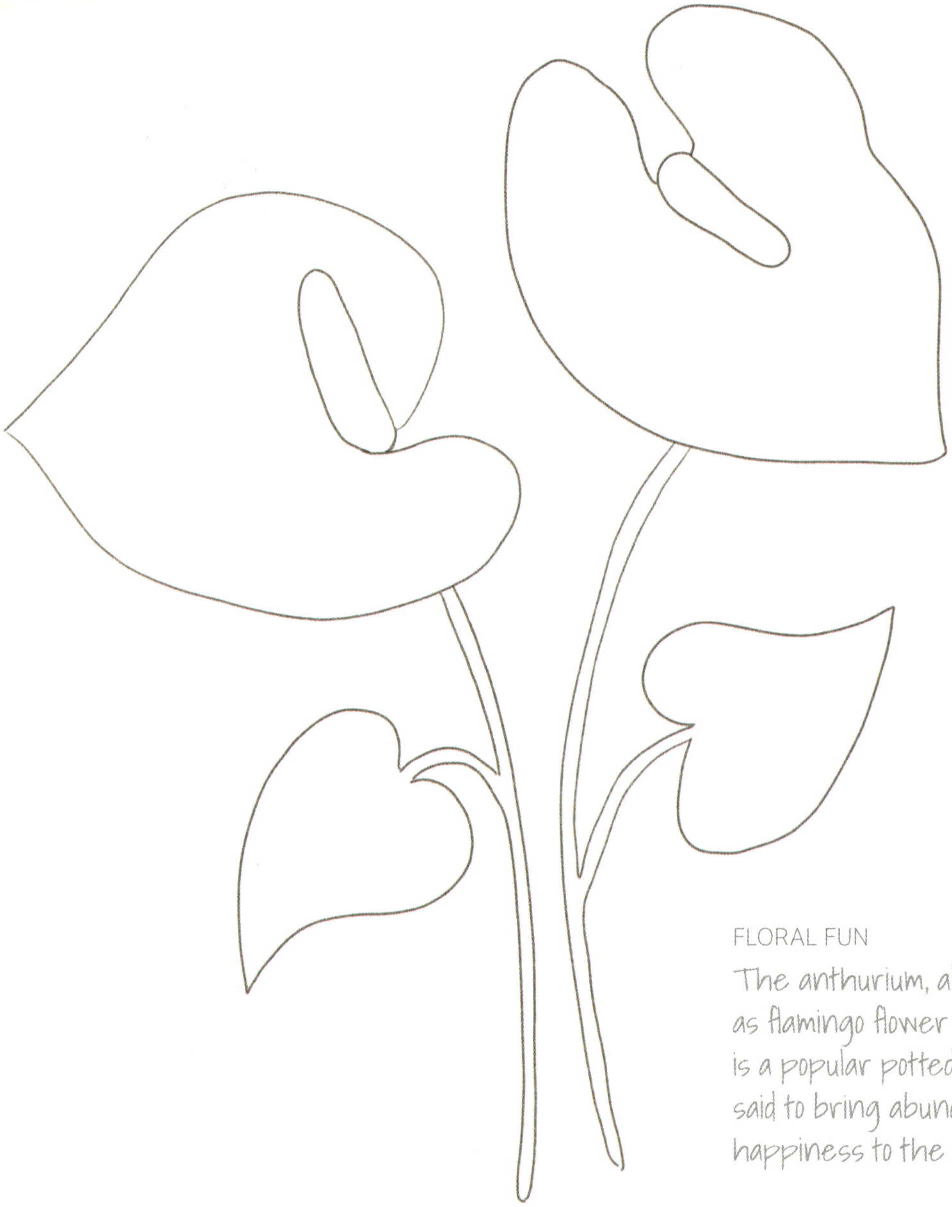

BRUSHES

- Large brush (8)

COLOR PALETTE

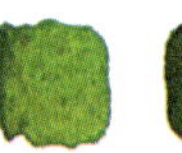

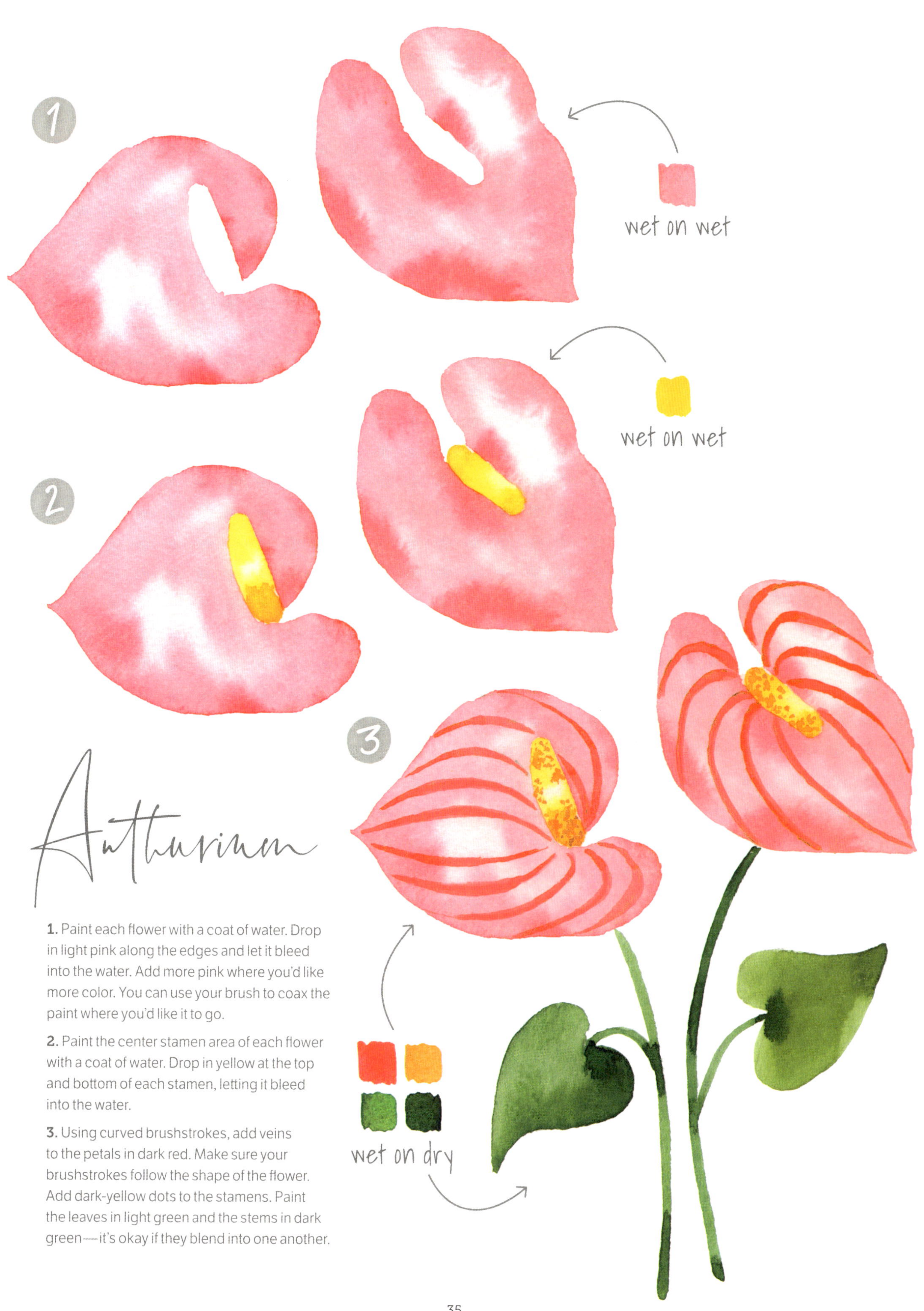

Anthurium

1. Paint each flower with a coat of water. Drop in light pink along the edges and let it bleed into the water. Add more pink where you'd like more color. You can use your brush to coax the paint where you'd like it to go.

2. Paint the center stamen area of each flower with a coat of water. Drop in yellow at the top and bottom of each stamen, letting it bleed into the water.

3. Using curved brushstrokes, add veins to the petals in dark red. Make sure your brushstrokes follow the shape of the flower. Add dark-yellow dots to the stamens. Paint the leaves in light green and the stems in dark green—it's okay if they blend into one another.

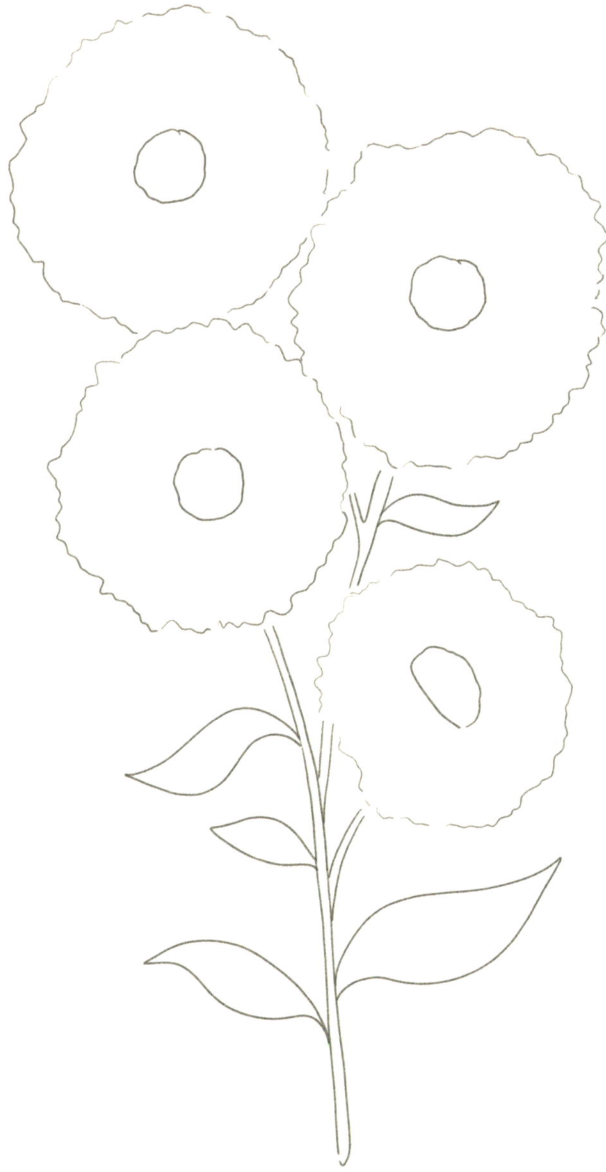

According to Greek mythology, asters were created from the tears of the goddess Astraea, who cried because of a lack of stars in the dark sky. They are known to represent love.

BRUSHES

- Large brush (8)

COLOR PALETTE

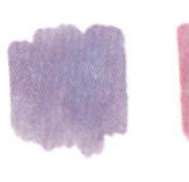
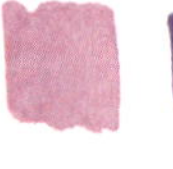

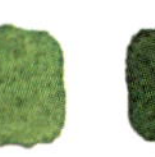
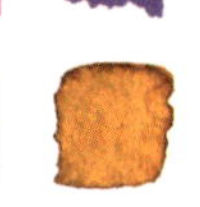

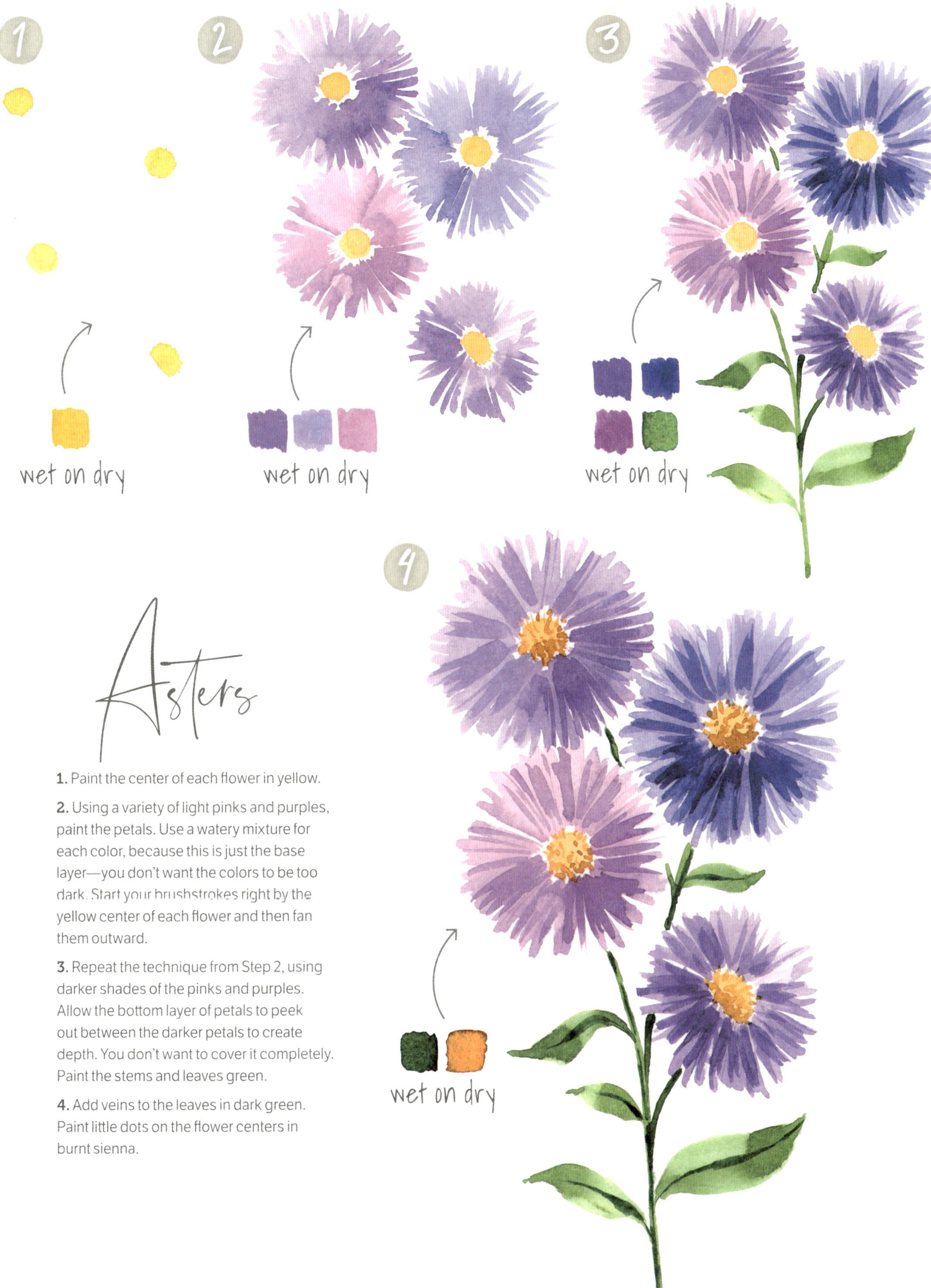

Asters

1. Paint the center of each flower in yellow.

2. Using a variety of light pinks and purples, paint the petals. Use a watery mixture for each color, because this is just the base layer—you don't want the colors to be too dark. Start your brushstrokes right by the yellow center of each flower and then fan them outward.

3. Repeat the technique from Step 2, using darker shades of the pinks and purples. Allow the bottom layer of petals to peek out between the darker petals to create depth. You don't want to cover it completely. Paint the stems and leaves green.

4. Add veins to the leaves in dark green. Paint little dots on the flower centers in burnt sienna.

FLORAL FUN

Banksia is also known as Australian honeysuckle and is said to symbolize new beginnings.

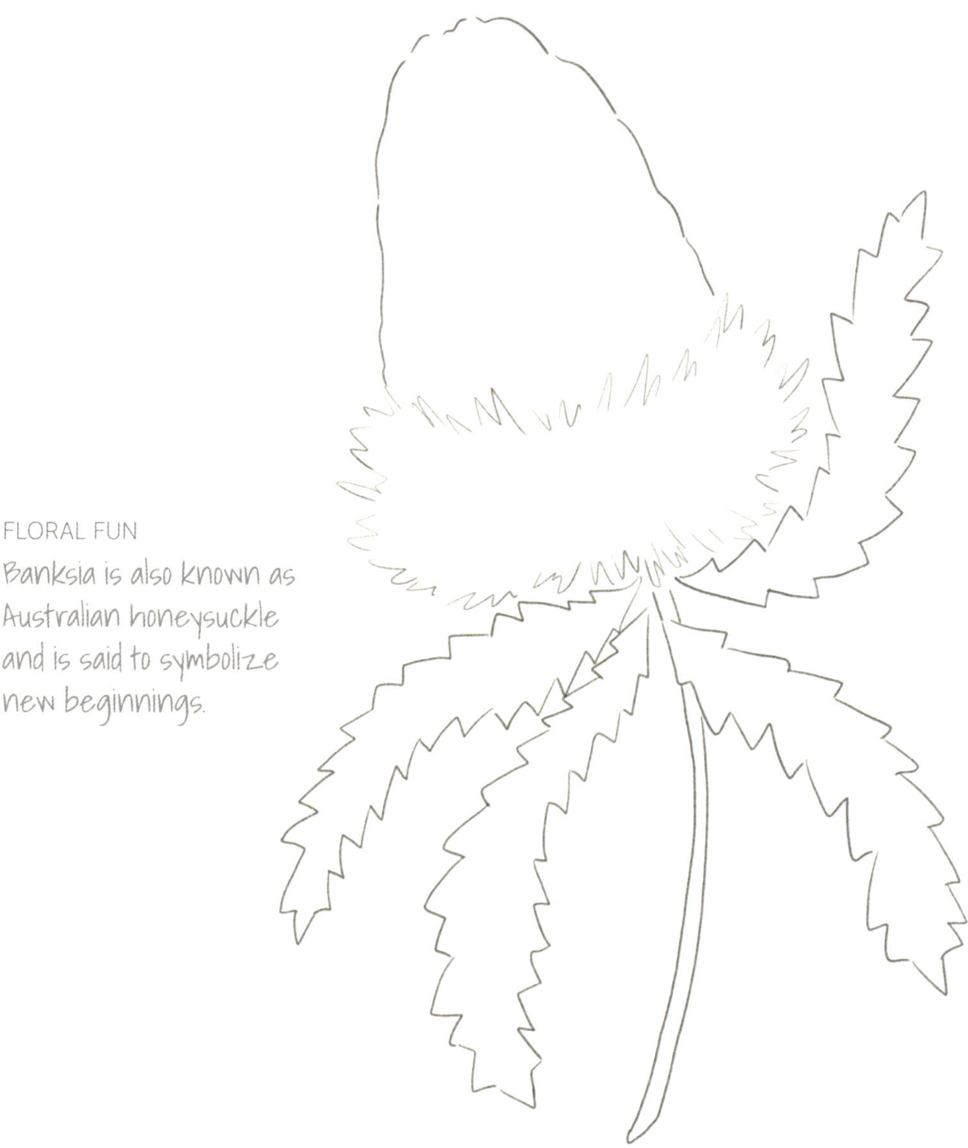

BRUSHES

- Large brush (8)

COLOR PALETTE

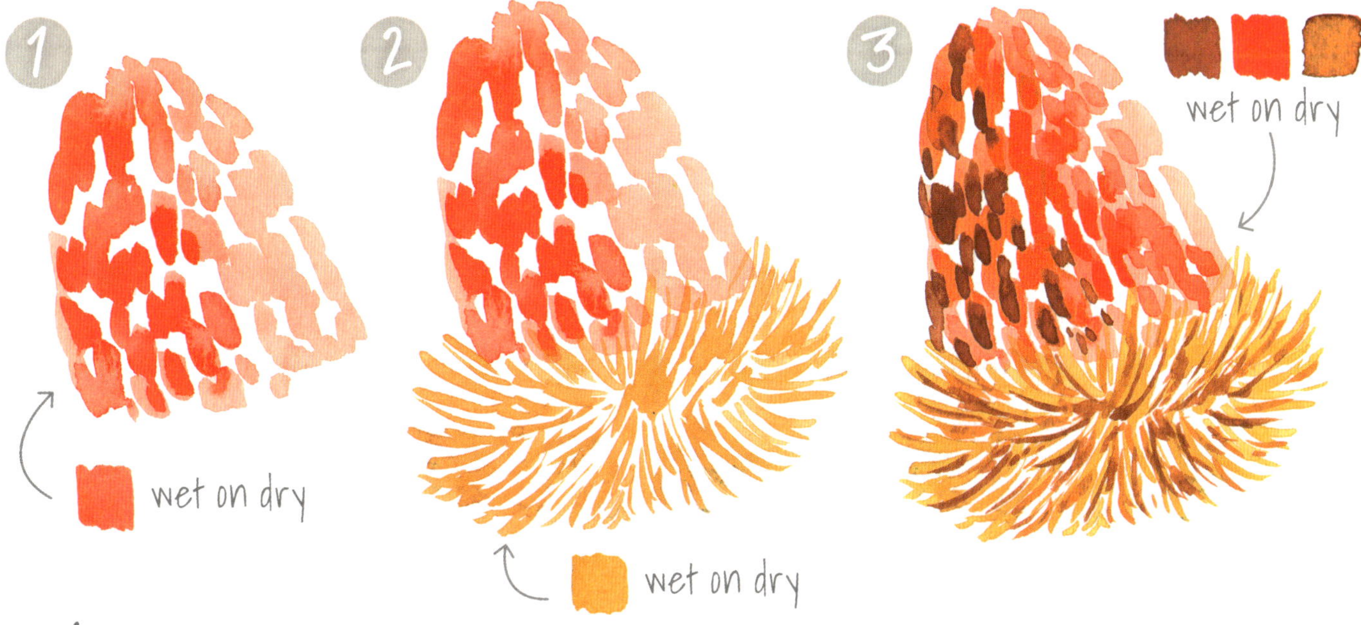

Banksia

1. Paint the top of the flower, using a watery mix of orange. Concentrate the darkest orange on the left side.

2. Paint the bottom of the flower in light orange, using thin feathery brushstrokes. Start your brushstrokes at the center and feather them outward.

3. Darken the left side of the flower even further with darker oranges and reds. On the bottom part, add some darker feathery brushstrokes.

4. Paint the stem brown. Paint the leaves green, concentrating the darkest green at the bottoms of the leaves. Notice that the leaves have pointed edges.

5. Add detail to the stem and leaves with dark brown and dark green.

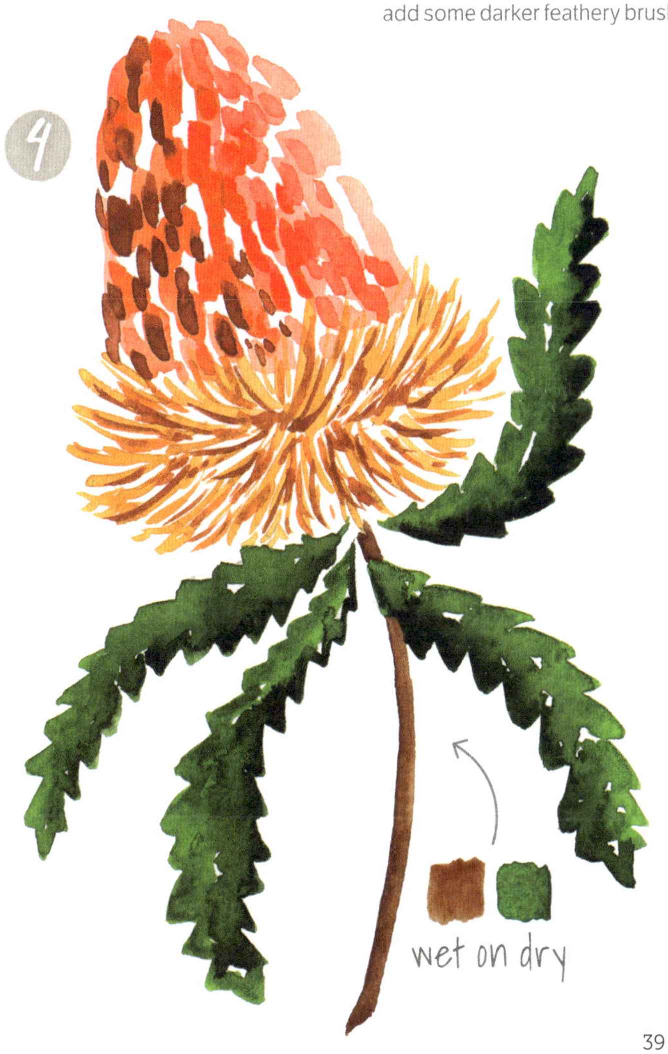

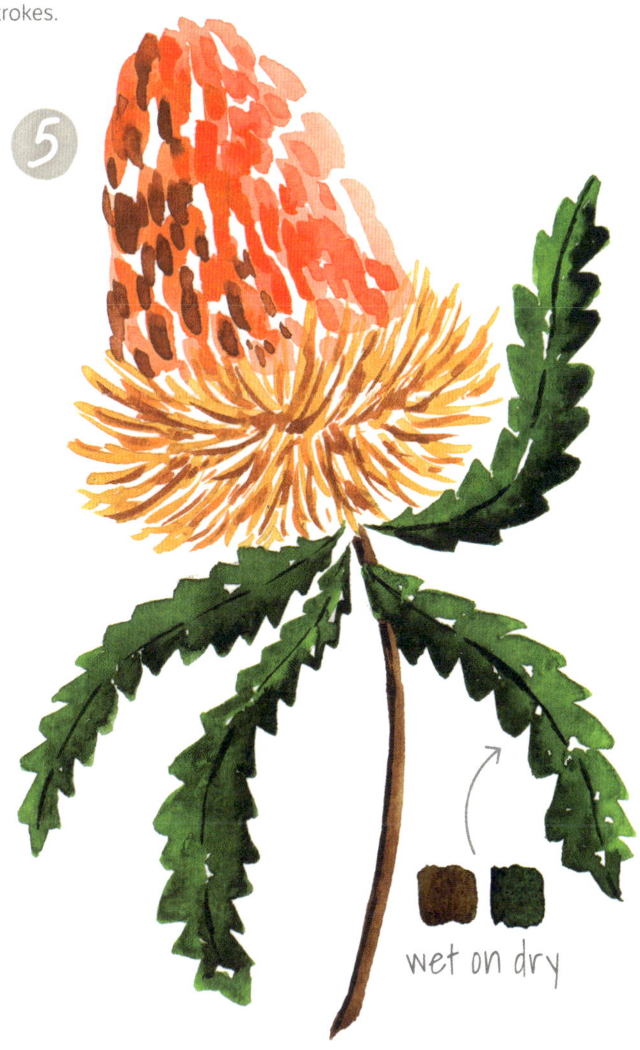

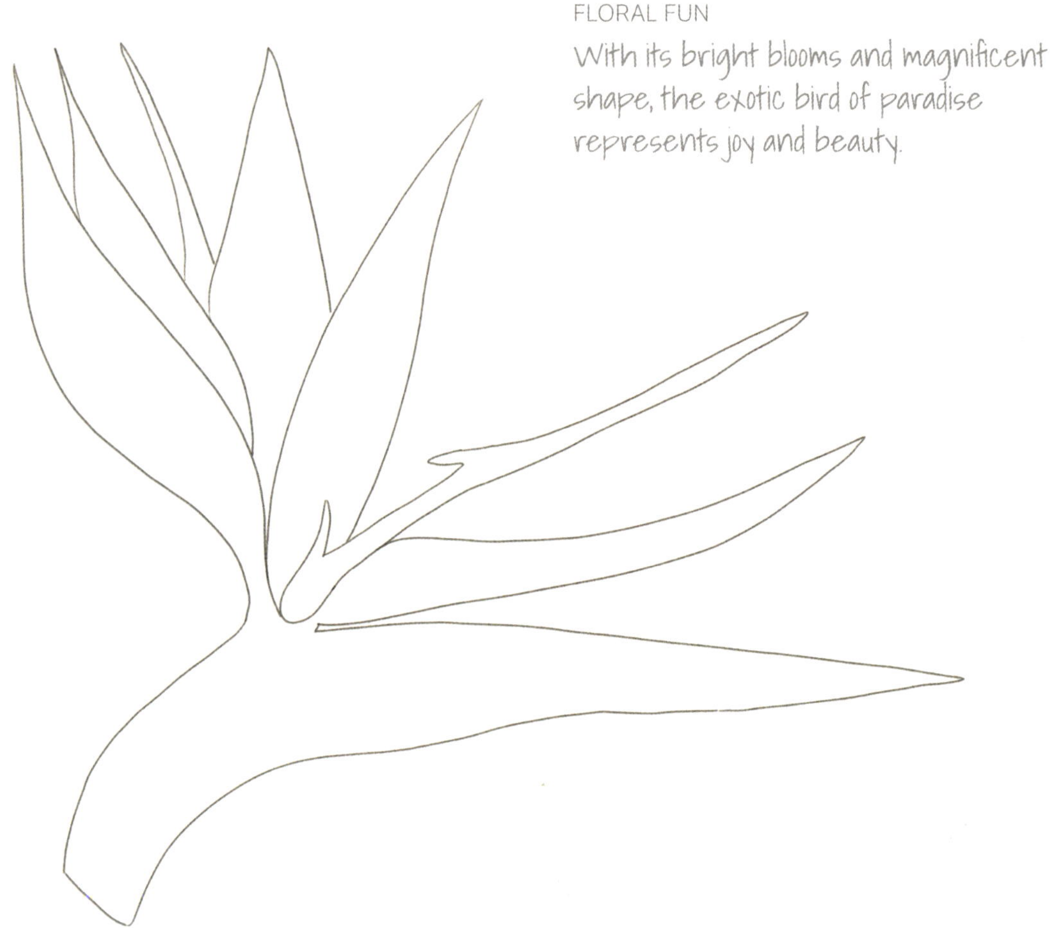

With its bright blooms and magnificent shape, the exotic bird of paradise represents joy and beauty.

BRUSHES
• Medium/large brush (6, 8)

COLOR PALETTE

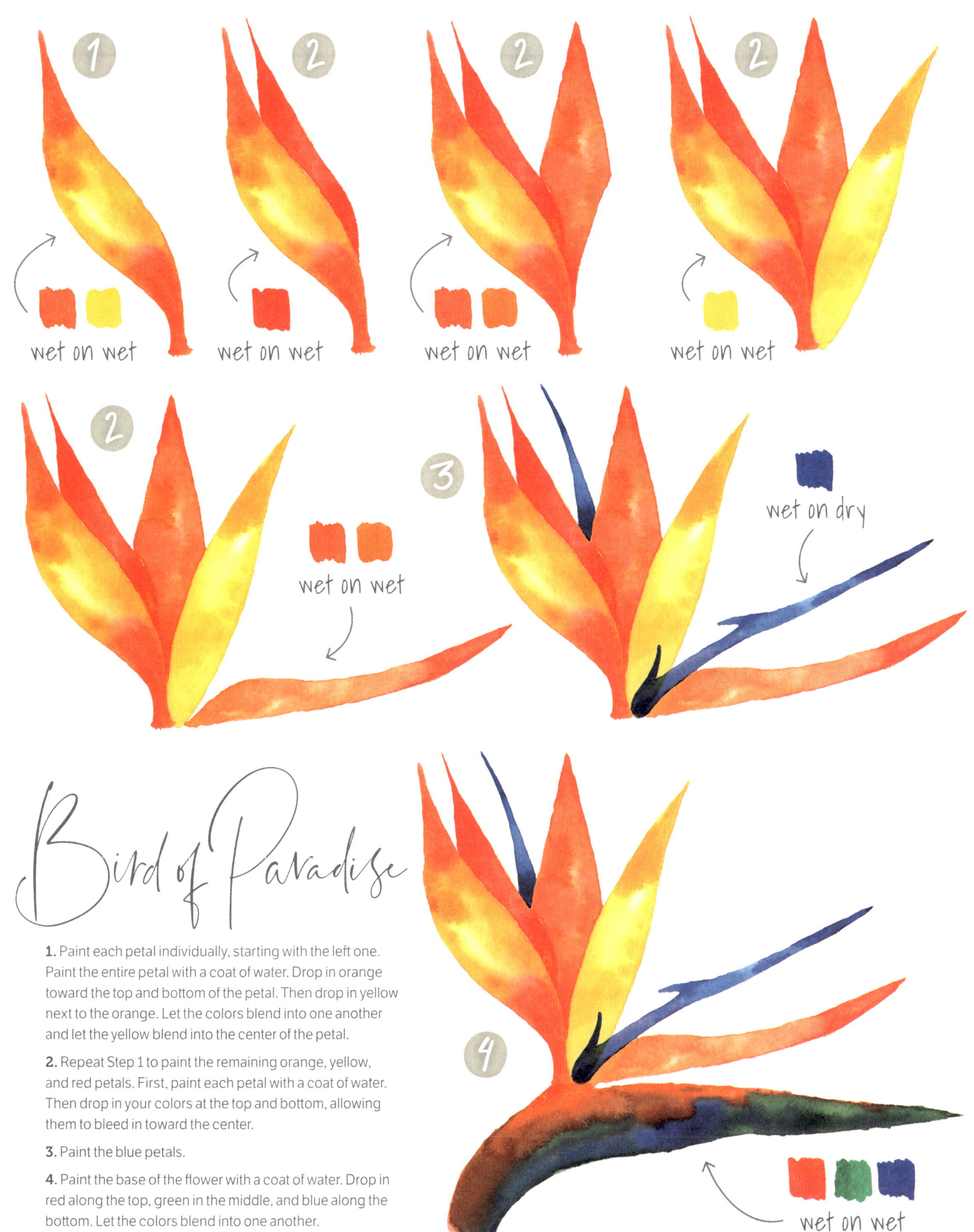

Bird of Paradise

1. Paint each petal individually, starting with the left one. Paint the entire petal with a coat of water. Drop in orange toward the top and bottom of the petal. Then drop in yellow next to the orange. Let the colors blend into one another and let the yellow blend into the center of the petal.

2. Repeat Step 1 to paint the remaining orange, yellow, and red petals. First, paint each petal with a coat of water. Then drop in your colors at the top and bottom, allowing them to bleed in toward the center.

3. Paint the blue petals.

4. Paint the base of the flower with a coat of water. Drop in red along the top, green in the middle, and blue along the bottom. Let the colors blend into one another.

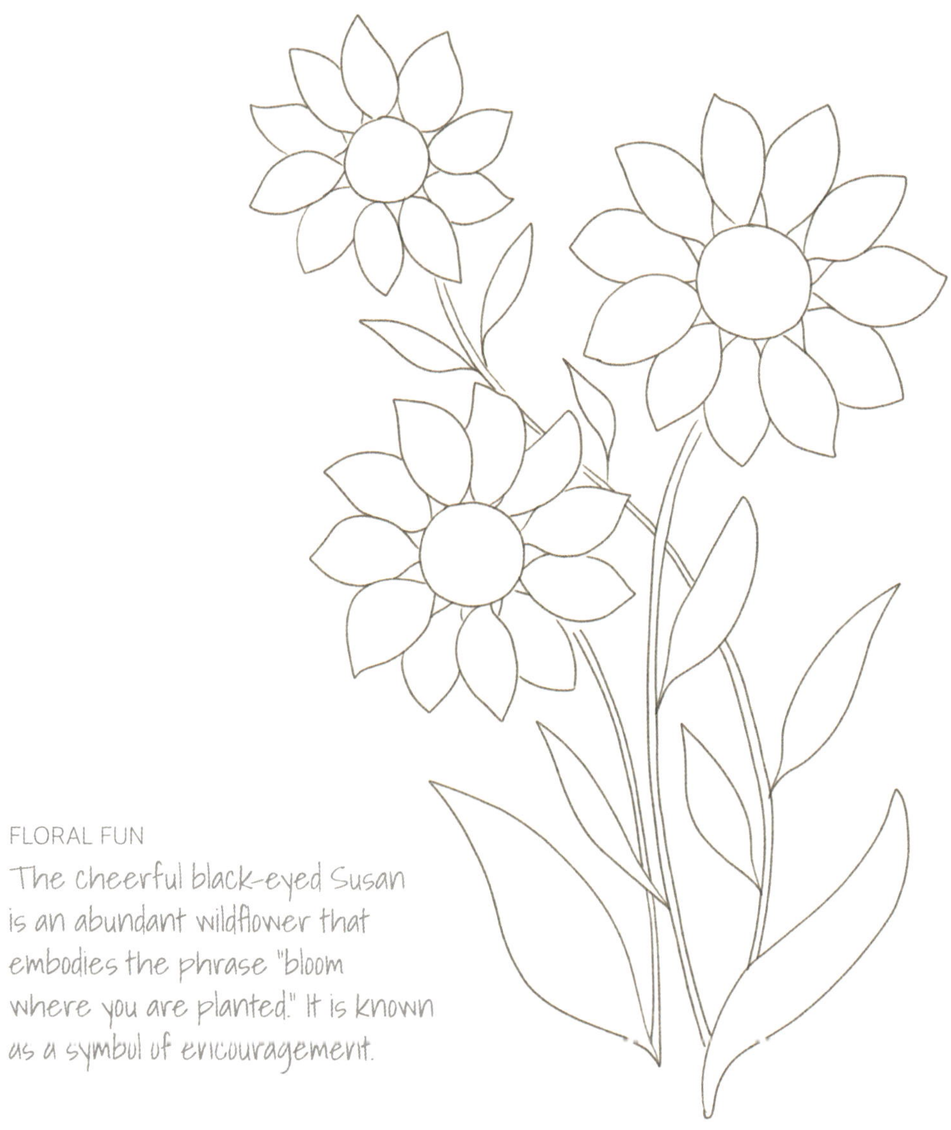

The cheerful black-eyed Susan is an abundant wildflower that embodies the phrase "bloom where you are planted." It is known as a symbol of encouragement.

BRUSHES
• Large brush (8)

COLOR PALETTE

Black-Eyed Susans

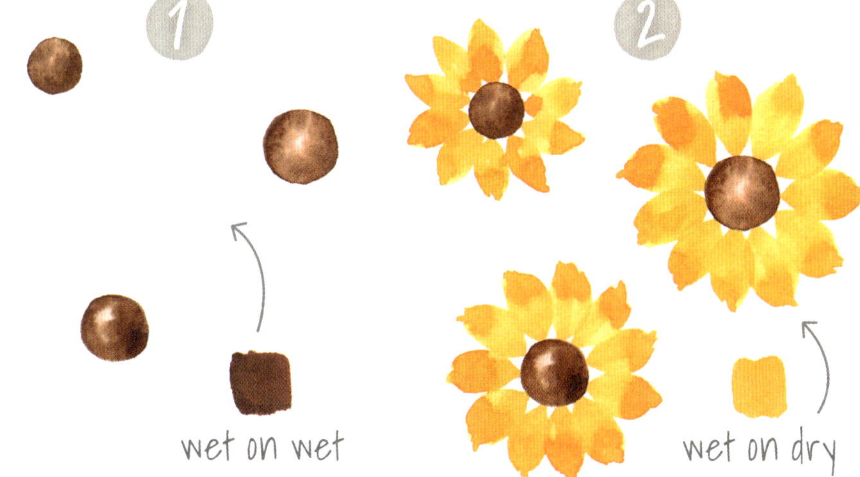

1. Paint the center of each flower with a coat of water. Drop in brown along the edges and let it bleed into the water.

2. Using the Loose Petals technique (page 21), paint each petal in yellow. Start each brushstroke right up against the brown center and then move out.

3. Paint the stems and leaves green.

4. Use the tip of your brush for this step so your lines are nice and thin. Paint tiny dark-brown dots around the edges of the flower centers. Next, paint short, curved lines at the base of each petal in dark yellow. Make sure your brushstrokes follow the shape of the petals. Finally, paint a center vein on each leaf in dark green.

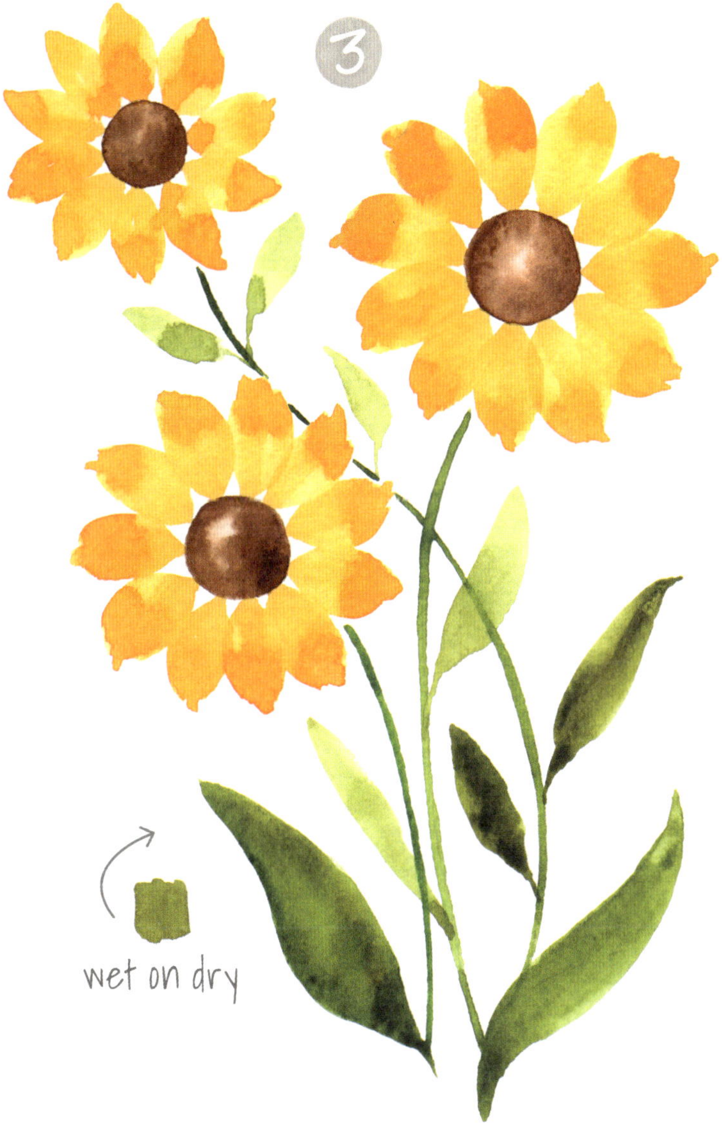

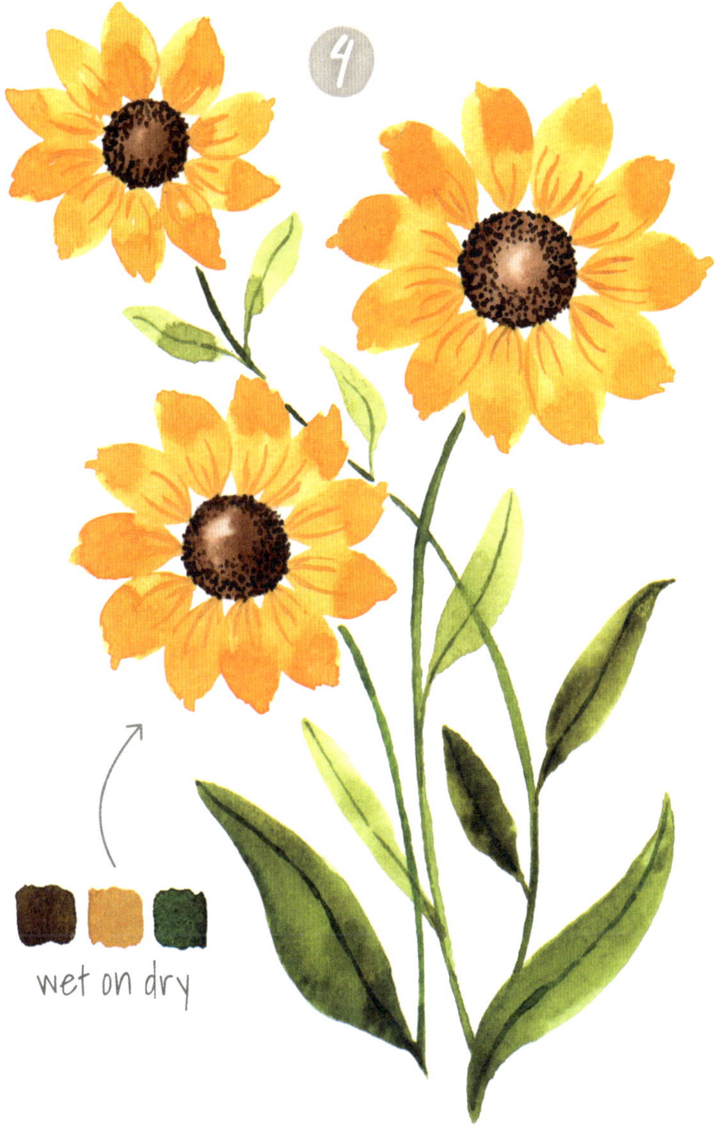

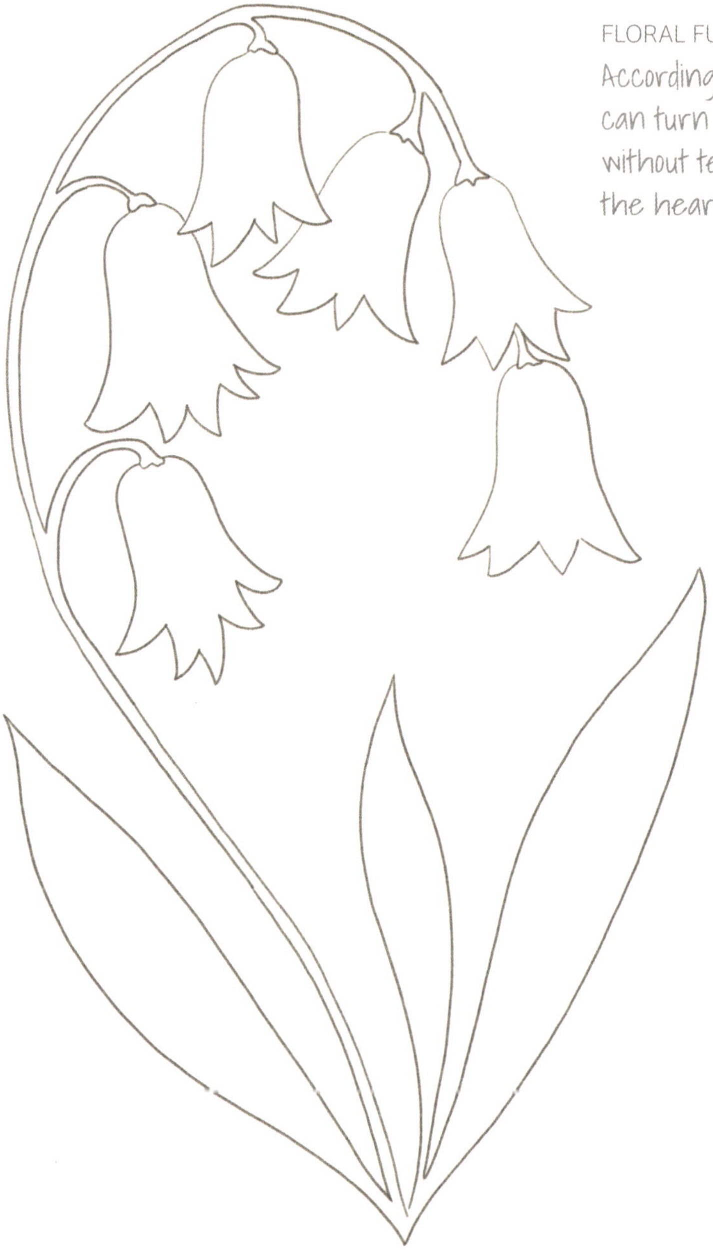

According to legend, if you can turn a bluebell inside out without tearing it, you will win the heart of your true love.

BRUSHES

- Medium/large brush (6, 8)

COLOR PALETTE

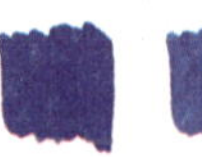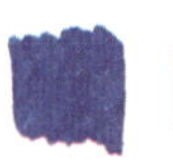
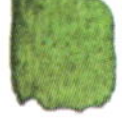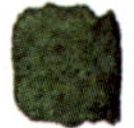

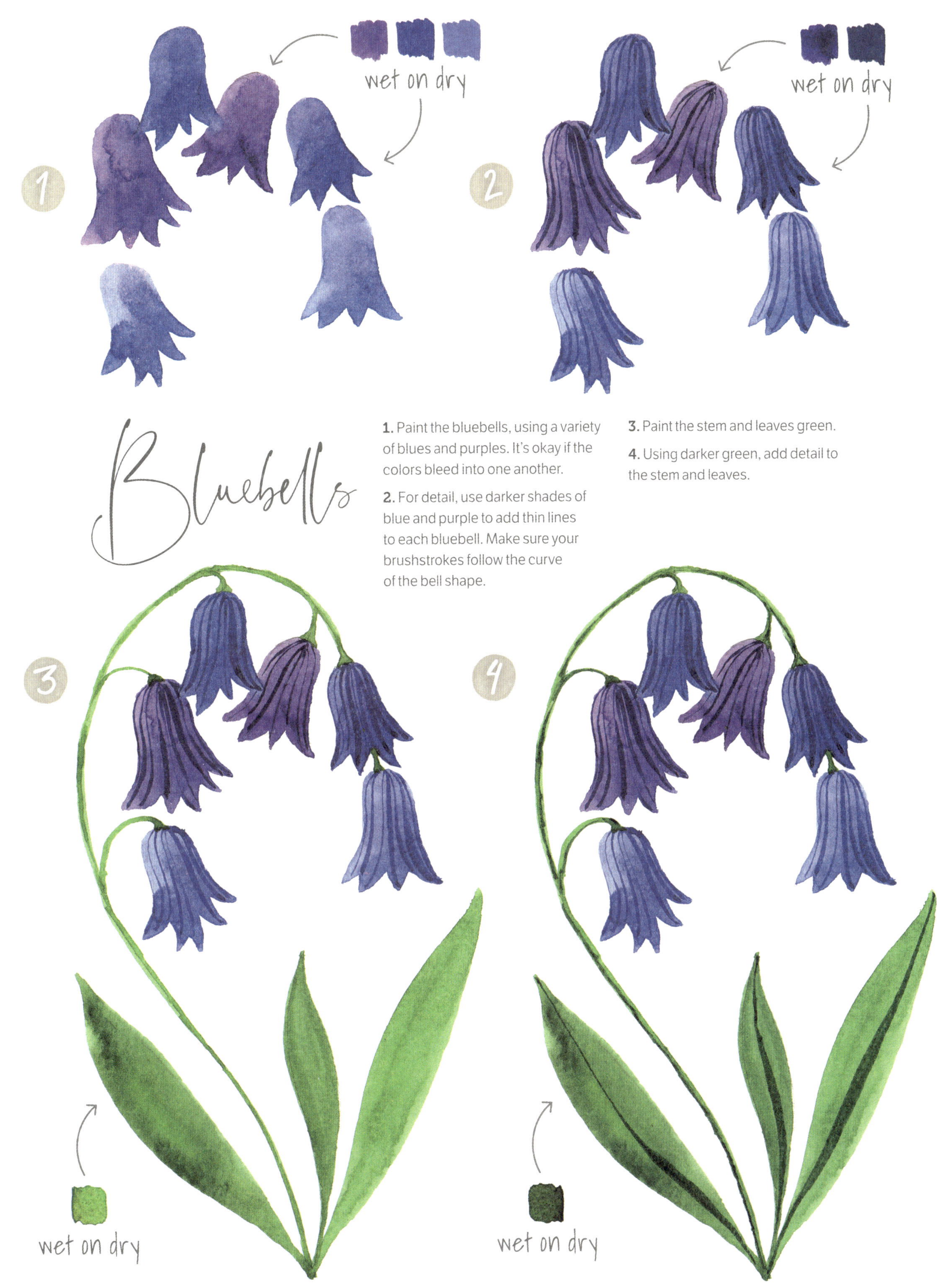

Bluebells

1. Paint the bluebells, using a variety of blues and purples. It's okay if the colors bleed into one another.

2. For detail, use darker shades of blue and purple to add thin lines to each bluebell. Make sure your brushstrokes follow the curve of the bell shape.

3. Paint the stem and leaves green.

4. Using darker green, add detail to the stem and leaves.

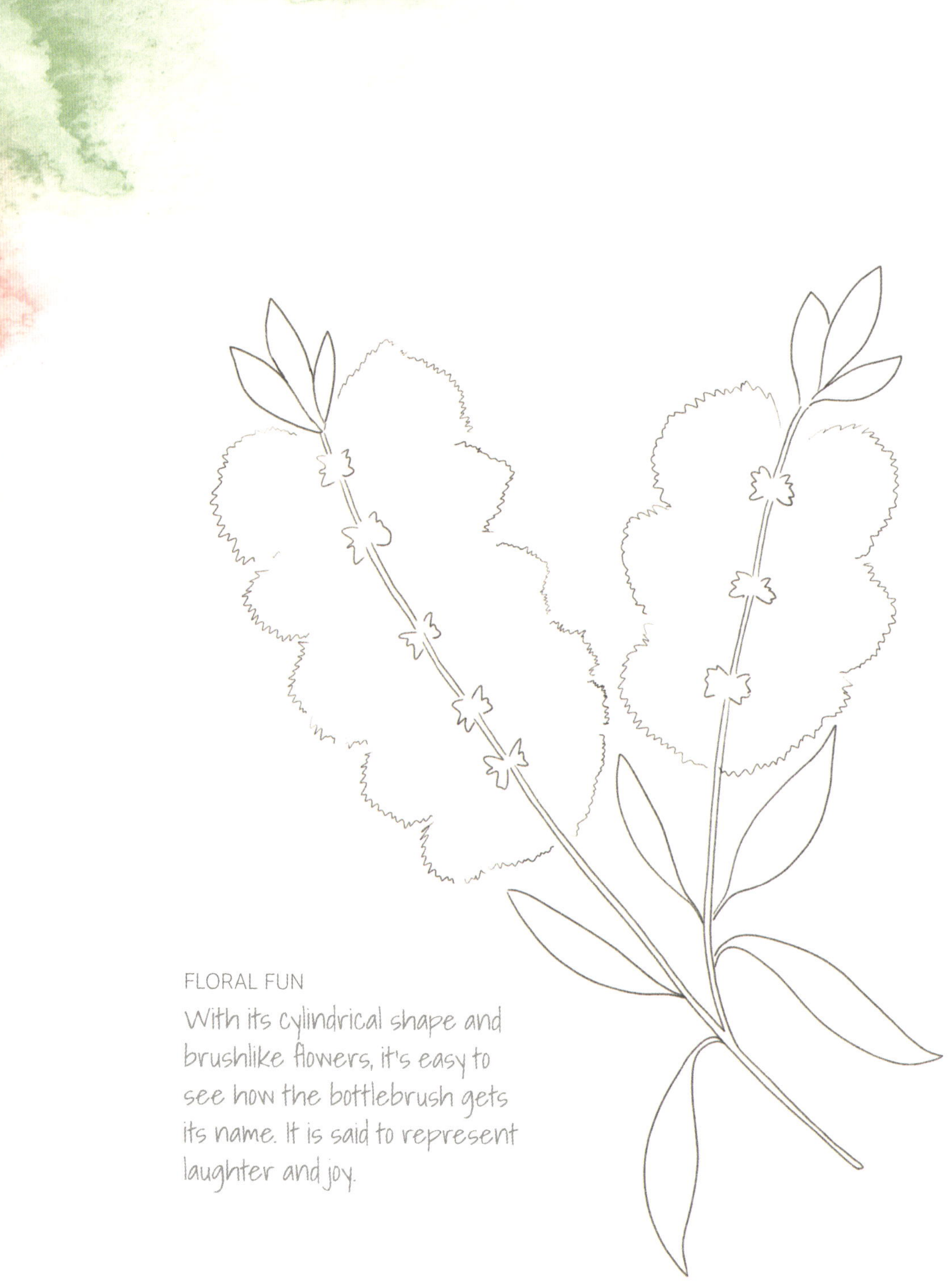

FLORAL FUN

With its cylindrical shape and brushlike flowers, it's easy to see how the bottlebrush gets its name. It is said to represent laughter and joy.

BRUSHES

• Large brush (8)

COLOR PALETTE

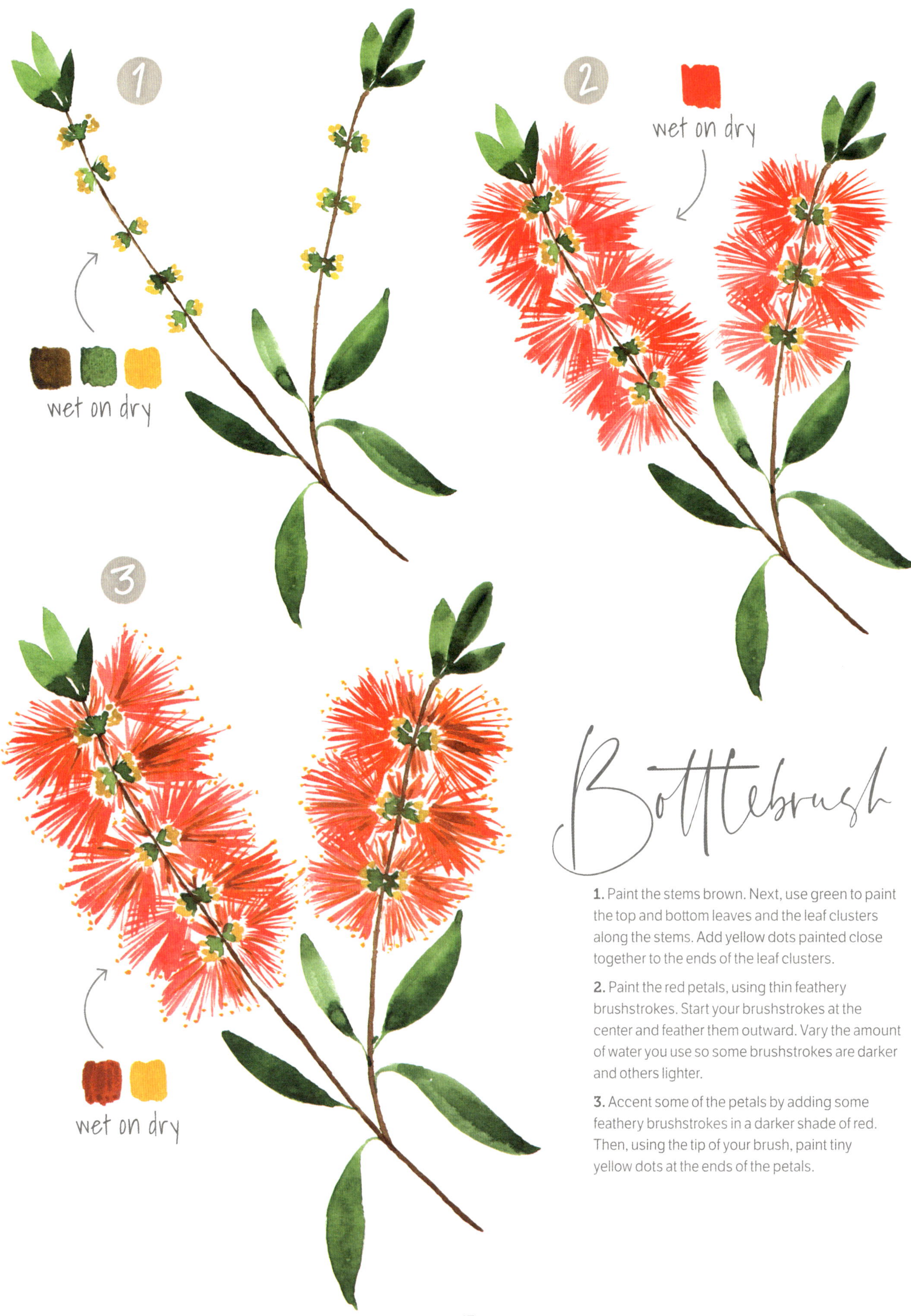

Bottlebrush

1. Paint the stems brown. Next, use green to paint the top and bottom leaves and the leaf clusters along the stems. Add yellow dots painted close together to the ends of the leaf clusters.

2. Paint the red petals, using thin feathery brushstrokes. Start your brushstrokes at the center and feather them outward. Vary the amount of water you use so some brushstrokes are darker and others lighter.

3. Accent some of the petals by adding some feathery brushstrokes in a darker shade of red. Then, using the tip of your brush, paint tiny yellow dots at the ends of the petals.

The beautiful bougainvillea is used to create floral garlands worn in Hawaii, and symbolizes welcome.

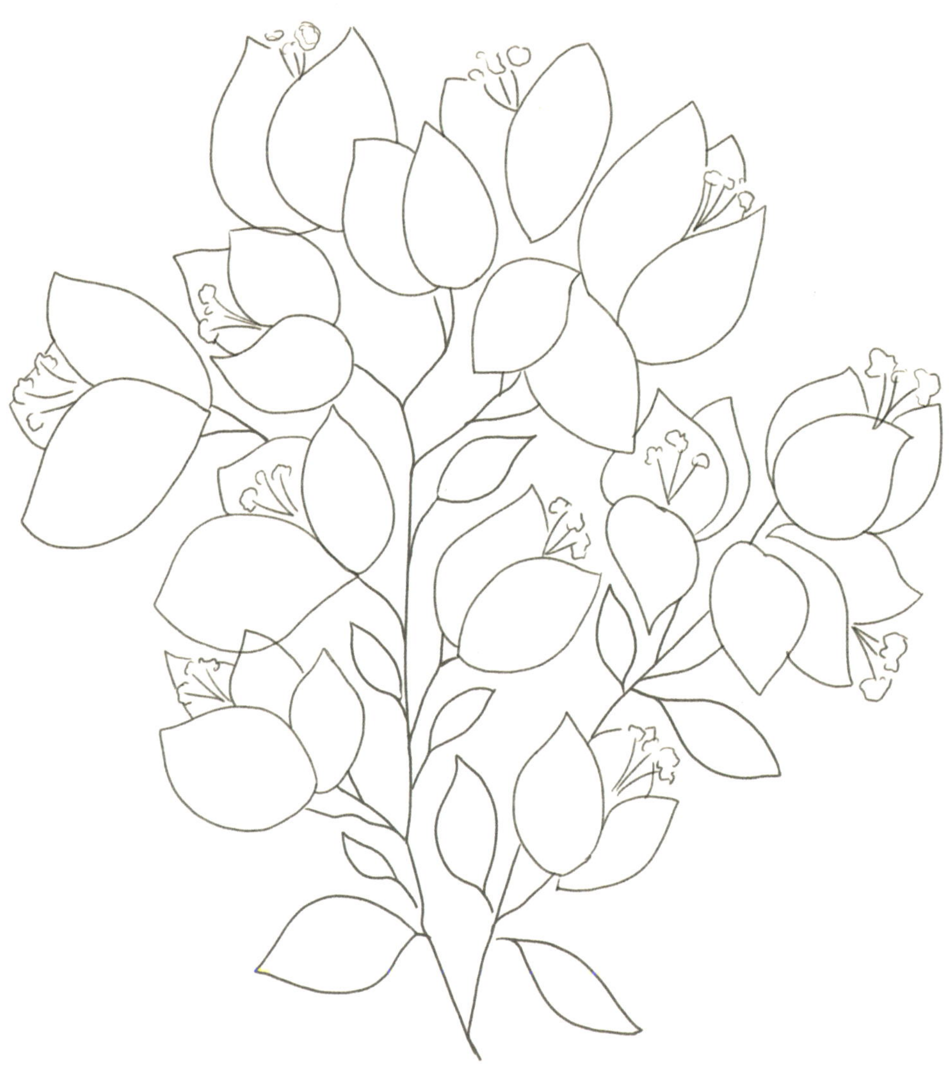

BRUSHES

- Medium/large brush (6, 8)

COLOR PALETTE

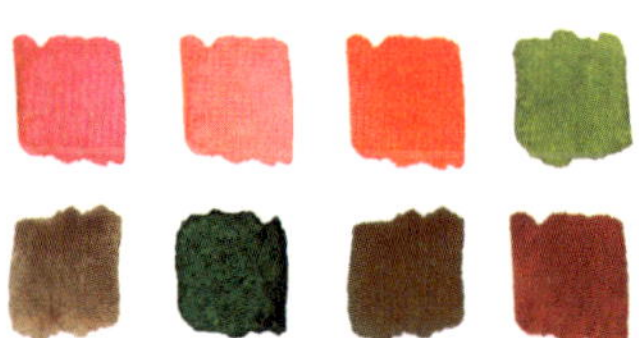

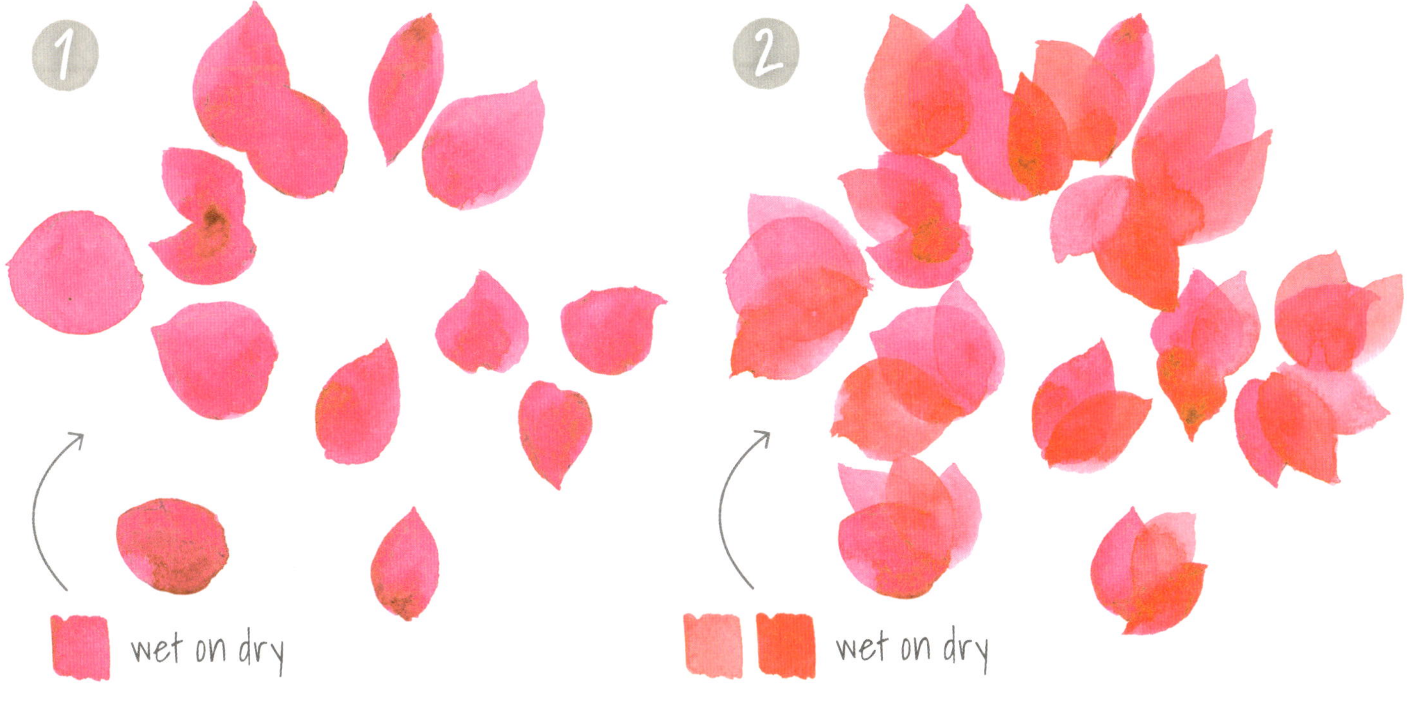

Bougainvillea

1. To capture the translucence of bougainvillea petals, paint each flower layer by layer. First, paint a few petals in pink. Let dry.

2. Paint a few more petals in shades of red. Make sure your colors are light enough that the pink petals you painted in Step 1 show through. Let dry. Repeat this technique until you've added enough petals for each flower.

3. Paint the stem brown and the leaves green.

4. Add detail to the stem and leaves with darker shades of brown and green. Using dark red, paint the stamens near the center of each flower.

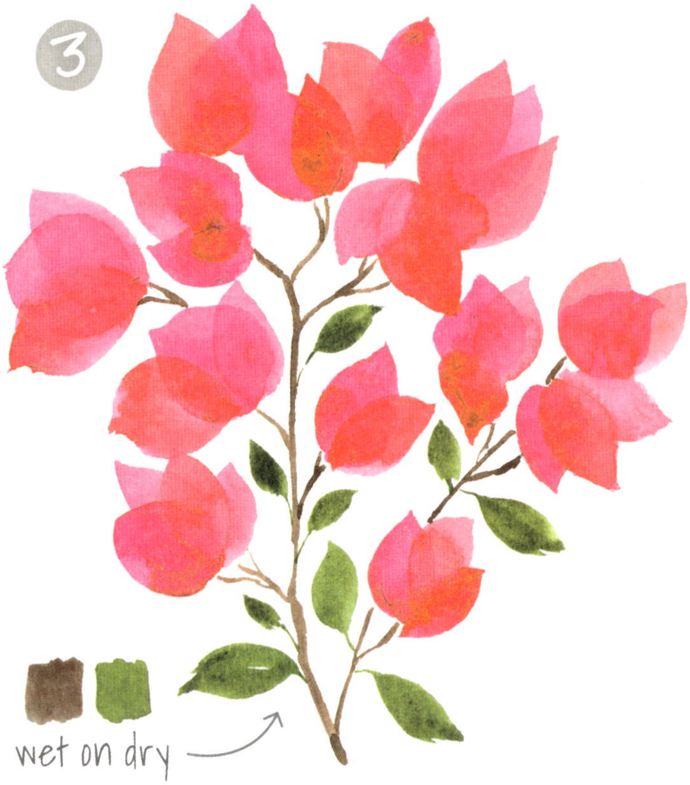

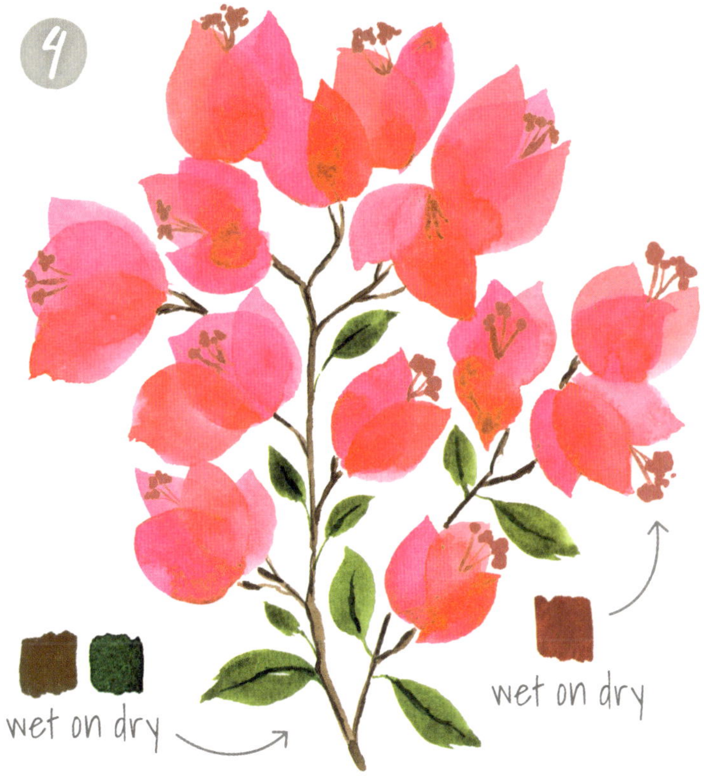

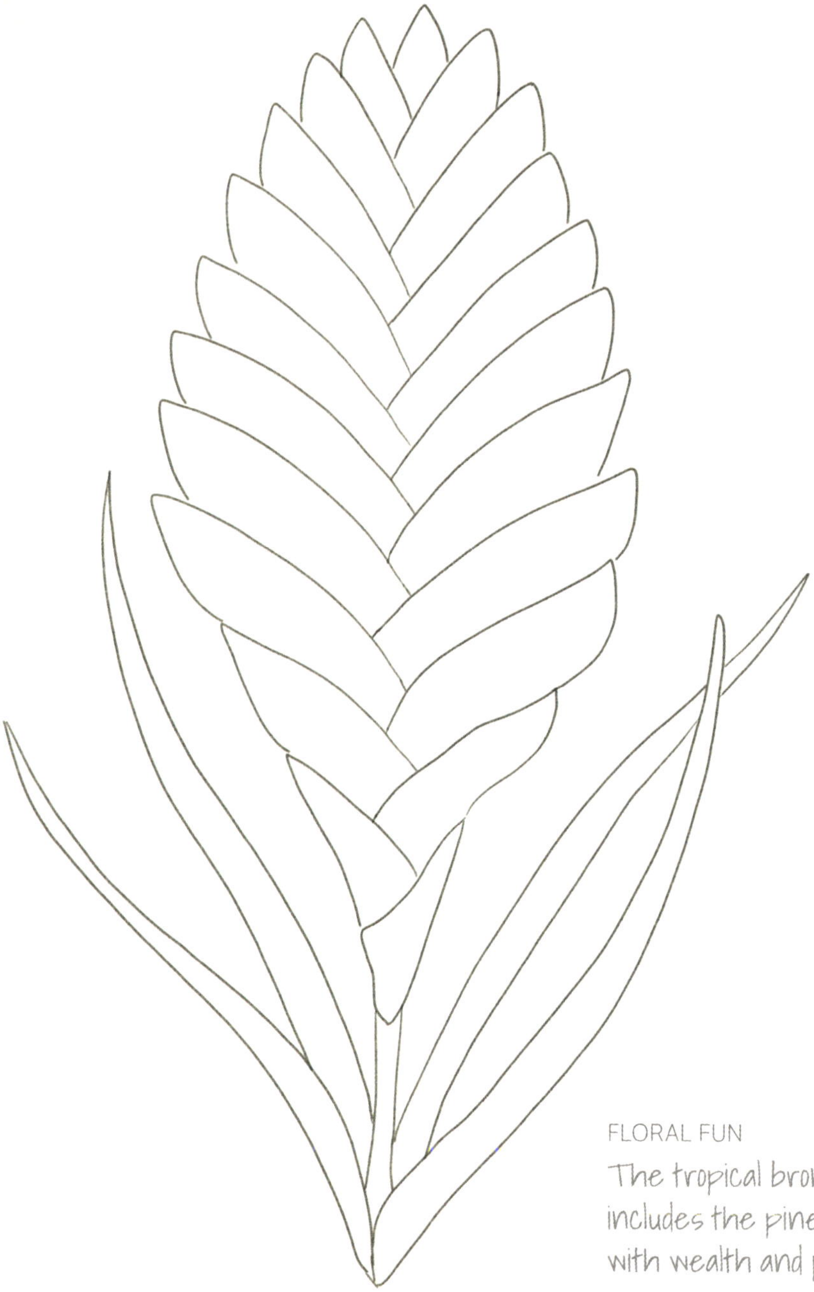

BRUSHES

- Large brush (8)

COLOR PALETTE

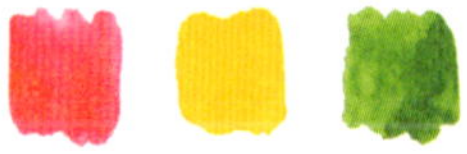

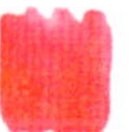  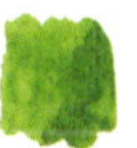

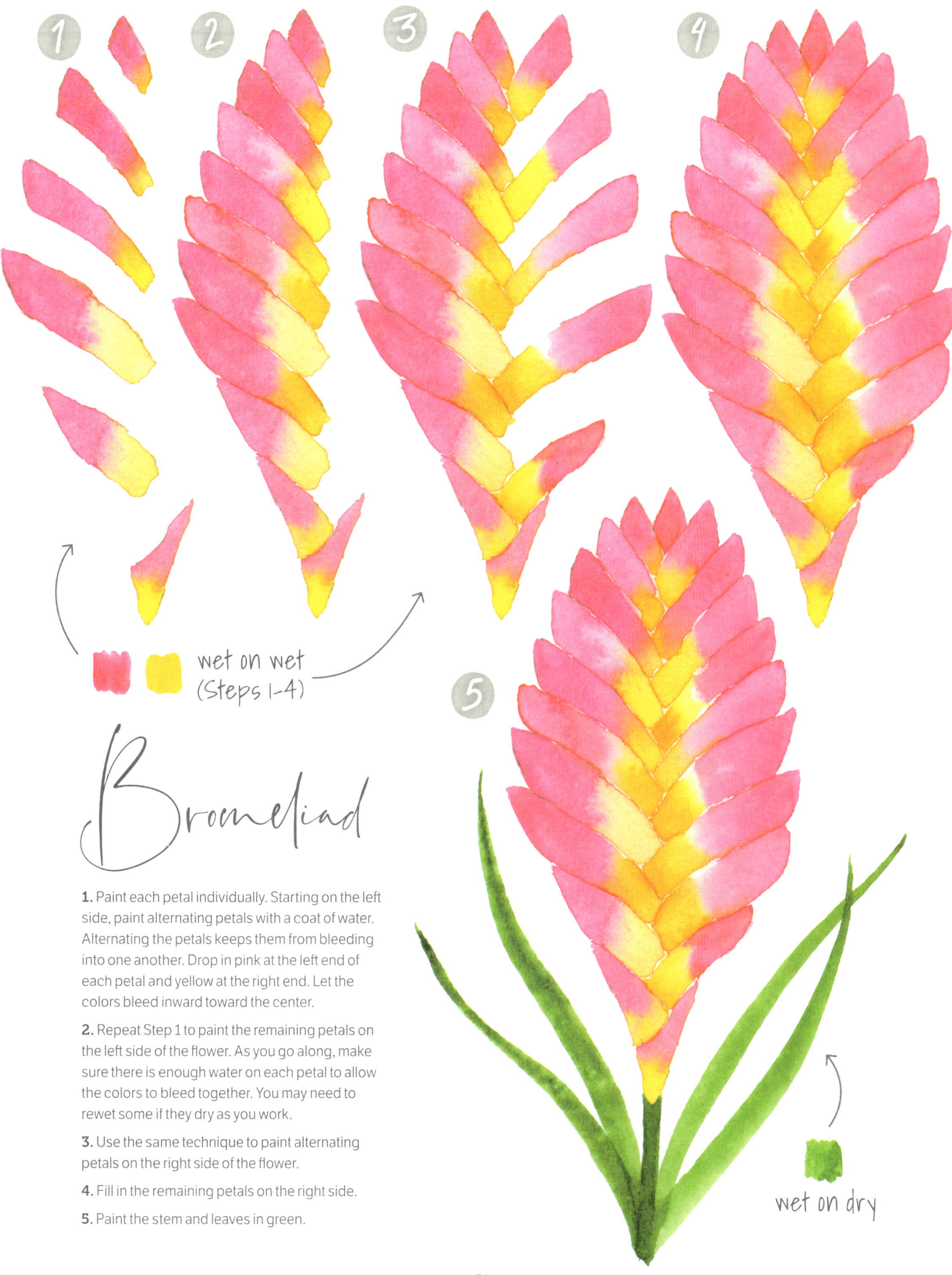

Bromeliad

1. Paint each petal individually. Starting on the left side, paint alternating petals with a coat of water. Alternating the petals keeps them from bleeding into one another. Drop in pink at the left end of each petal and yellow at the right end. Let the colors bleed inward toward the center.

2. Repeat Step 1 to paint the remaining petals on the left side of the flower. As you go along, make sure there is enough water on each petal to allow the colors to bleed together. You may need to rewet some if they dry as you work.

3. Use the same technique to paint alternating petals on the right side of the flower.

4. Fill in the remaining petals on the right side.

5. Paint the stem and leaves in green.

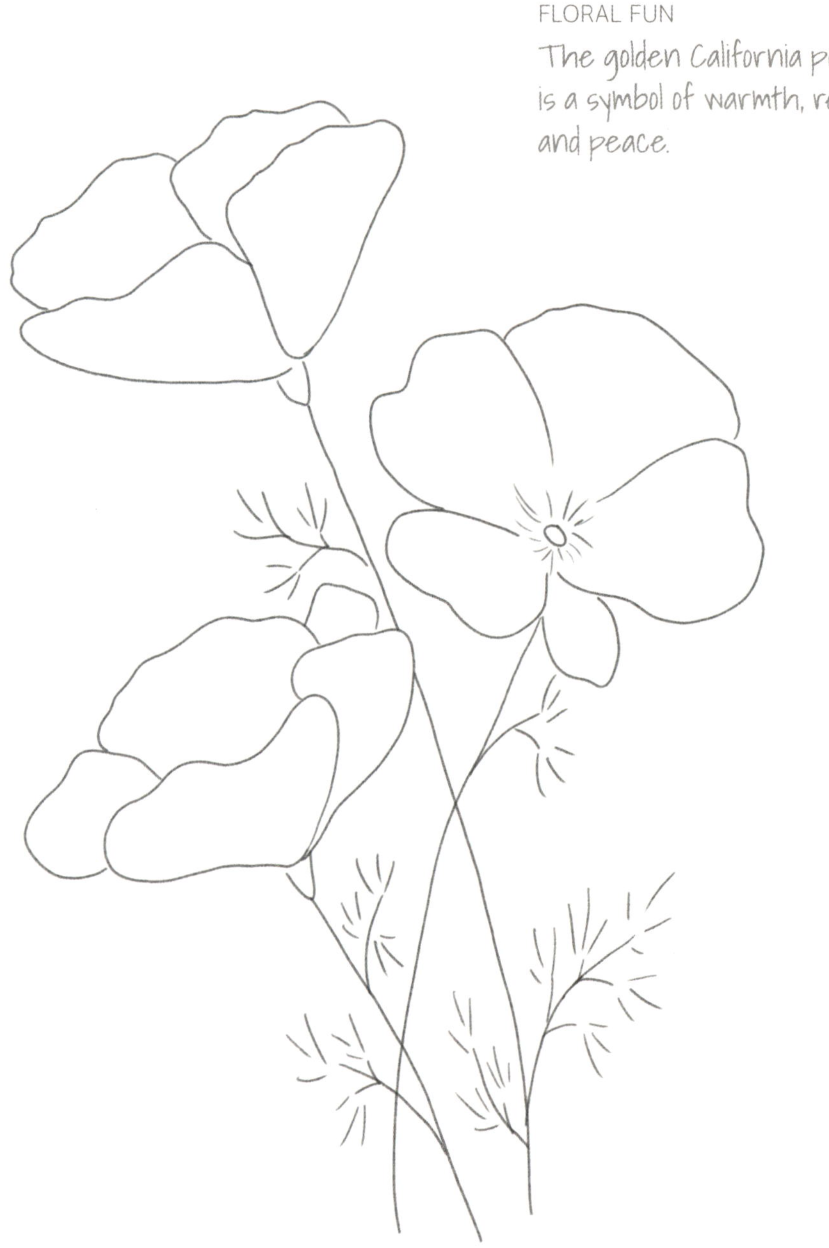

BRUSHES

- Large brush (8)

COLOR PALETTE

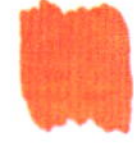  
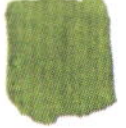  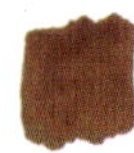

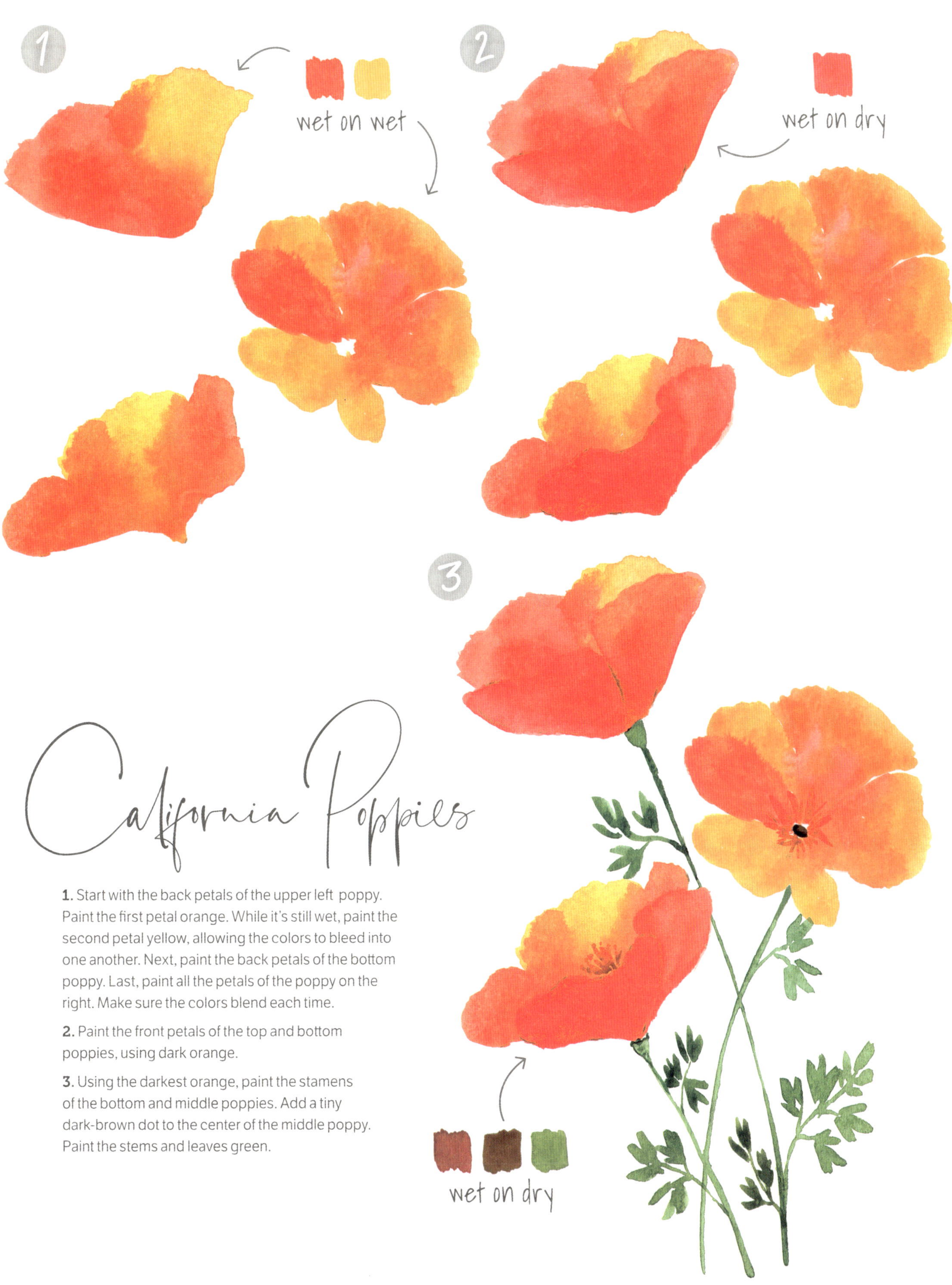

California Poppies

1. Start with the back petals of the upper left poppy. Paint the first petal orange. While it's still wet, paint the second petal yellow, allowing the colors to bleed into one another. Next, paint the back petals of the bottom poppy. Last, paint all the petals of the poppy on the right. Make sure the colors blend each time.

2. Paint the front petals of the top and bottom poppies, using dark orange.

3. Using the darkest orange, paint the stamens of the bottom and middle poppies. Add a tiny dark-brown dot to the center of the middle poppy. Paint the stems and leaves green.

The impressive camellia is a symbol of love and affection. White means respect; pink, adoration; and red, passion.

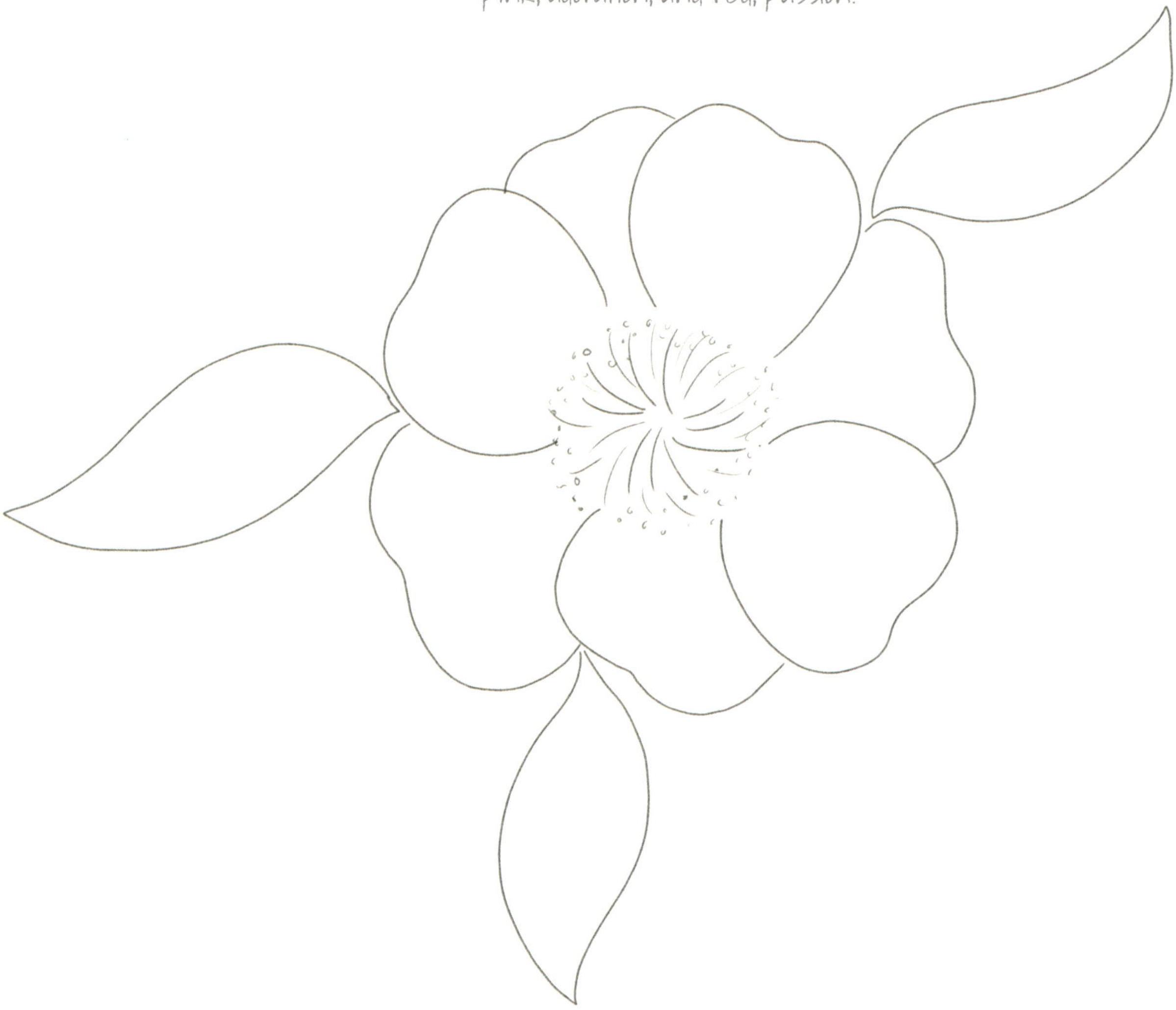

BRUSHES

- Medium/large brush (6, 10)

COLOR PALETTE

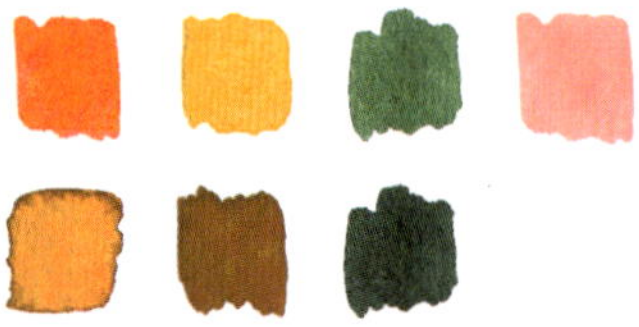

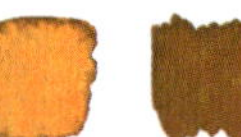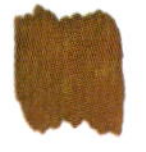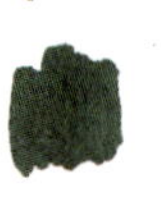

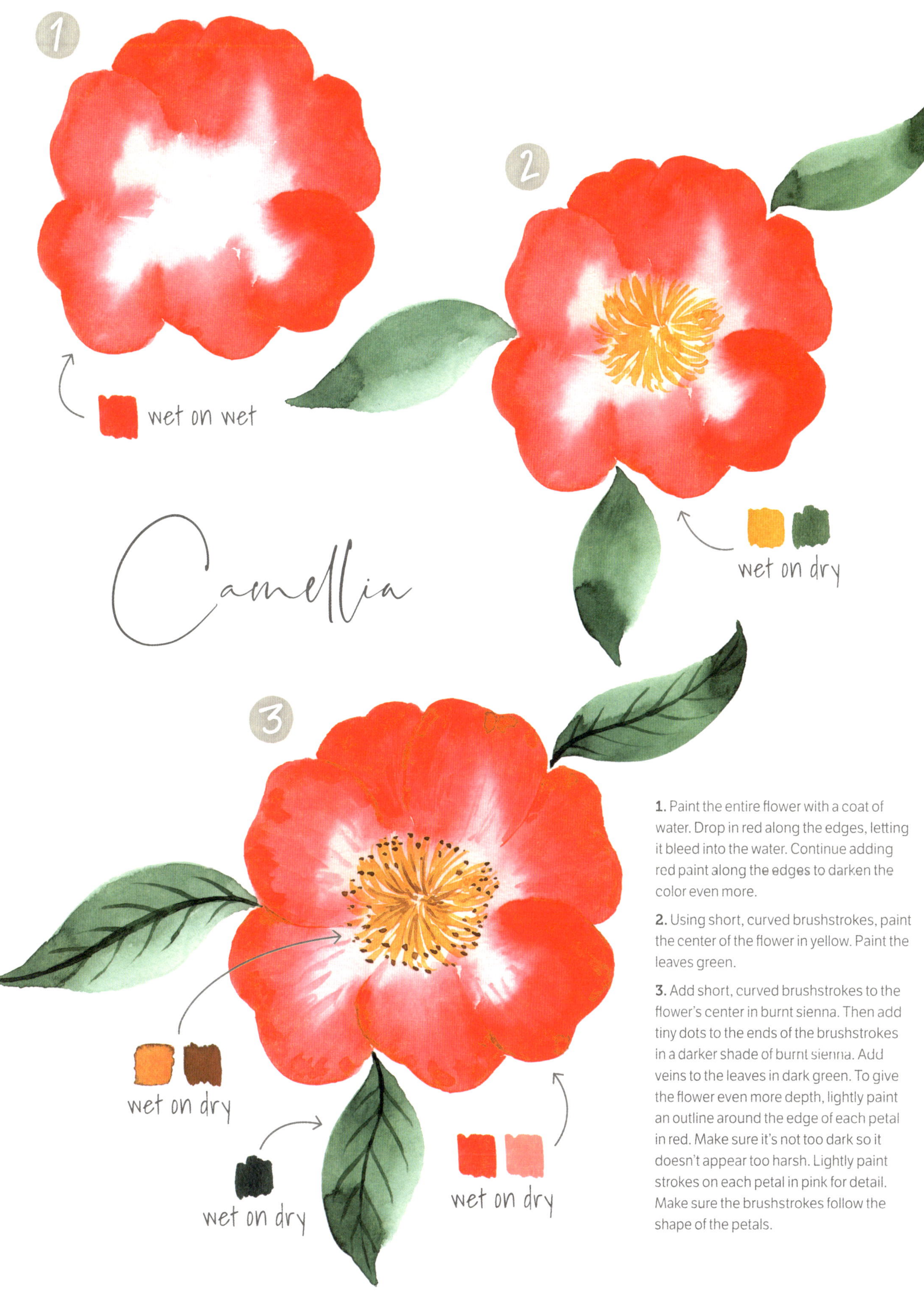

1. Paint the entire flower with a coat of water. Drop in red along the edges, letting it bleed into the water. Continue adding red paint along the edges to darken the color even more.

2. Using short, curved brushstrokes, paint the center of the flower in yellow. Paint the leaves green.

3. Add short, curved brushstrokes to the flower's center in burnt sienna. Then add tiny dots to the ends of the brushstrokes in a darker shade of burnt sienna. Add veins to the leaves in dark green. To give the flower even more depth, lightly paint an outline around the edge of each petal in red. Make sure it's not too dark so it doesn't appear too harsh. Lightly paint strokes on each petal in pink for detail. Make sure the brushstrokes follow the shape of the petals.

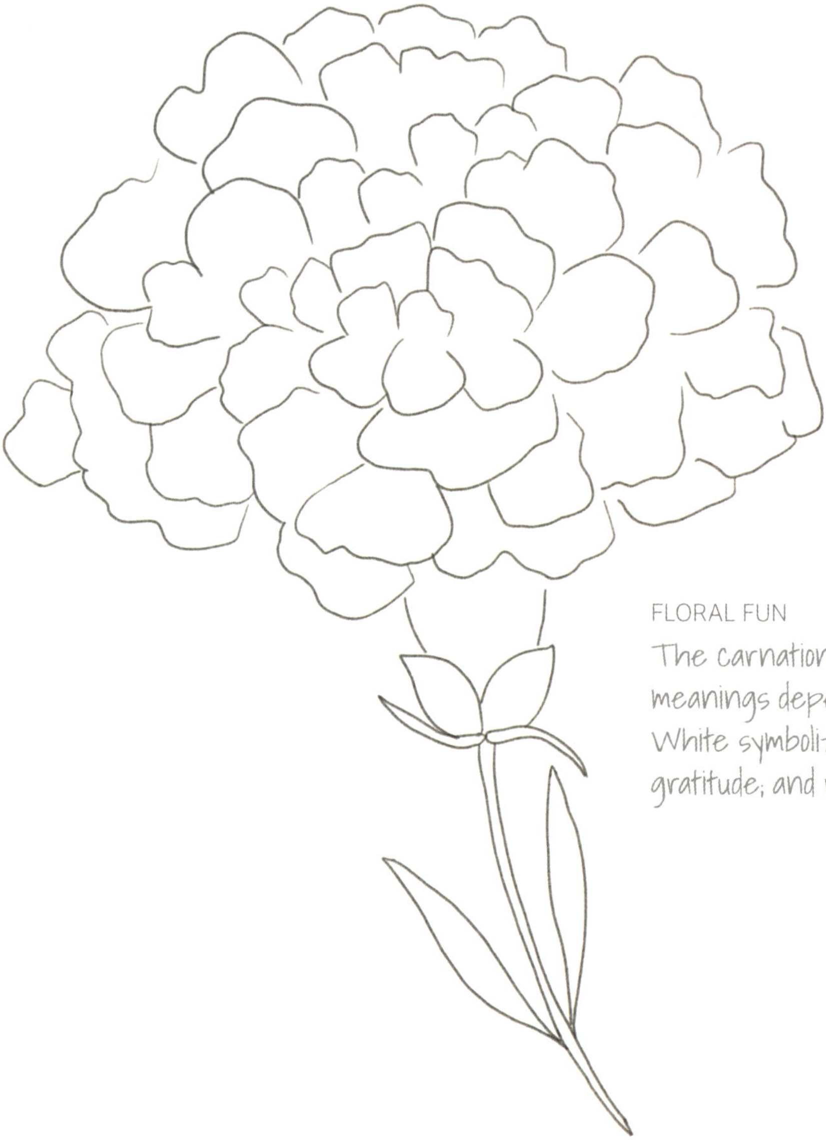

BRUSHES

- Large brush (8)

COLOR PALETTE

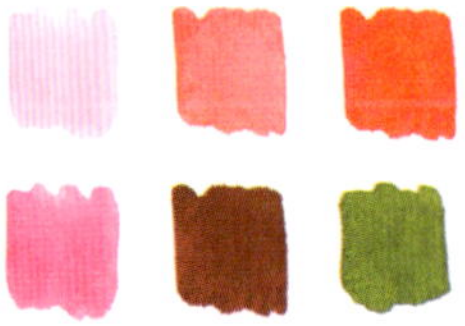

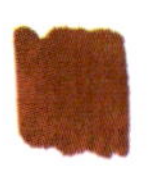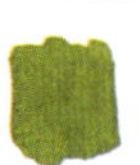

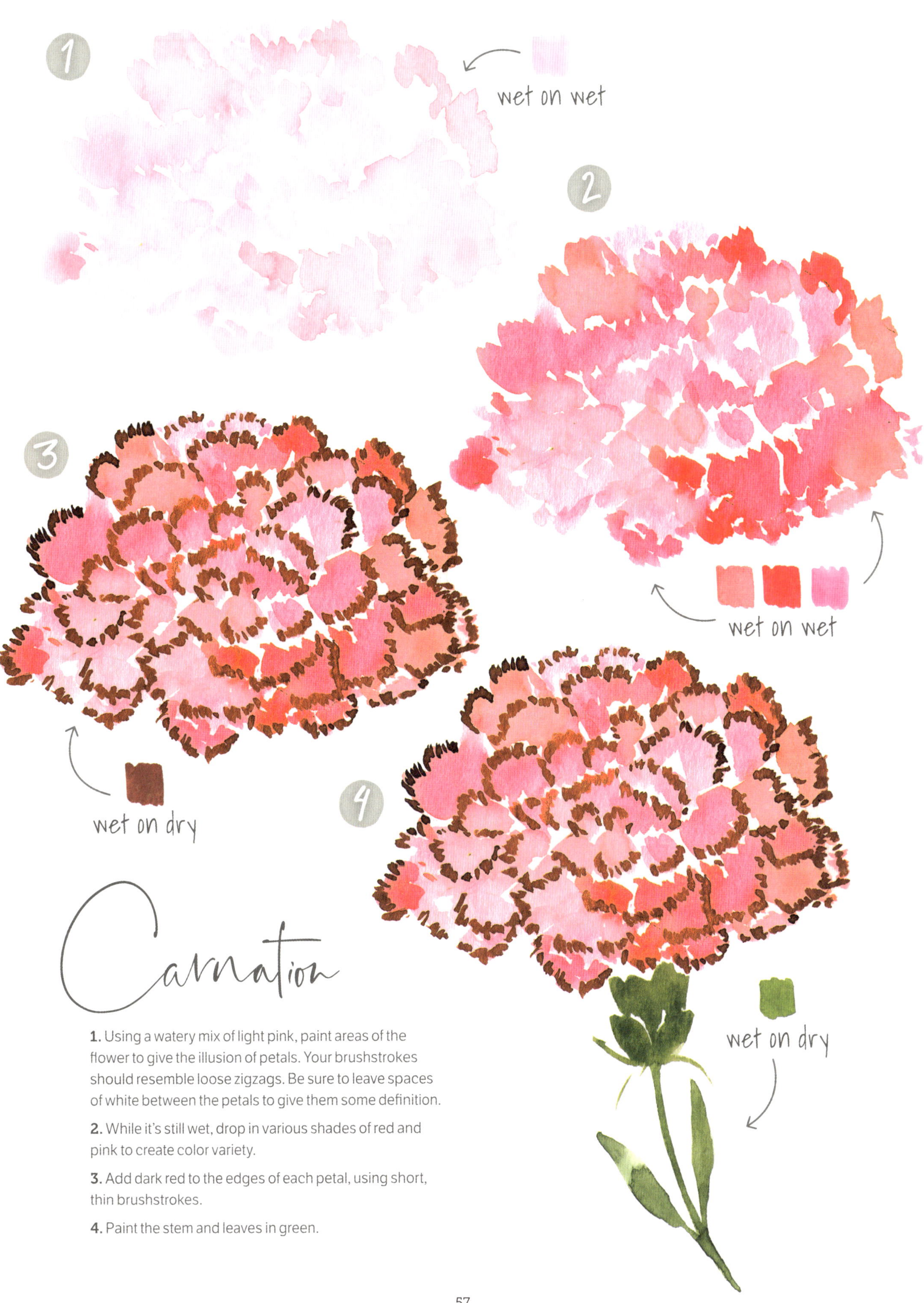

Carnation

1. Using a watery mix of light pink, paint areas of the flower to give the illusion of petals. Your brushstrokes should resemble loose zigzags. Be sure to leave spaces of white between the petals to give them some definition.

2. While it's still wet, drop in various shades of red and pink to create color variety.

3. Add dark red to the edges of each petal, using short, thin brushstrokes.

4. Paint the stem and leaves in green.

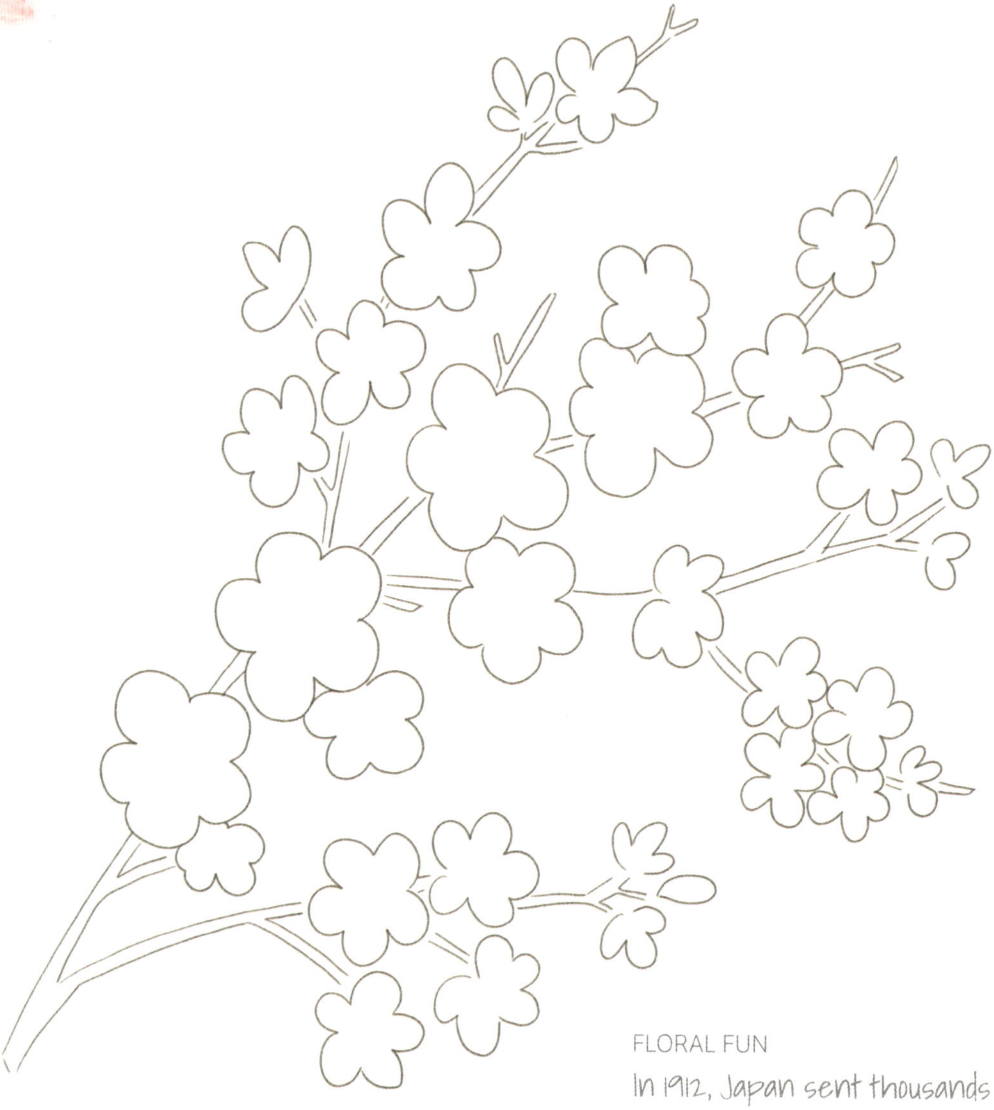

FLORAL FUN

In 1912, Japan sent thousands of cherry blossoms to the United States as a symbol of friendship.

BRUSHES

• Medium/large brush (6, 8)

COLOR PALETTE

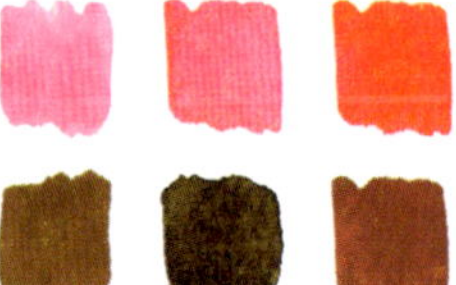

Cherry Blossom

1. Paint each flower in light shades of pink, leaving the center white. While the petals are still wet, lightly drop red paint into the center of each flower, letting the color bleed into the petals.

2. Paint the stems brown.

3. Using dark red, paint the stamens and add a small dot to the center of each flower. Add detail to the stems in dark brown.

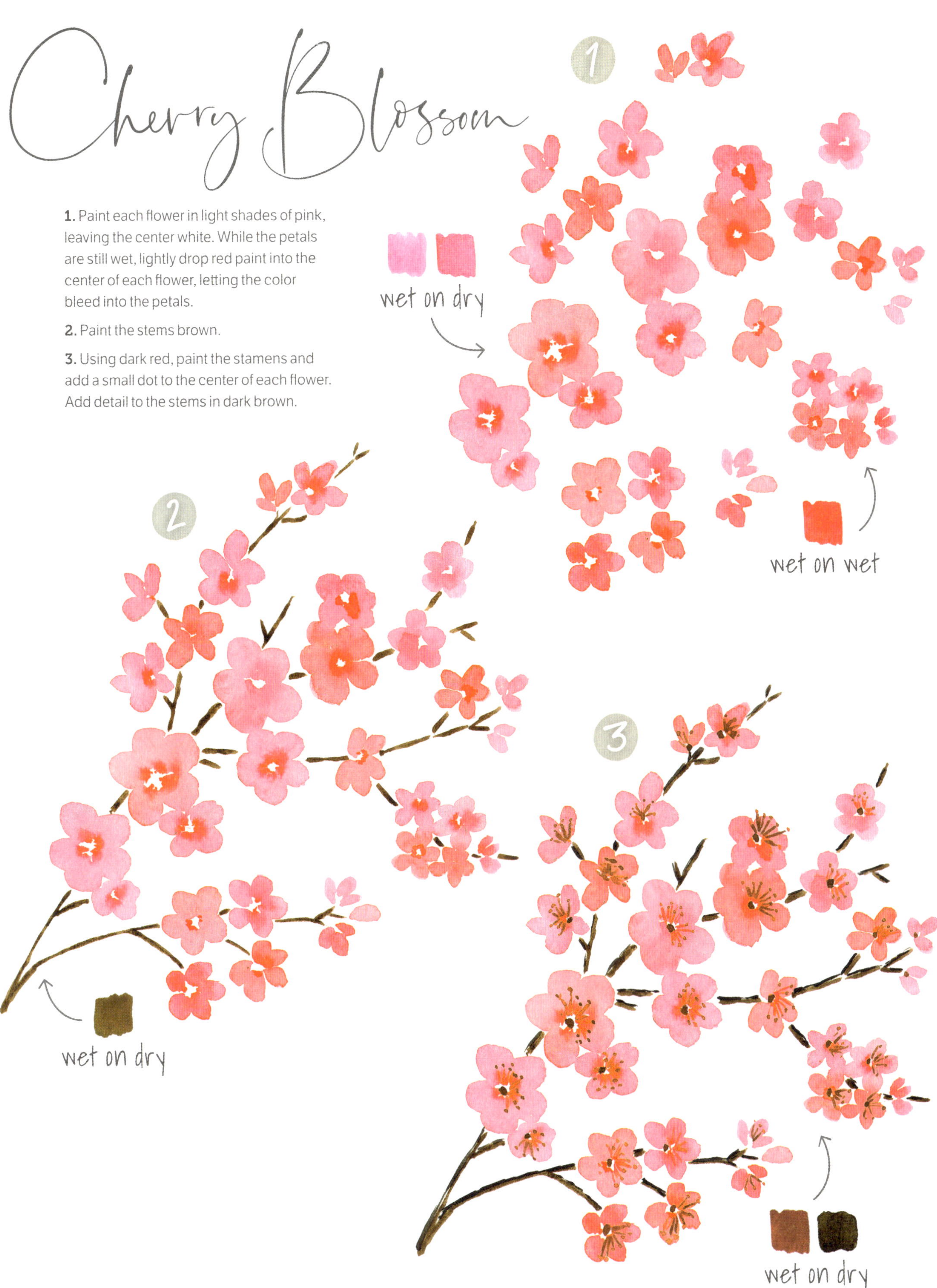

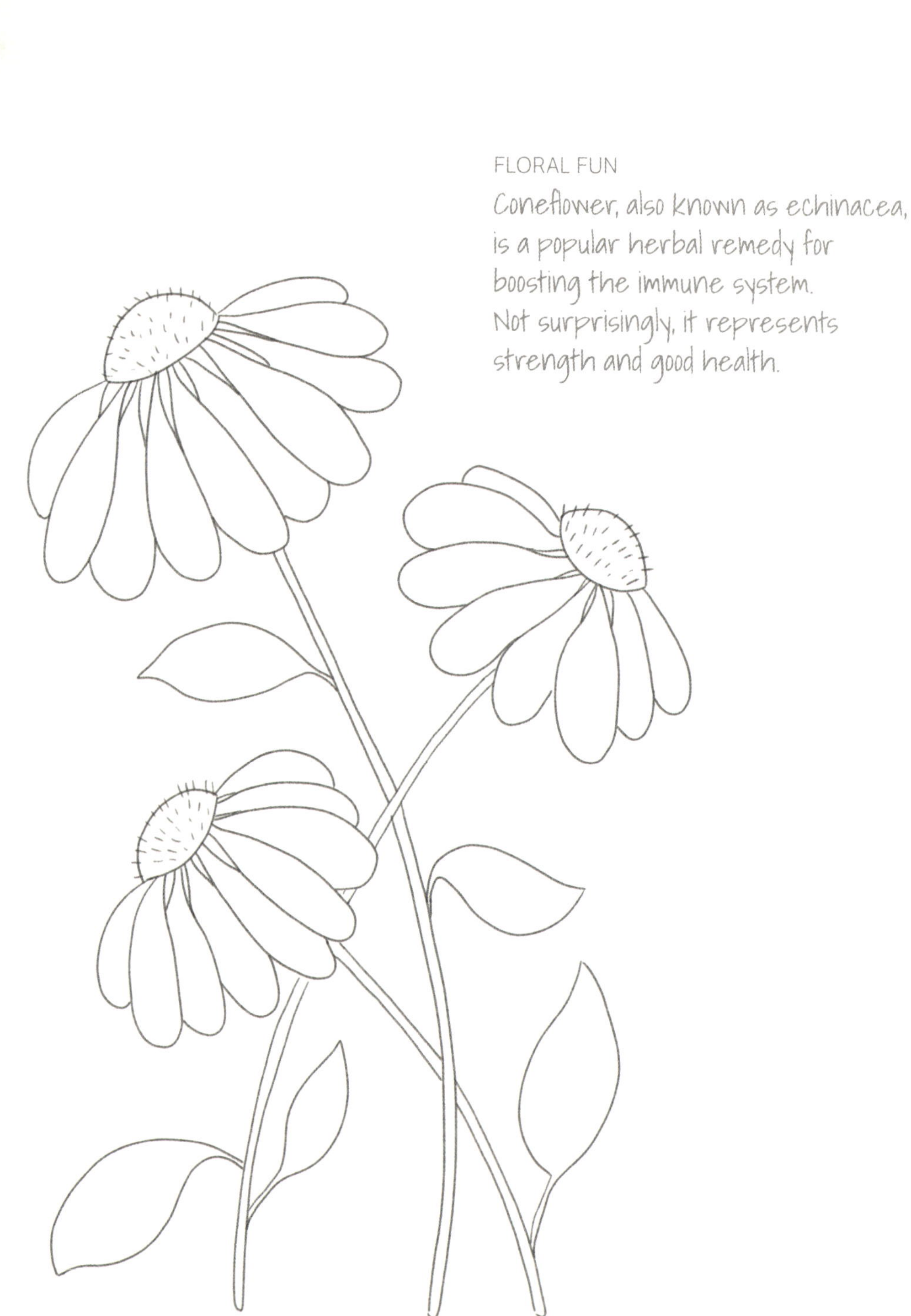

BRUSHES

- Medium/large brush (6, 8)

COLOR PALETTE

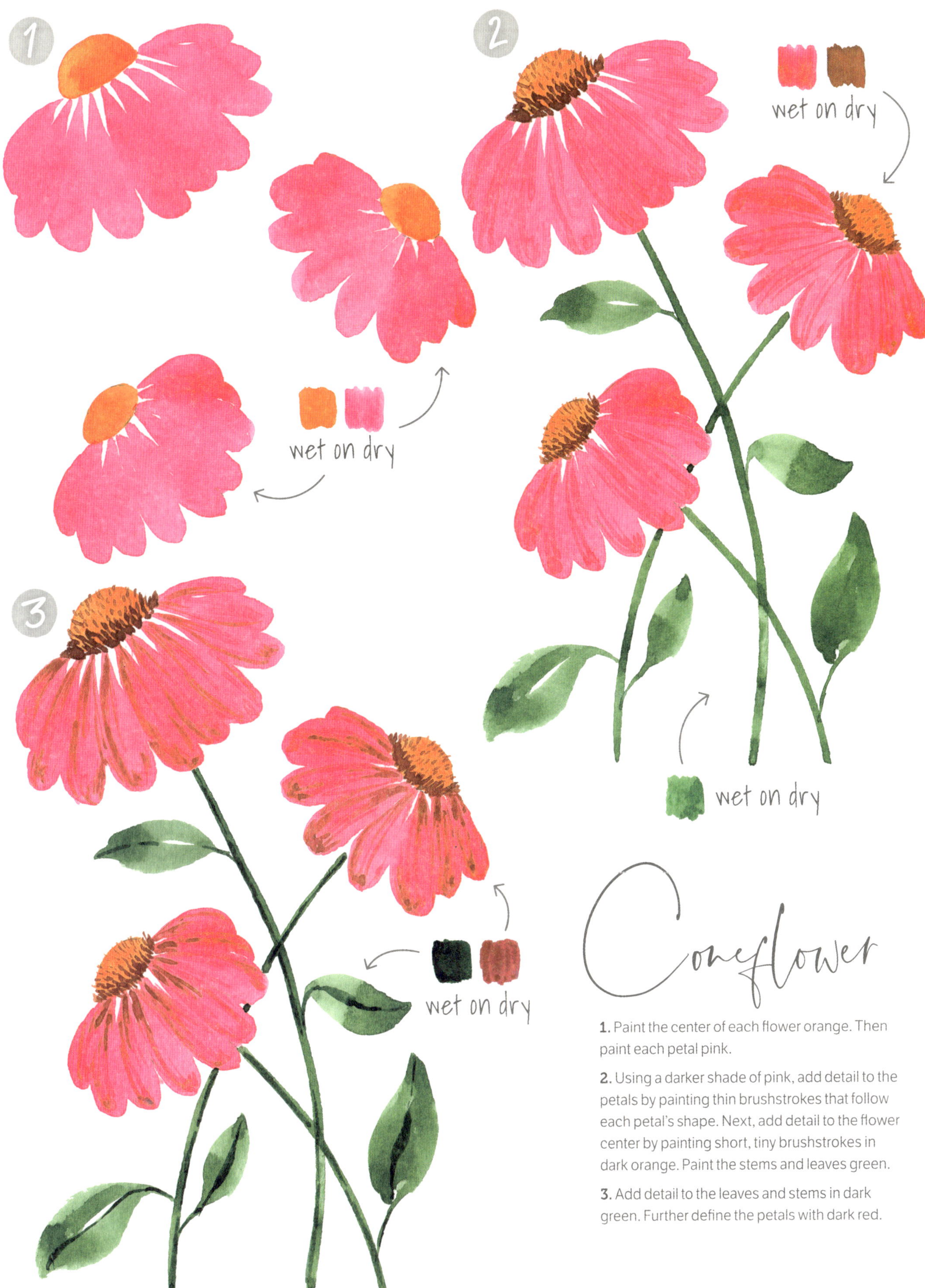

Coneflower

1. Paint the center of each flower orange. Then paint each petal pink.

2. Using a darker shade of pink, add detail to the petals by painting thin brushstrokes that follow each petal's shape. Next, add detail to the flower center by painting short, tiny brushstrokes in dark orange. Paint the stems and leaves green.

3. Add detail to the leaves and stems in dark green. Further define the petals with dark red.

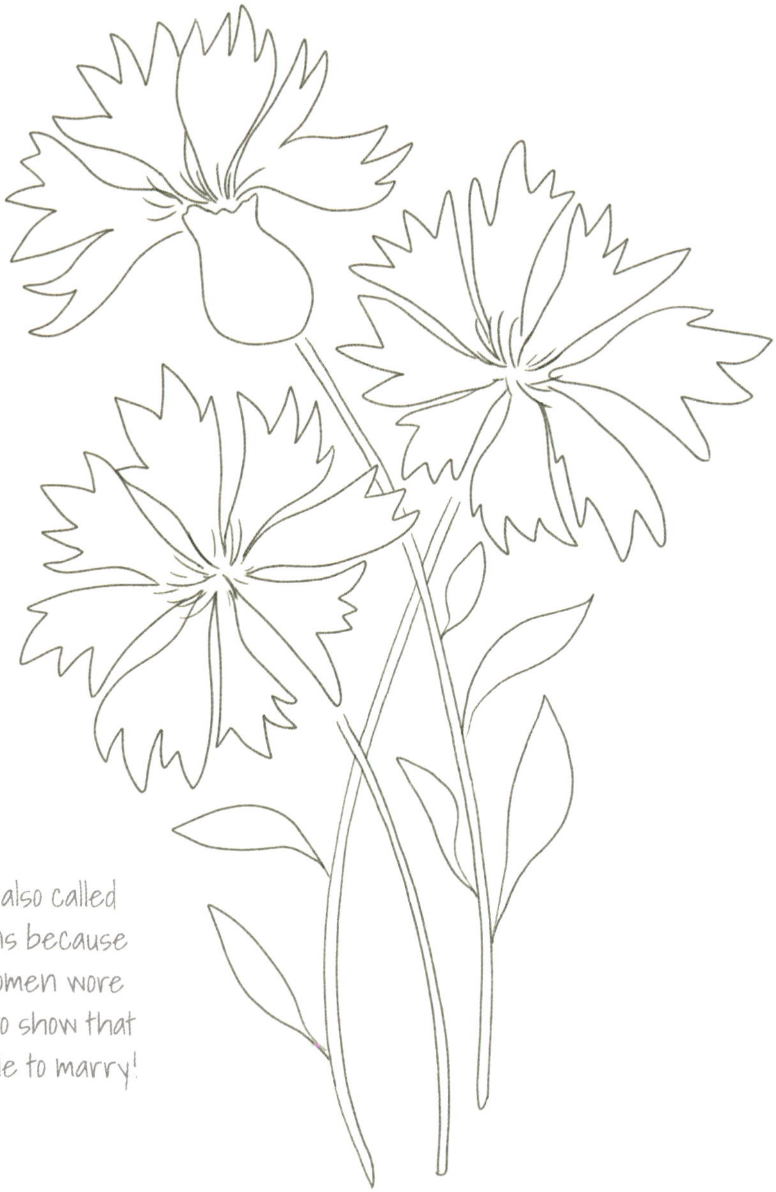

BRUSHES

- Large brush (8)

COLOR PALETTE

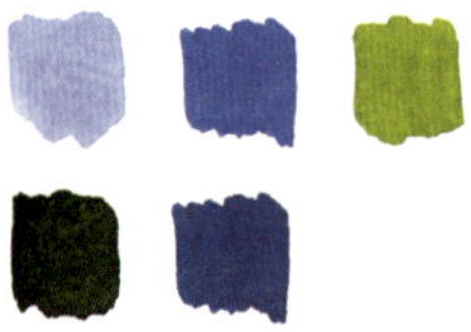

 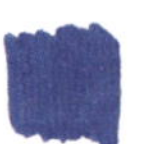 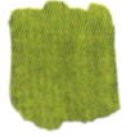

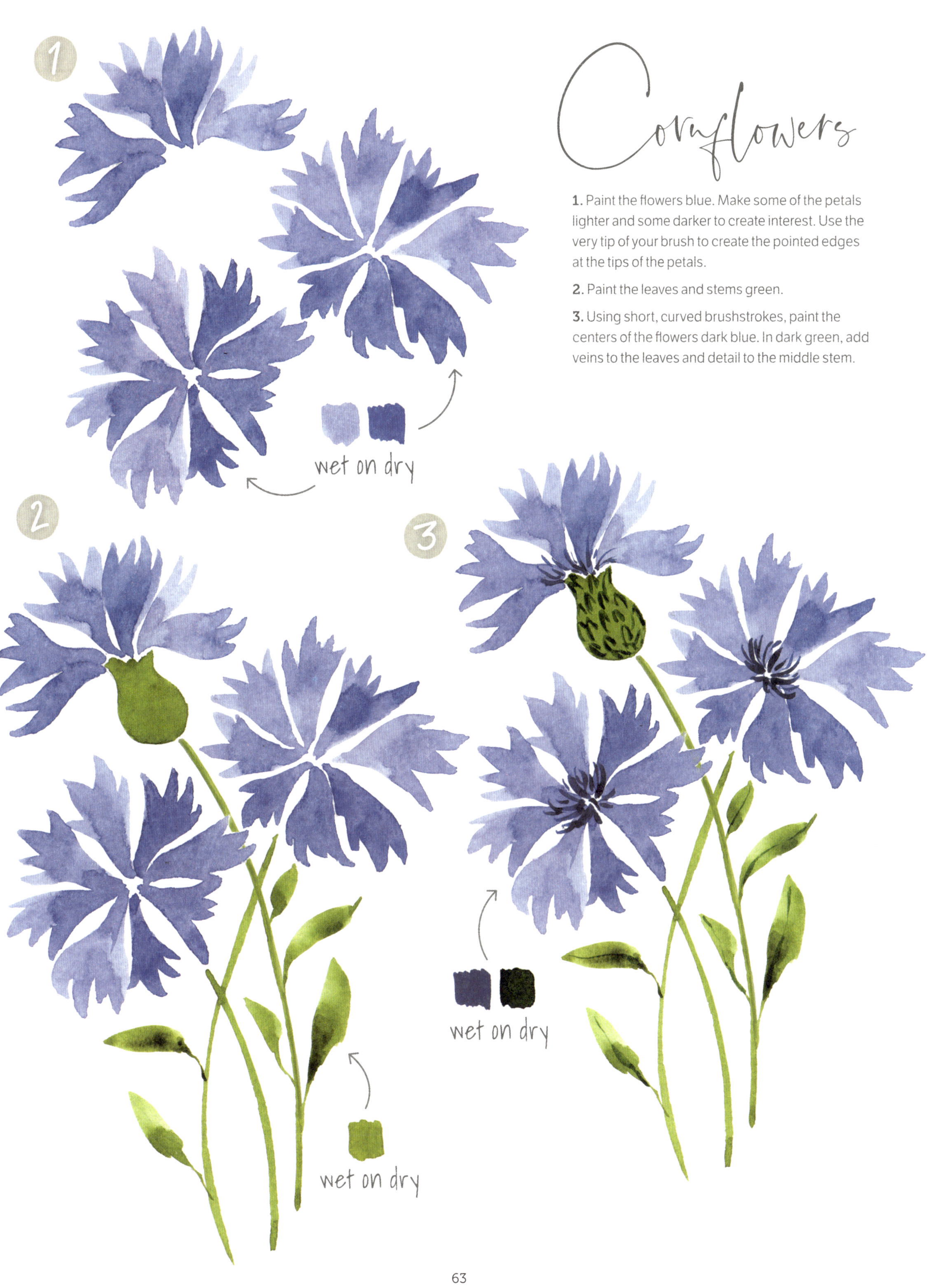

Cornflowers

1. Paint the flowers blue. Make some of the petals lighter and some darker to create interest. Use the very tip of your brush to create the pointed edges at the tips of the petals.

2. Paint the leaves and stems green.

3. Using short, curved brushstrokes, paint the centers of the flowers dark blue. In dark green, add veins to the leaves and detail to the middle stem.

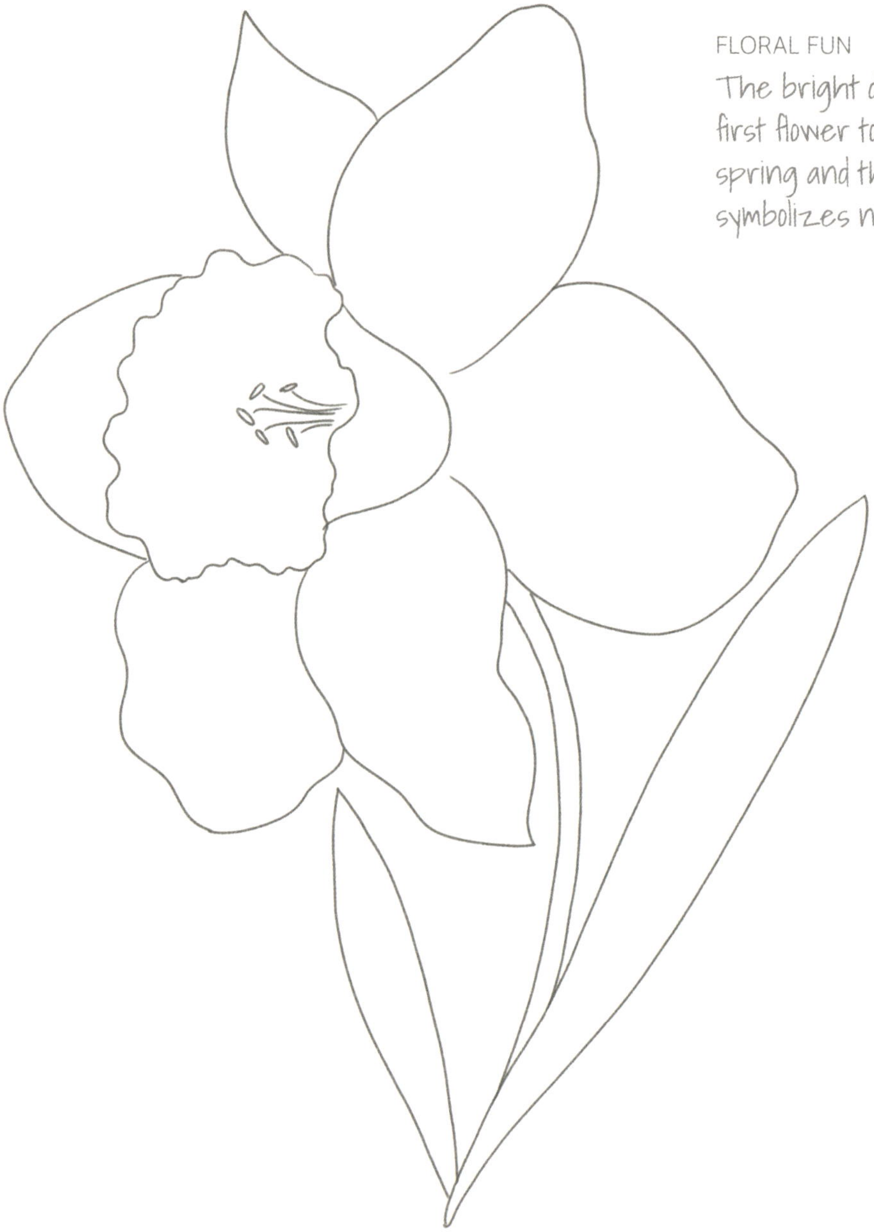

BRUSHES

- Medium/large brush (6, 10)

COLOR PALETTE

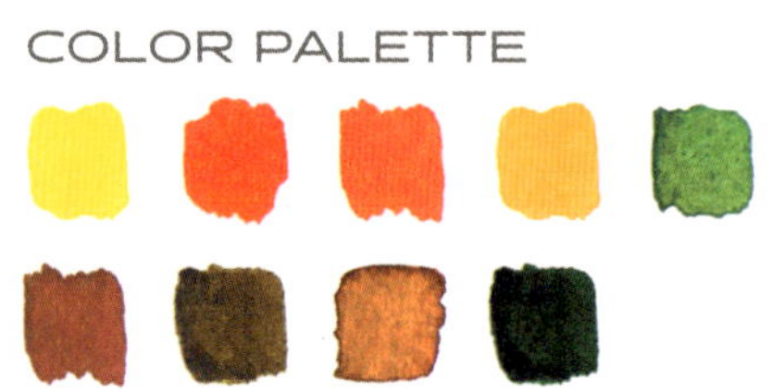

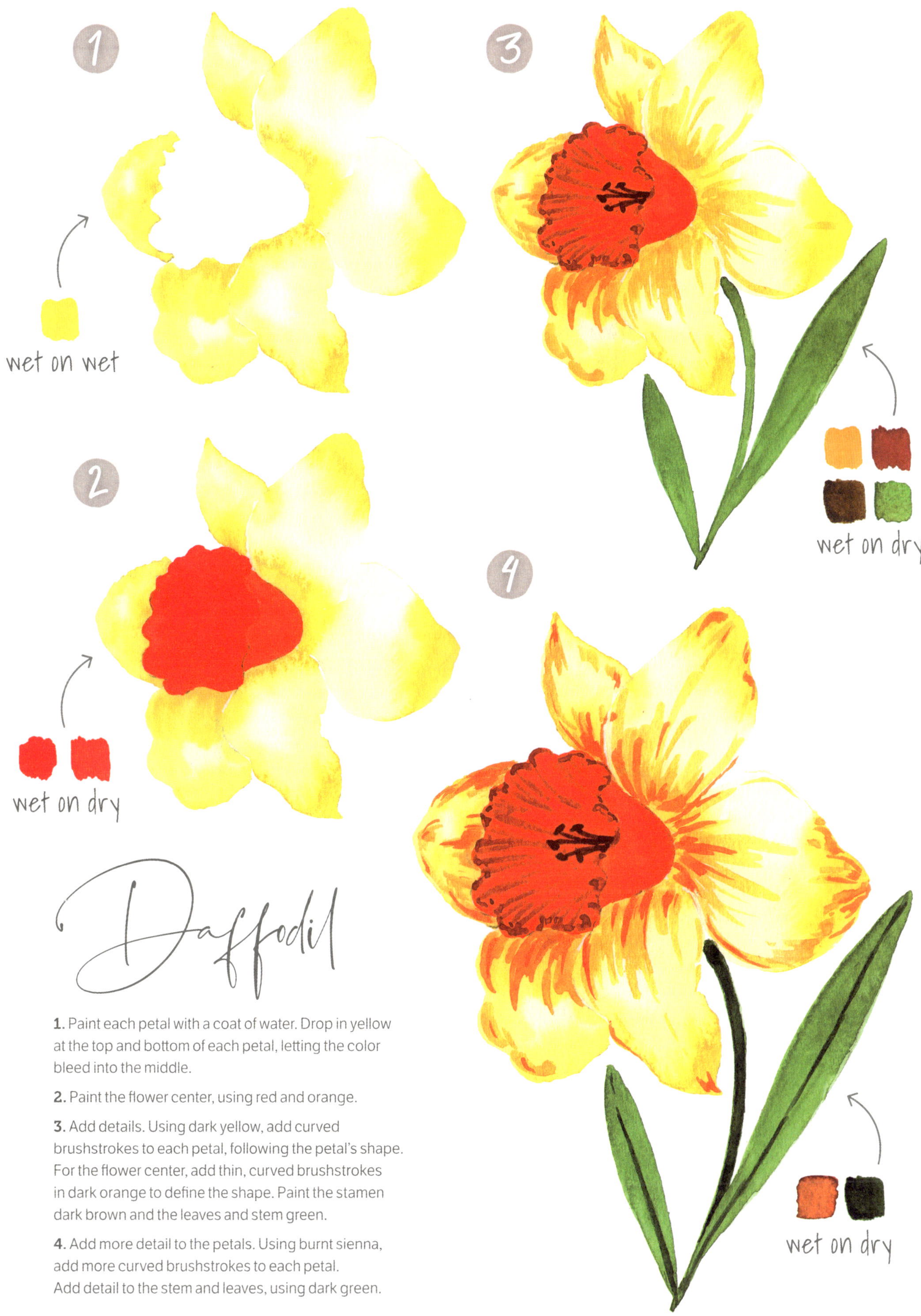

Daffodil

1. Paint each petal with a coat of water. Drop in yellow at the top and bottom of each petal, letting the color bleed into the middle.

2. Paint the flower center, using red and orange.

3. Add details. Using dark yellow, add curved brushstrokes to each petal, following the petal's shape. For the flower center, add thin, curved brushstrokes in dark orange to define the shape. Paint the stamen dark brown and the leaves and stem green.

4. Add more detail to the petals. Using burnt sienna, add more curved brushstrokes to each petal. Add detail to the stem and leaves, using dark green.

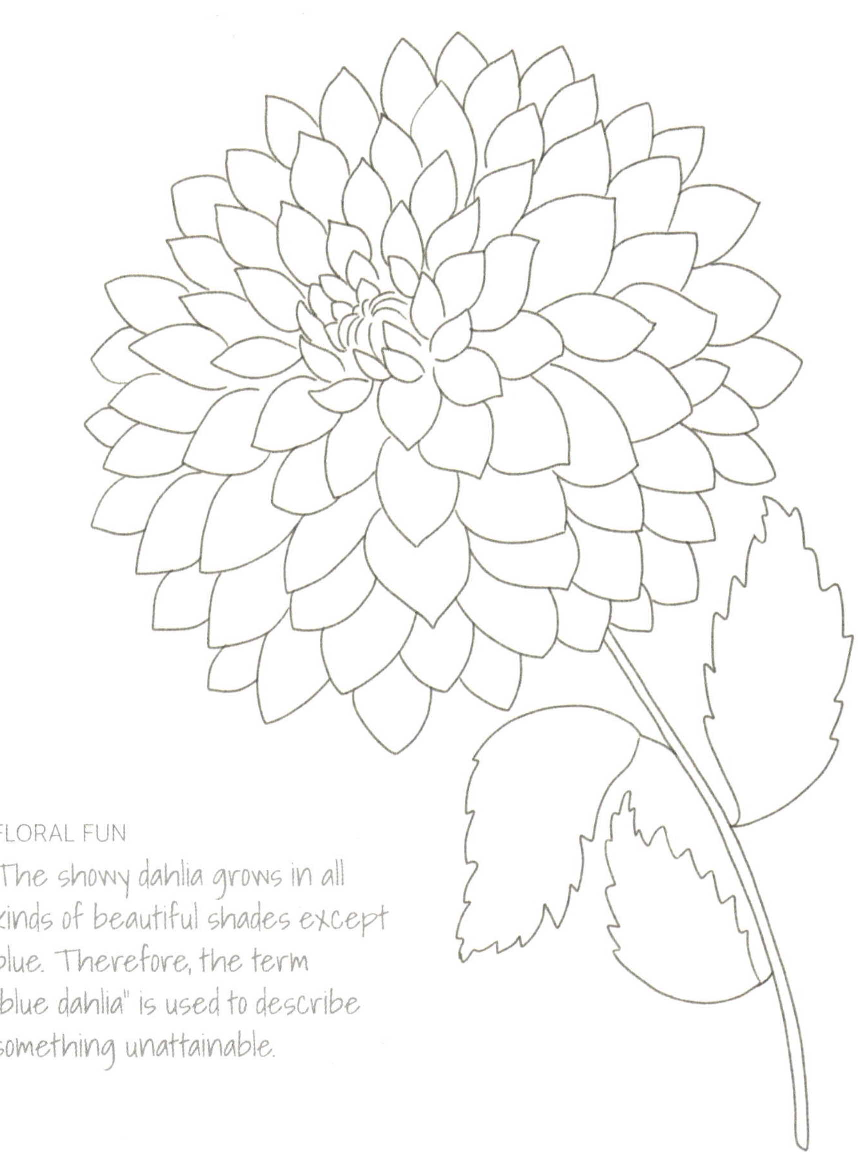

FLORAL FUN

The showy dahlia grows in all kinds of beautiful shades except blue. Therefore, the term "blue dahlia" is used to describe something unattainable.

BRUSHES
• Large brush (8, 10)

COLOR PALETTE

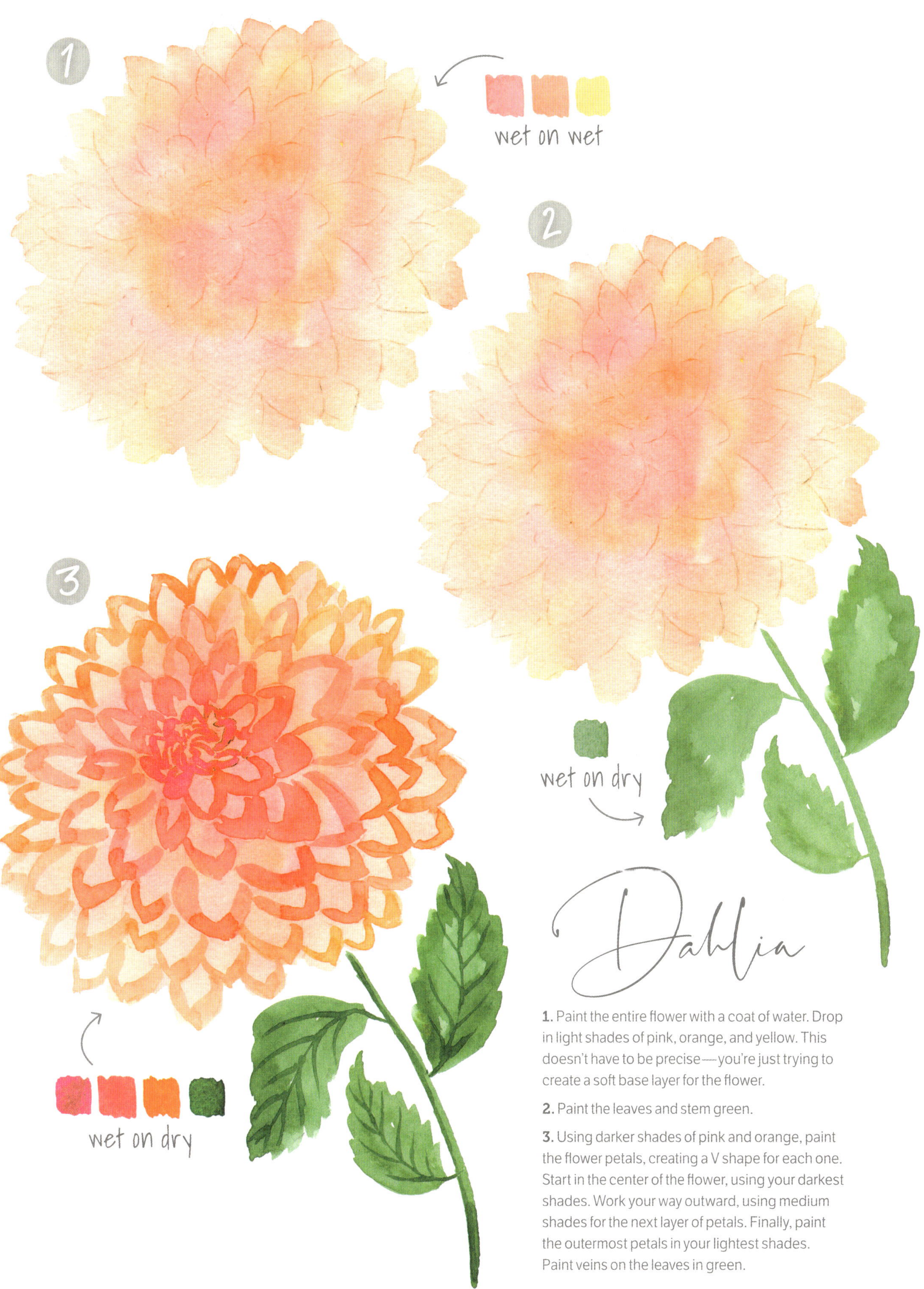

1. Paint the entire flower with a coat of water. Drop in light shades of pink, orange, and yellow. This doesn't have to be precise—you're just trying to create a soft base layer for the flower.

2. Paint the leaves and stem green.

3. Using darker shades of pink and orange, paint the flower petals, creating a V shape for each one. Start in the center of the flower, using your darkest shades. Work your way outward, using medium shades for the next layer of petals. Finally, paint the outermost petals in your lightest shades. Paint veins on the leaves in green.

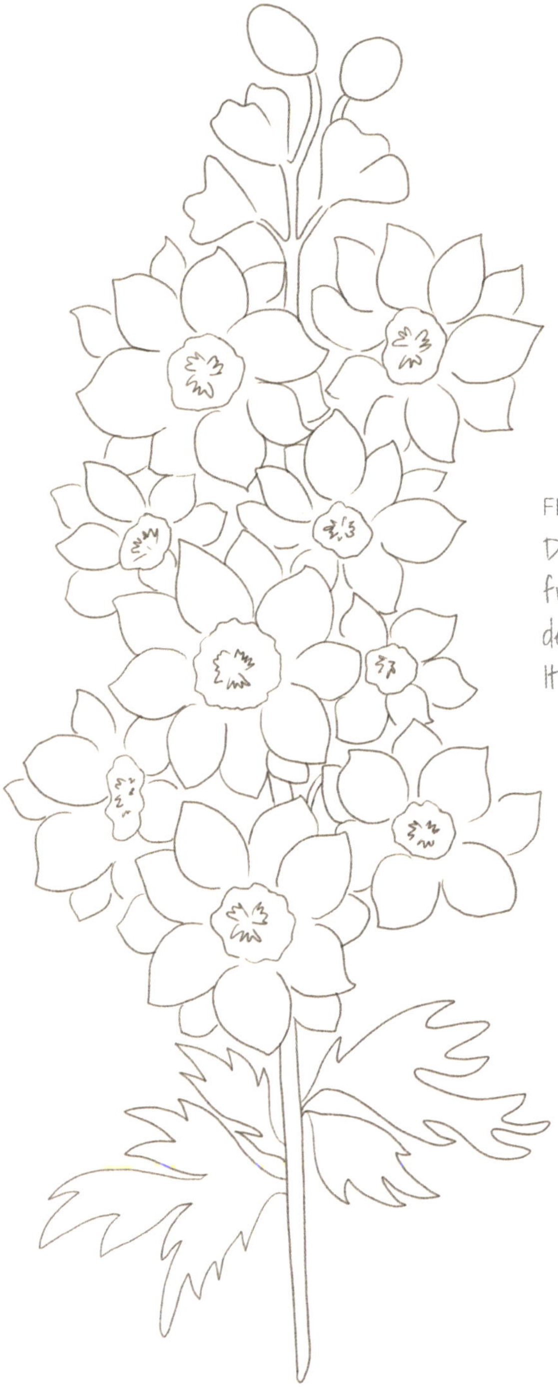

BRUSHES

- Large brush (8)

COLOR PALETTE

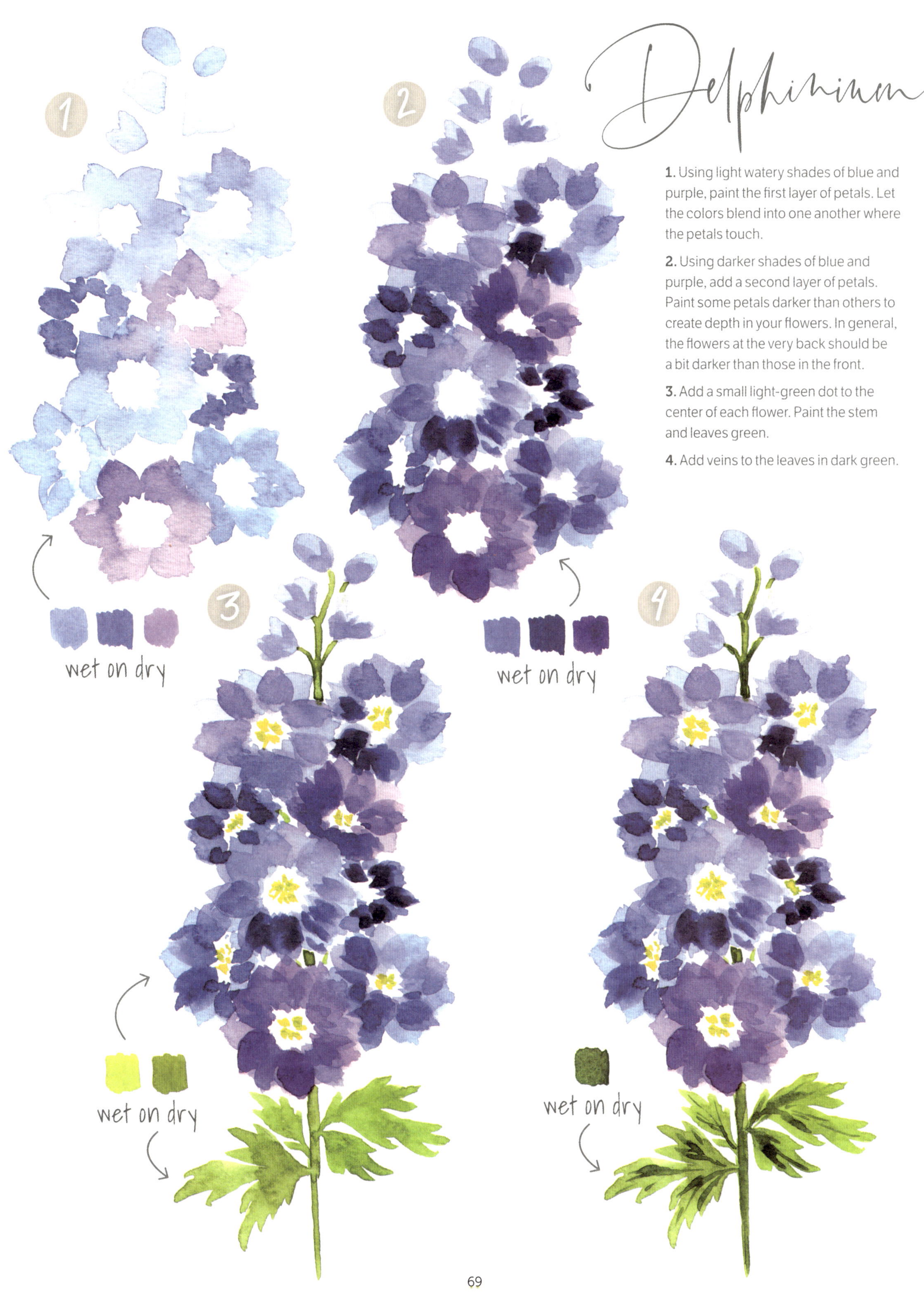

1. Using light watery shades of blue and purple, paint the first layer of petals. Let the colors blend into one another where the petals touch.

2. Using darker shades of blue and purple, add a second layer of petals. Paint some petals darker than others to create depth in your flowers. In general, the flowers at the very back should be a bit darker than those in the front.

3. Add a small light-green dot to the center of each flower. Paint the stem and leaves green.

4. Add veins to the leaves in dark green.

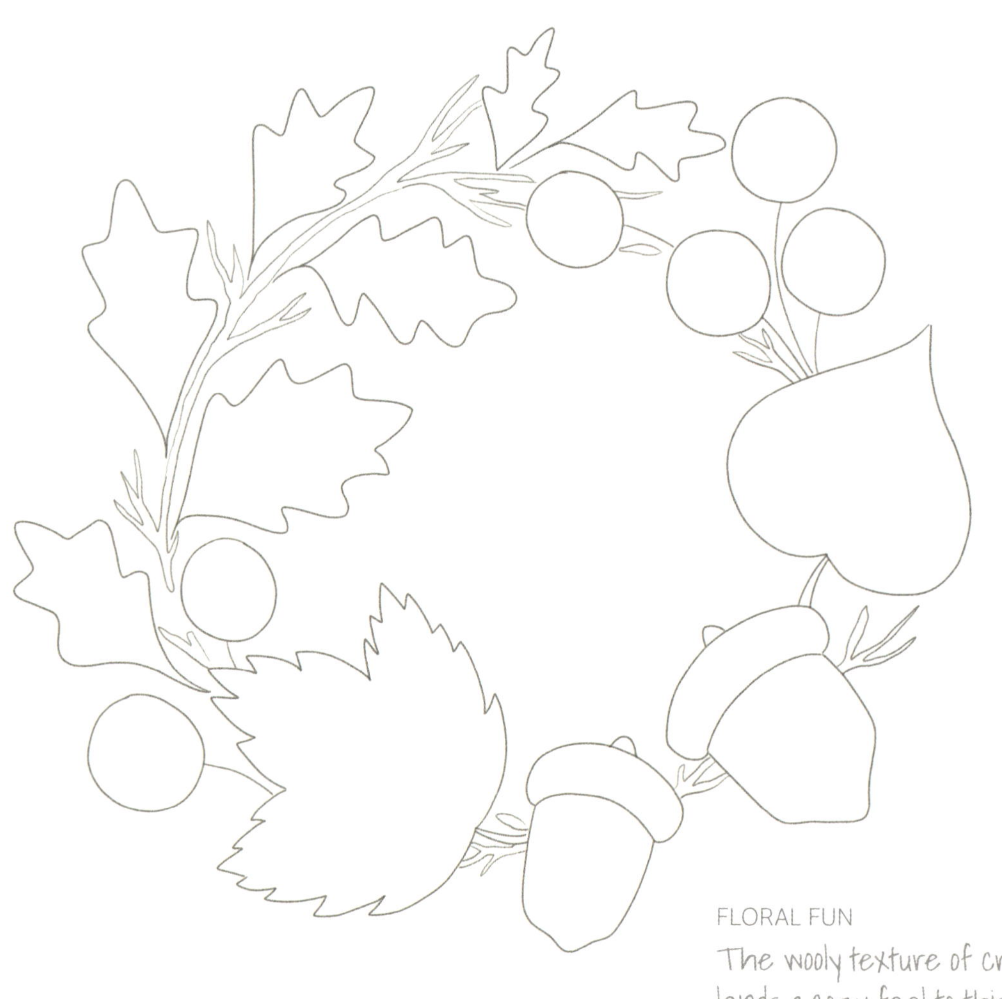

The wooly texture of craspedia lends a cozy feel to this fall wreath when combined with repeating autumn leaves and acorns.

BRUSHES
- Medium/large brush (6, 8)

COLOR PALETTE

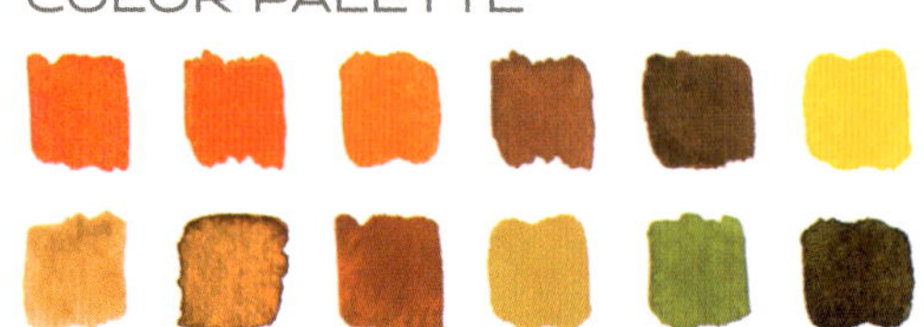

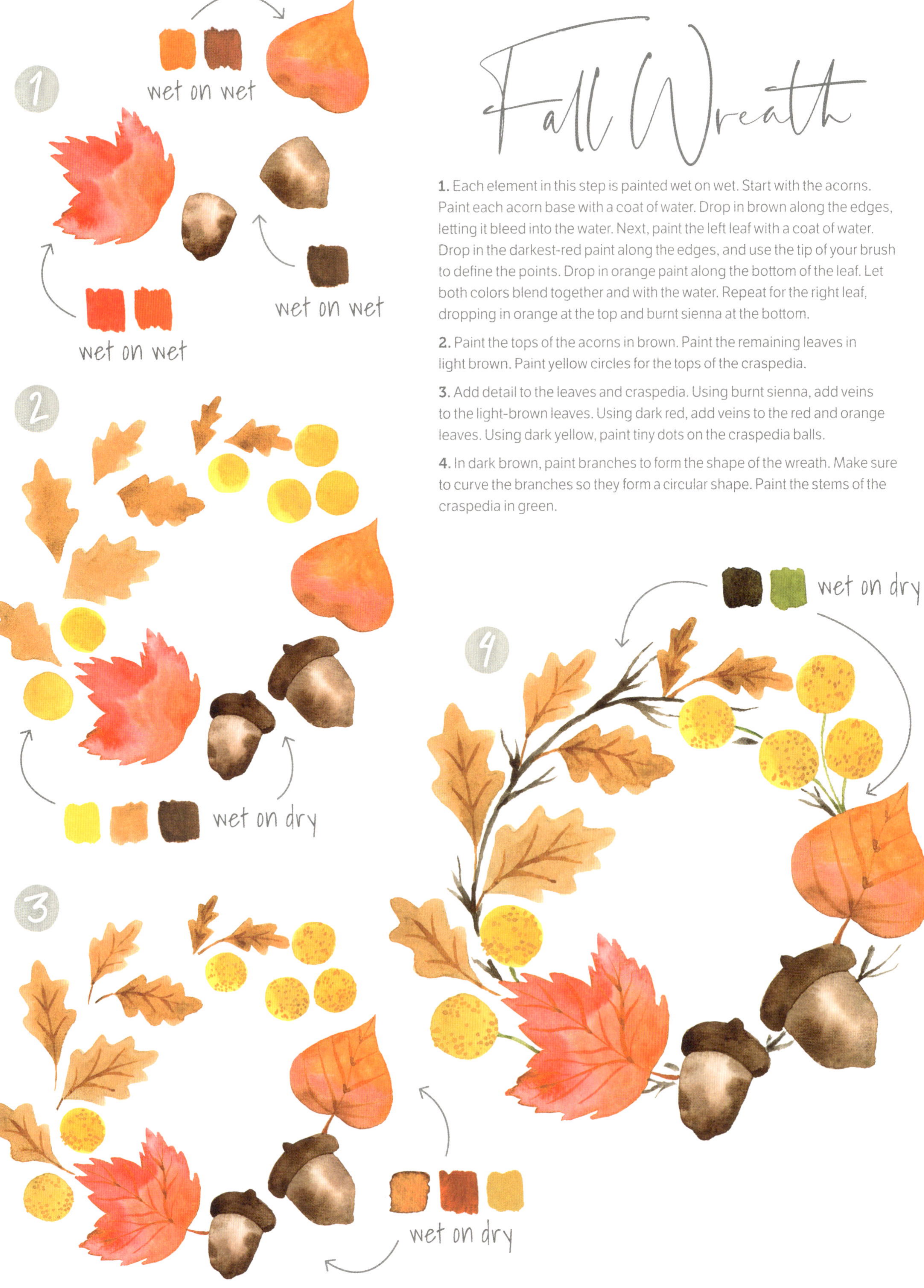

Fall Wreath

1. Each element in this step is painted wet on wet. Start with the acorns. Paint each acorn base with a coat of water. Drop in brown along the edges, letting it bleed into the water. Next, paint the left leaf with a coat of water. Drop in the darkest-red paint along the edges, and use the tip of your brush to define the points. Drop in orange paint along the bottom of the leaf. Let both colors blend together and with the water. Repeat for the right leaf, dropping in orange at the top and burnt sienna at the bottom.

2. Paint the tops of the acorns in brown. Paint the remaining leaves in light brown. Paint yellow circles for the tops of the craspedia.

3. Add detail to the leaves and craspedia. Using burnt sienna, add veins to the light-brown leaves. Using dark red, add veins to the red and orange leaves. Using dark yellow, paint tiny dots on the craspedia balls.

4. In dark brown, paint branches to form the shape of the wreath. Make sure to curve the branches so they form a circular shape. Paint the stems of the craspedia in green.

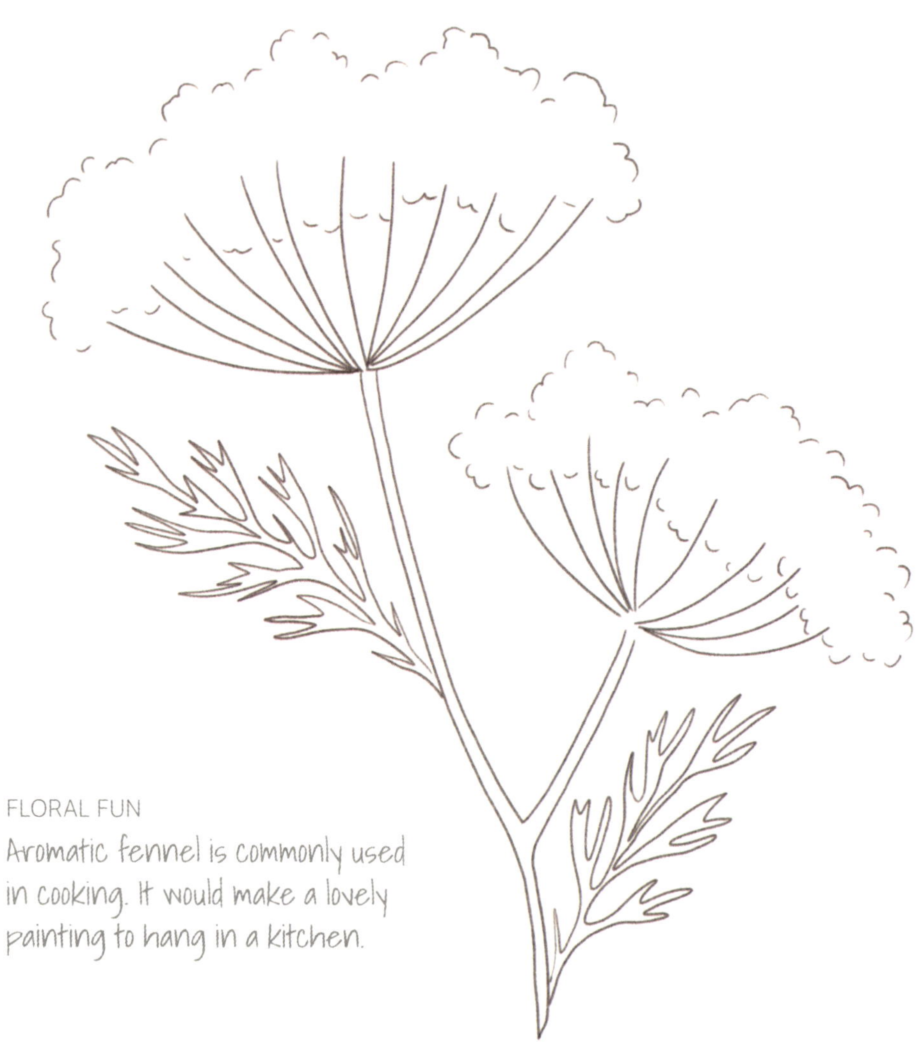

FLORAL FUN

Aromatic fennel is commonly used in cooking. It would make a lovely painting to hang in a kitchen.

BRUSHES

- Medium/large brush (6, 8)

COLOR PALETTE

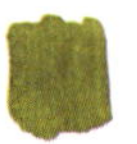 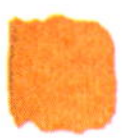 
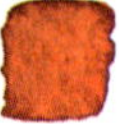 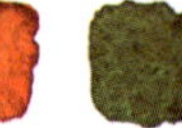

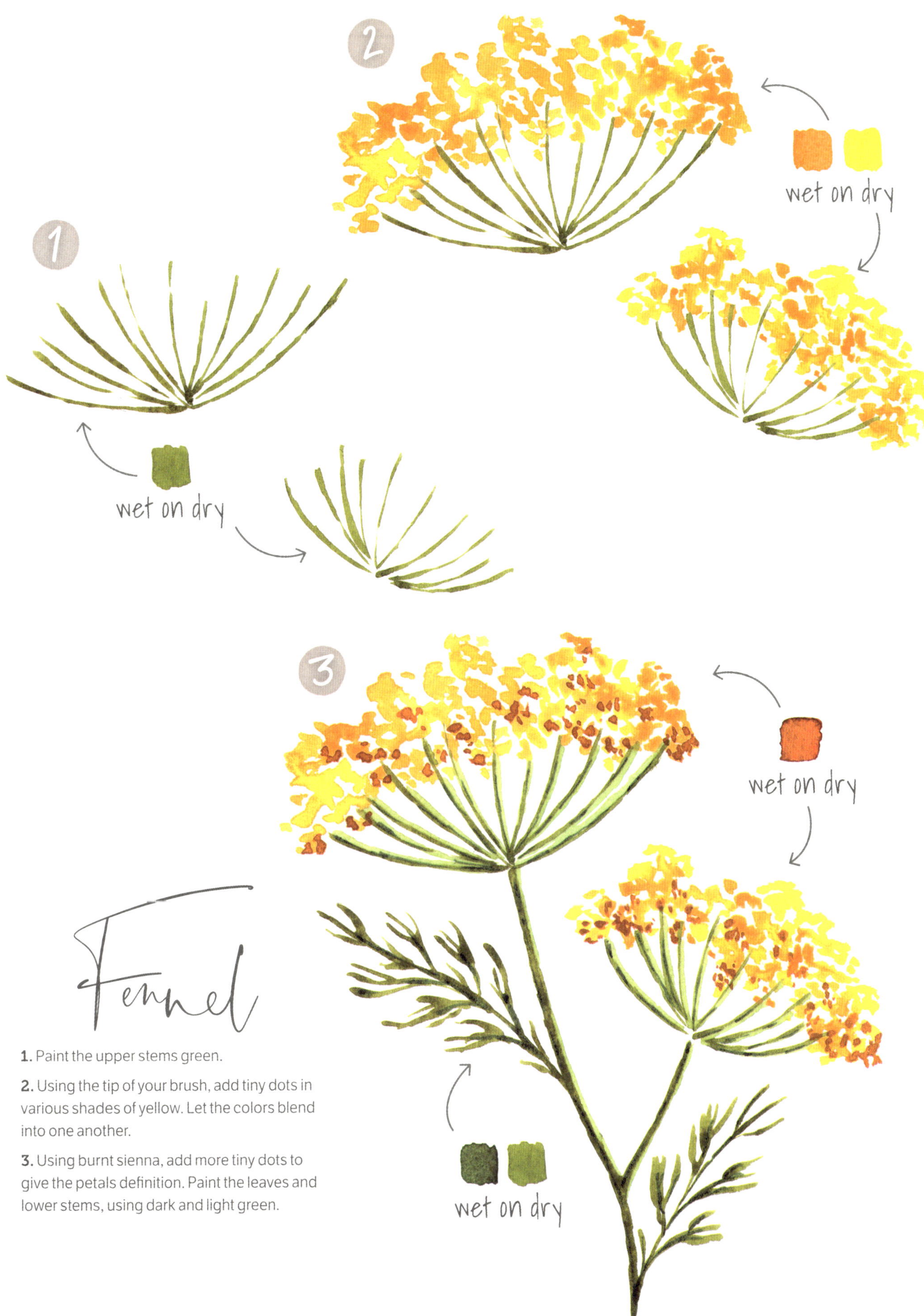

Fennel

1. Paint the upper stems green.

2. Using the tip of your brush, add tiny dots in various shades of yellow. Let the colors blend into one another.

3. Using burnt sienna, add more tiny dots to give the petals definition. Paint the leaves and lower stems, using dark and light green.

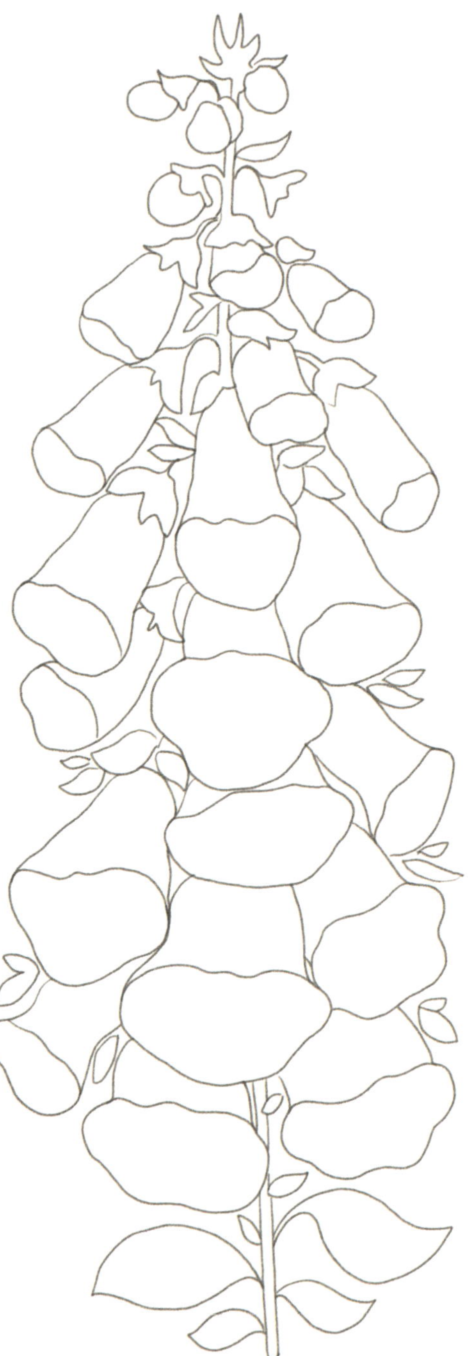

BRUSHES

- Medium brush (6)

COLOR PALETTE

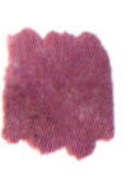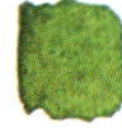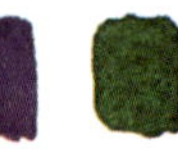

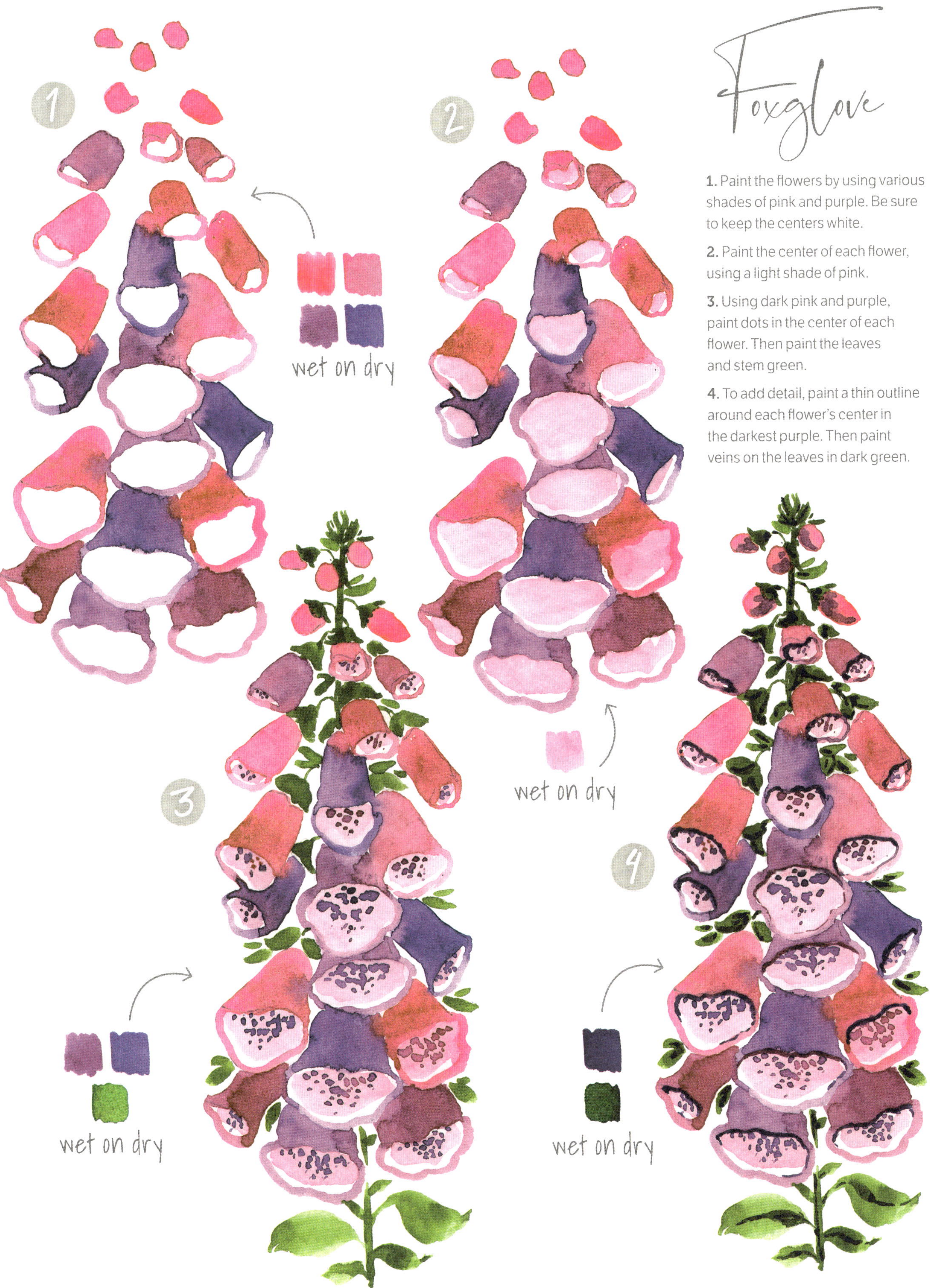

Foxglove

1. Paint the flowers by using various shades of pink and purple. Be sure to keep the centers white.

2. Paint the center of each flower, using a light shade of pink.

3. Using dark pink and purple, paint dots in the center of each flower. Then paint the leaves and stem green.

4. To add detail, paint a thin outline around each flower's center in the darkest purple. Then paint veins on the leaves in dark green.

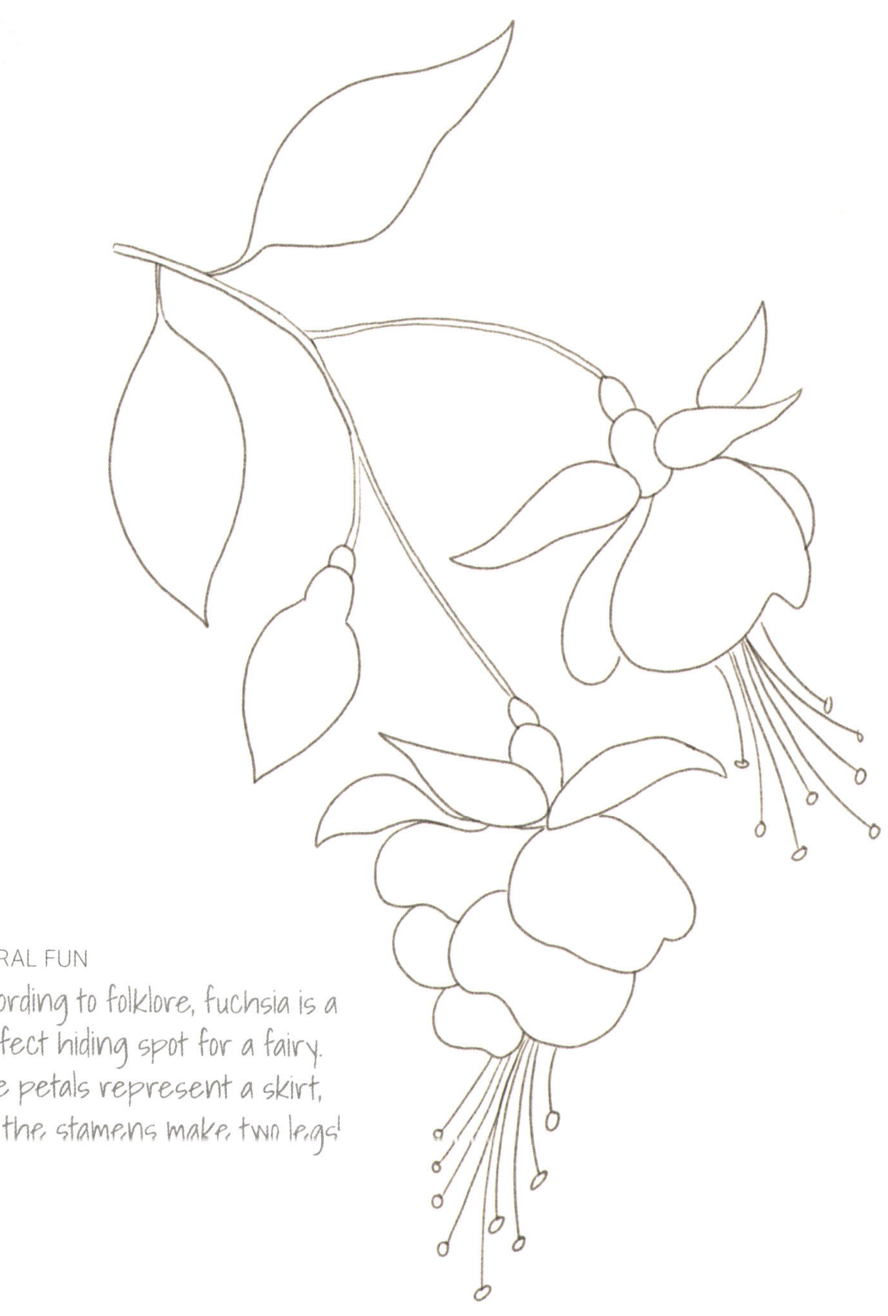

BRUSHES

- Medium brush (6)

COLOR PALETTE

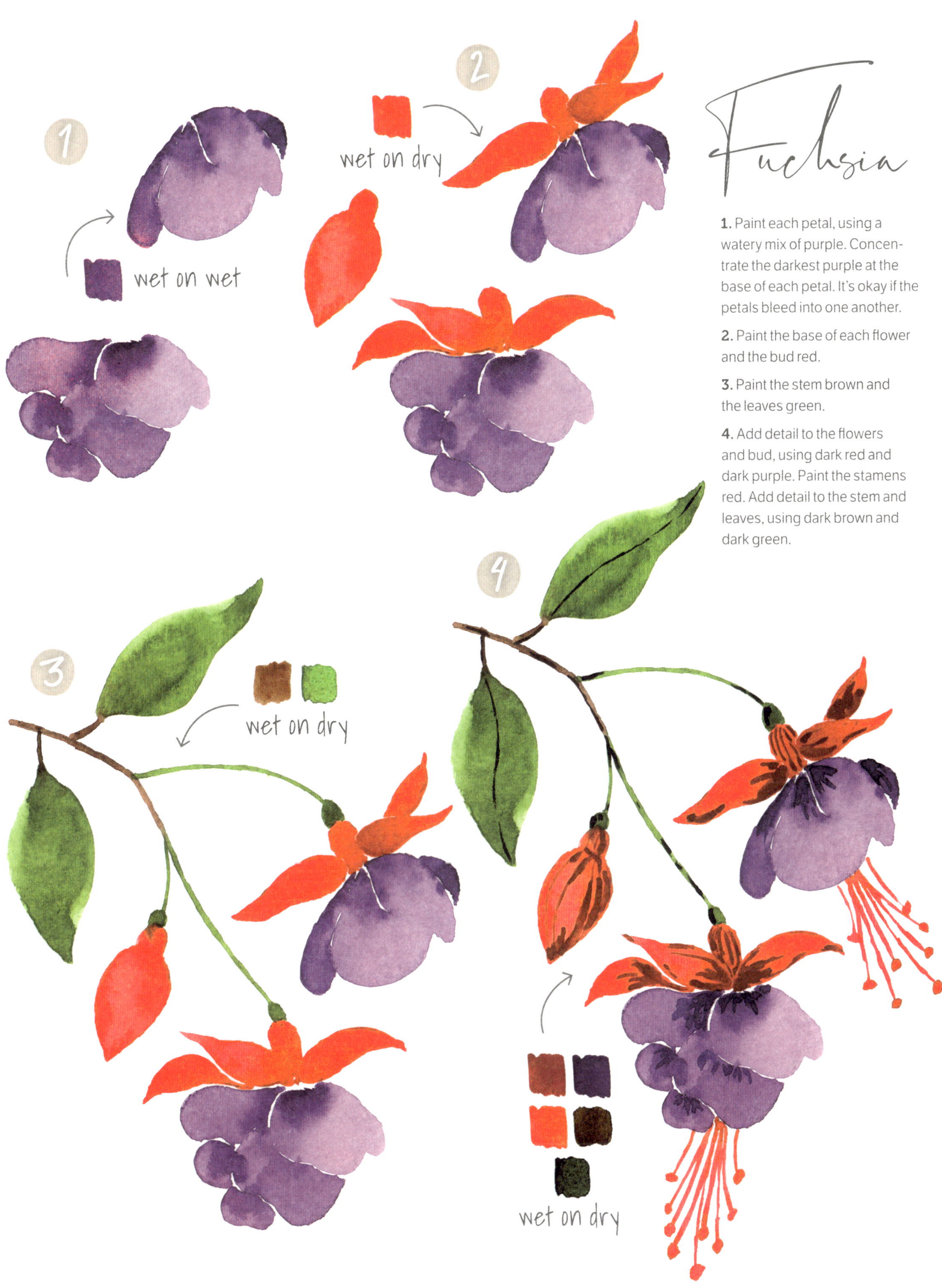

Fuchsia

1. Paint each petal, using a watery mix of purple. Concentrate the darkest purple at the base of each petal. It's okay if the petals bleed into one another.

2. Paint the base of each flower and the bud red.

3. Paint the stem brown and the leaves green.

4. Add detail to the flowers and bud, using dark red and dark purple. Paint the stamens red. Add detail to the stem and leaves, using dark brown and dark green.

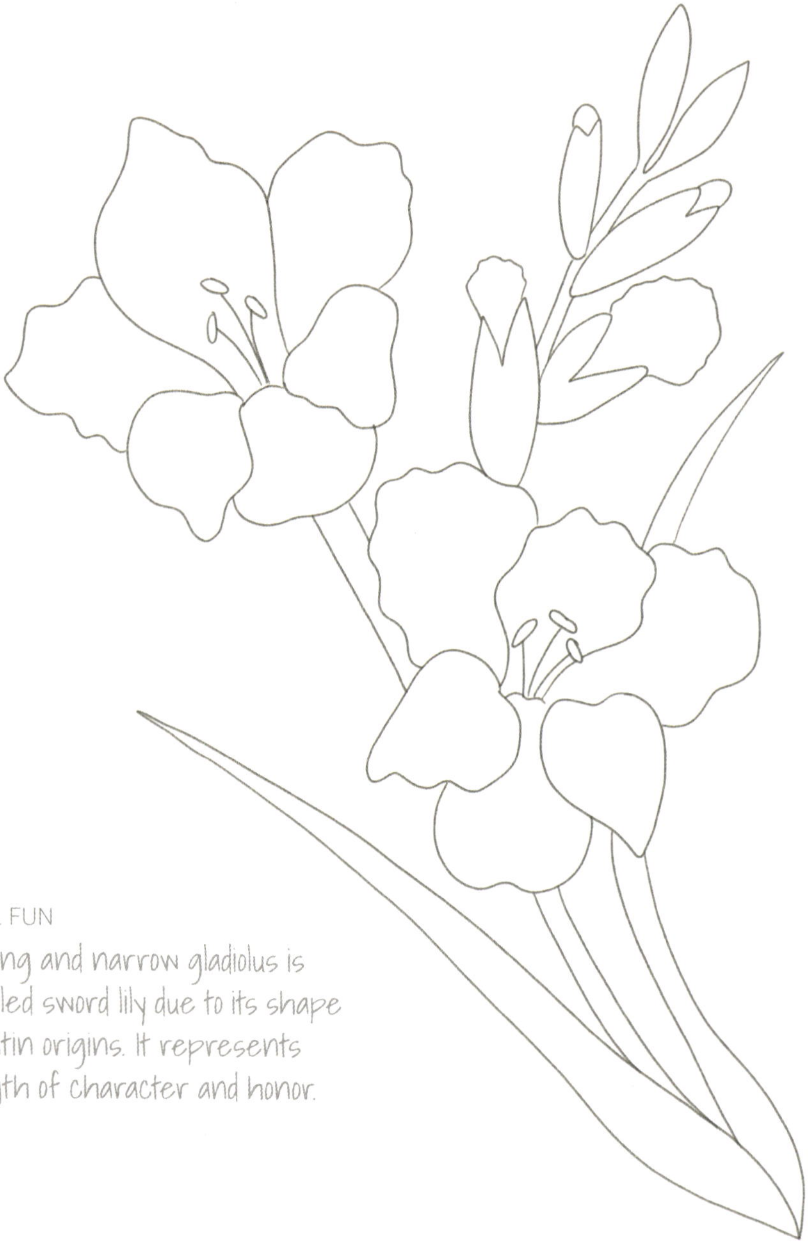

FLORAL FUN

The long and narrow gladiolus is also called sword lily due to its shape and Latin origins. It represents strength of character and honor.

BRUSHES

- Medium/large brush (6, 8)

COLOR PALETTE

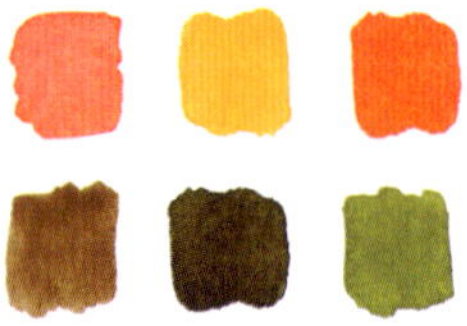

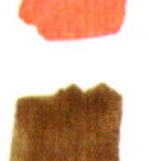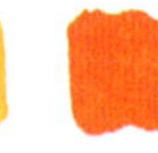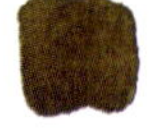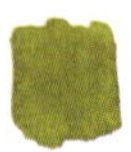

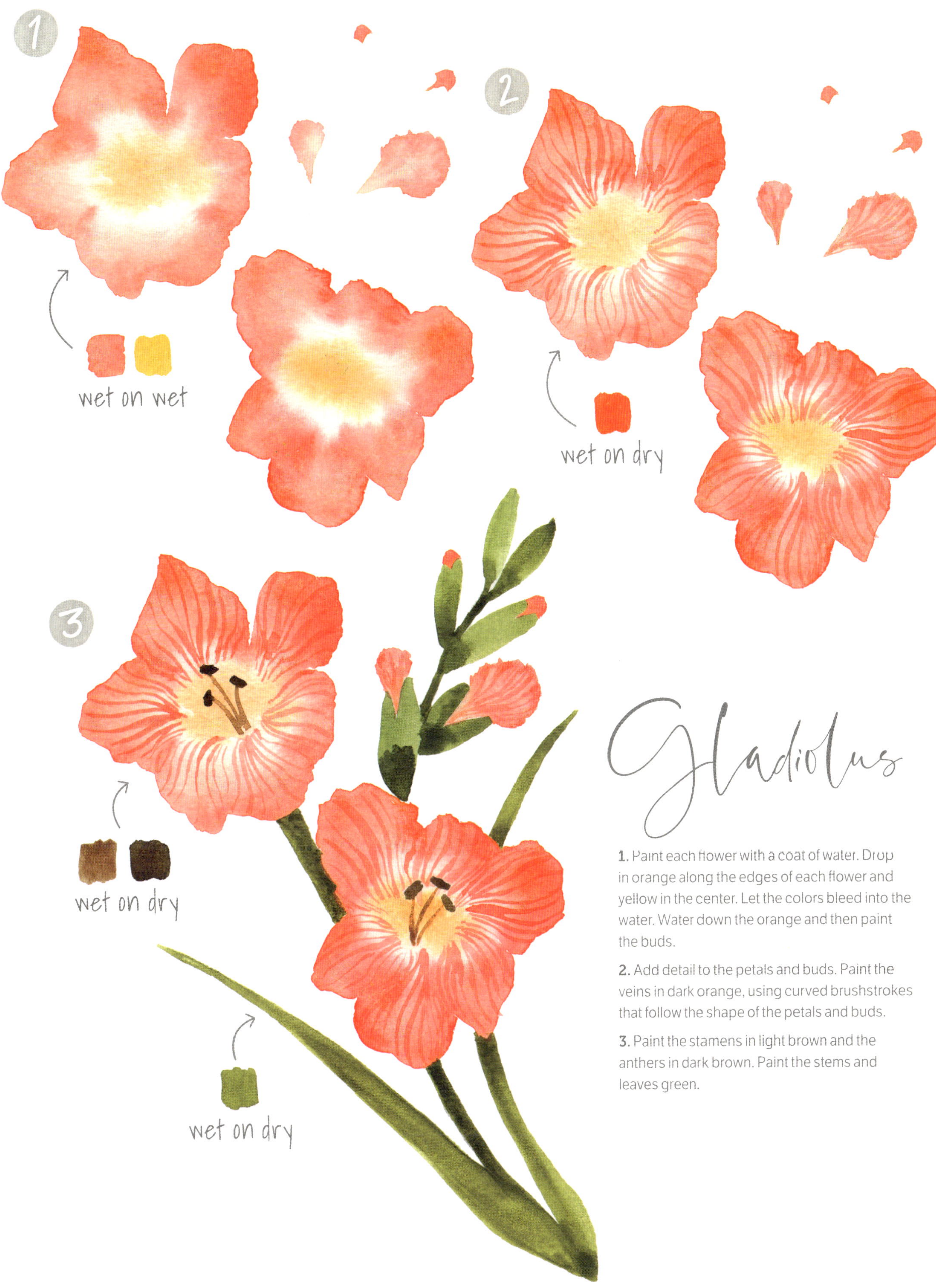

Gladiolus

1. Paint each flower with a coat of water. Drop in orange along the edges of each flower and yellow in the center. Let the colors bleed into the water. Water down the orange and then paint the buds.

2. Add detail to the petals and buds. Paint the veins in dark orange, using curved brushstrokes that follow the shape of the petals and buds.

3. Paint the stamens in light brown and the anthers in dark brown. Paint the stems and leaves green.

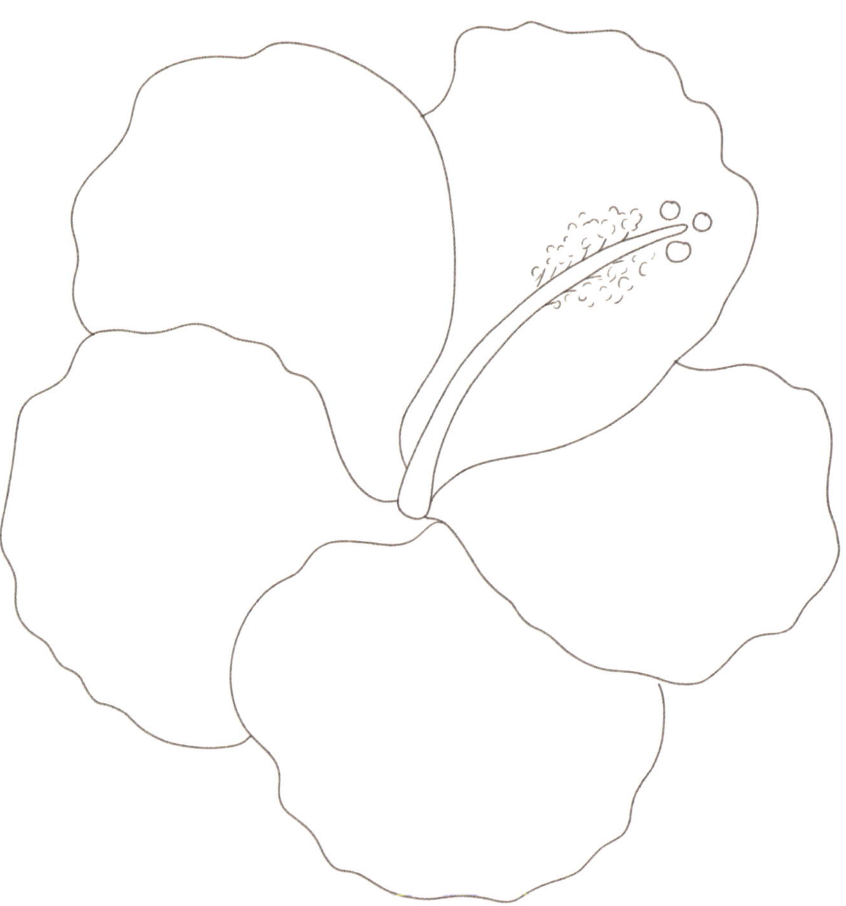

BRUSHES

• Medium/large brush (6, 10)

COLOR PALETTE

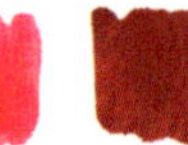

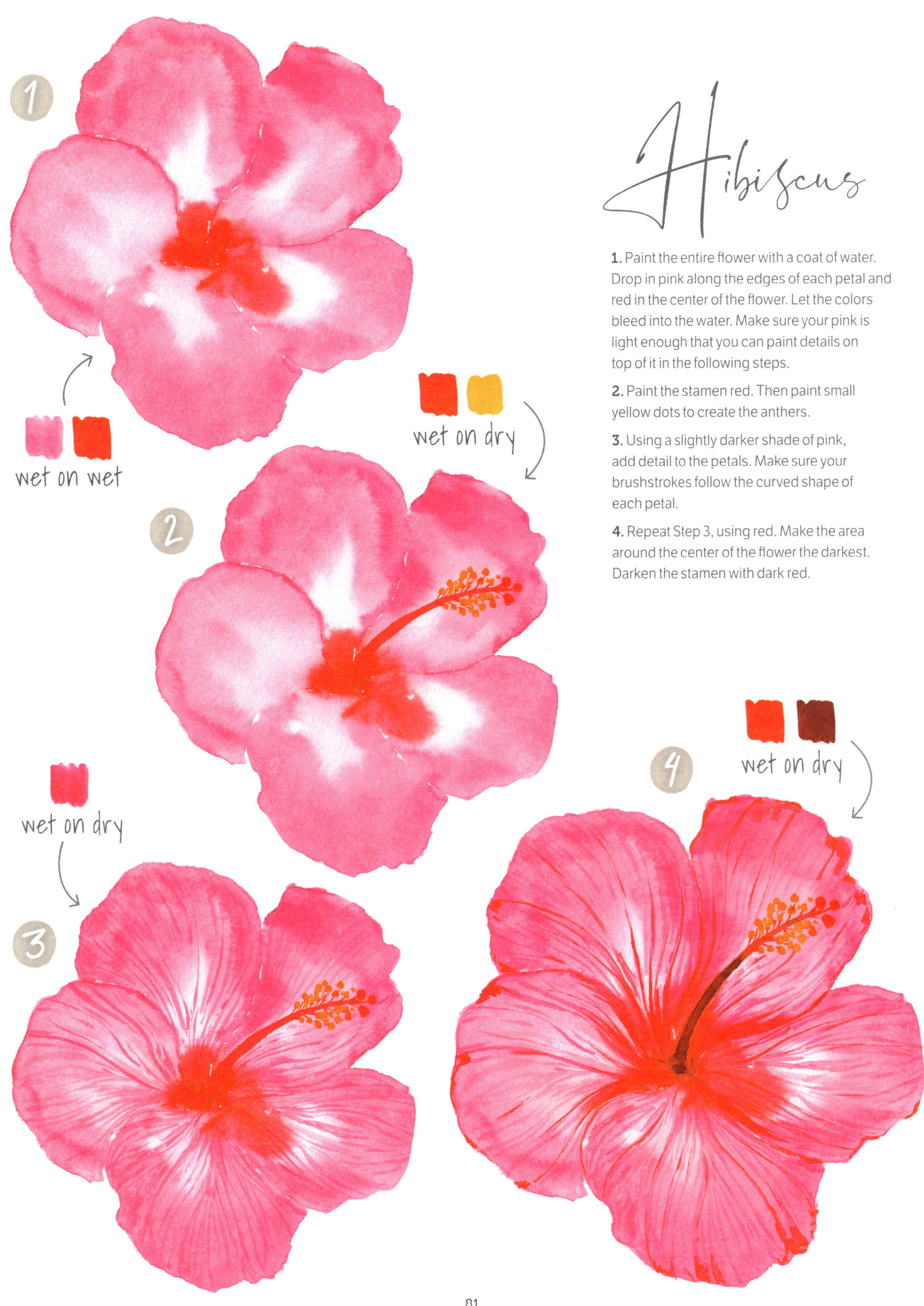

Hibiscus

1. Paint the entire flower with a coat of water. Drop in pink along the edges of each petal and red in the center of the flower. Let the colors bleed into the water. Make sure your pink is light enough that you can paint details on top of it in the following steps.

2. Paint the stamen red. Then paint small yellow dots to create the anthers.

3. Using a slightly darker shade of pink, add detail to the petals. Make sure your brushstrokes follow the curved shape of each petal.

4. Repeat Step 3, using red. Make the area around the center of the flower the darkest. Darken the stamen with dark red.

FLORAL FUN

Due to its showy nature (and the fact that it doesn't produce fruit), the Victorians deemed the hydrangea a showy or boastful plant. Other cultures associate it with heartfelt emotion and timeless beauty.

BRUSHES
• Medium/large brush (6, 10)

COLOR PALETTE

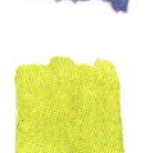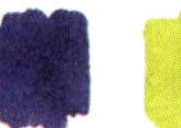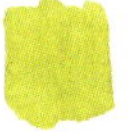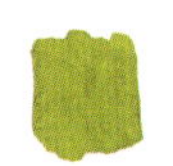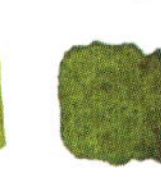

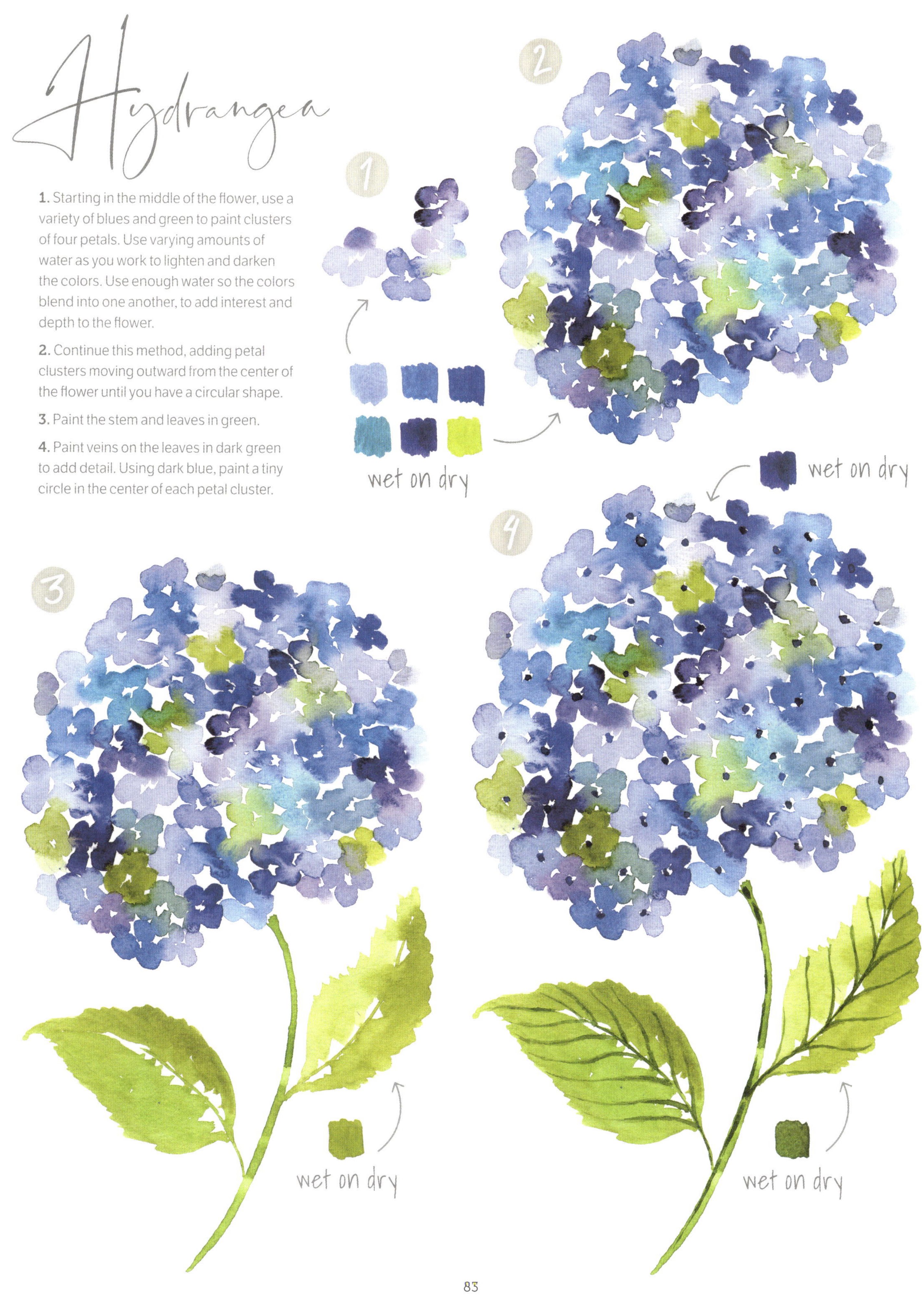

Hydrangea

1. Starting in the middle of the flower, use a variety of blues and green to paint clusters of four petals. Use varying amounts of water as you work to lighten and darken the colors. Use enough water so the colors blend into one another, to add interest and depth to the flower.

2. Continue this method, adding petal clusters moving outward from the center of the flower until you have a circular shape.

3. Paint the stem and leaves in green.

4. Paint veins on the leaves in dark green to add detail. Using dark blue, paint a tiny circle in the center of each petal cluster.

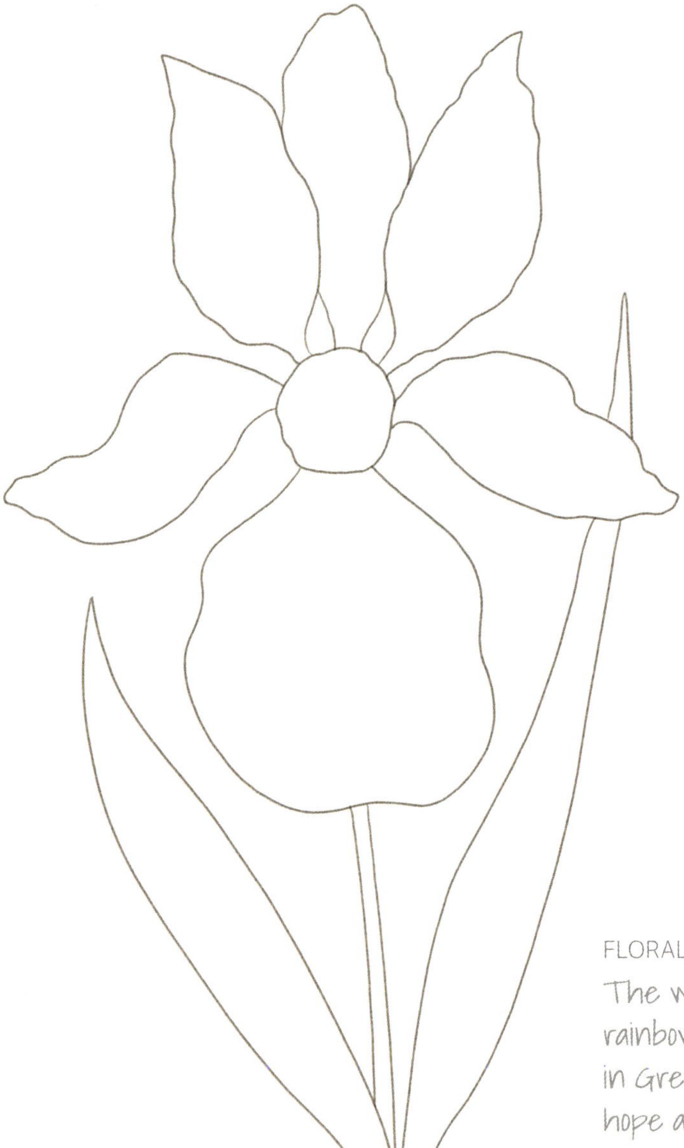

BRUSHES

- Medium/large brush (6, 8)

COLOR PALETTE

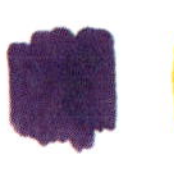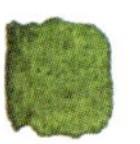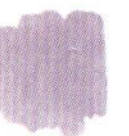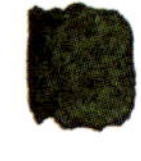

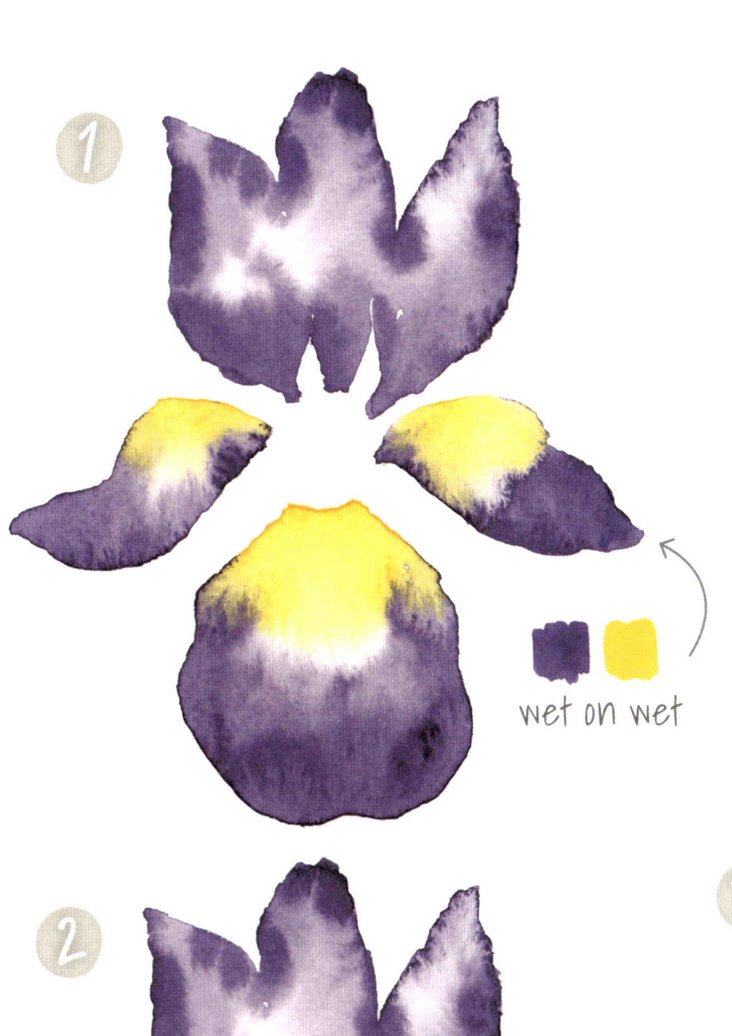

Iris

1. Paint the upper petals with a coat of water. Drop in purple along the edges and let it bleed inward. Now, paint the middle and lower petals with a coat of water. Drop in yellow toward the center of the flower and purple along the edges. Let the colors bleed inward.

2. Paint the center of the flower light purple. Paint the stem and leaves green.

3. Using dark purple, add veins and spots to the petals. Make sure your brushstrokes follow the curved shape of each petal. Add detail to the center of the flower in purple. Add veins to the leaves in dark green.

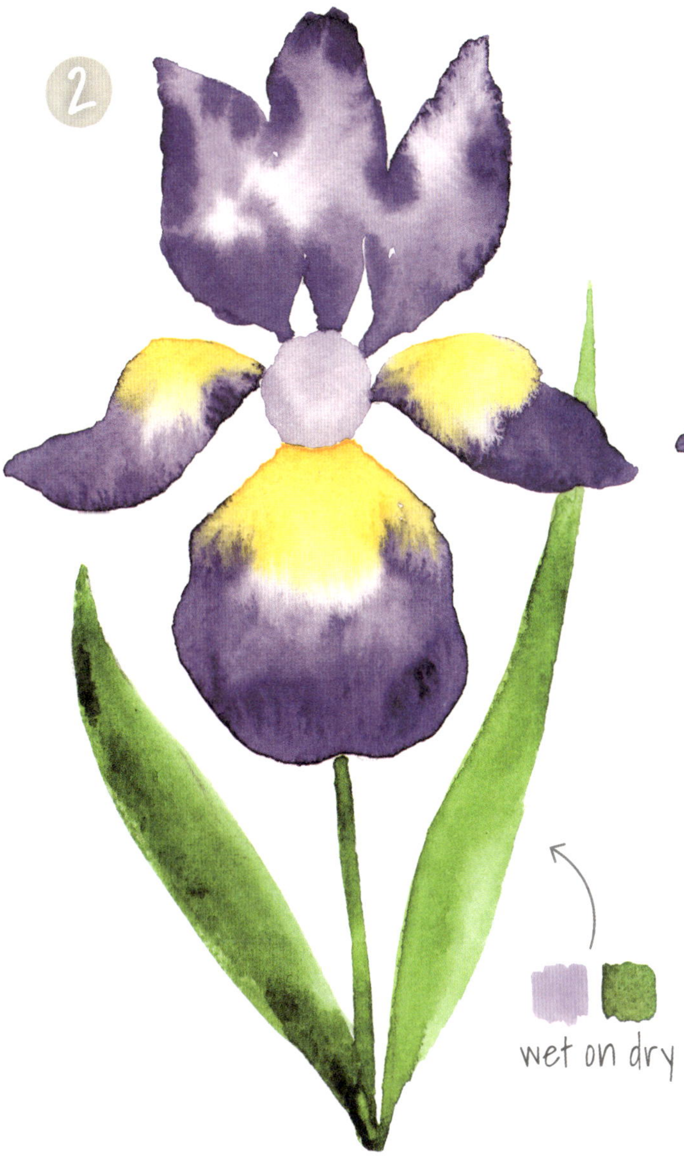

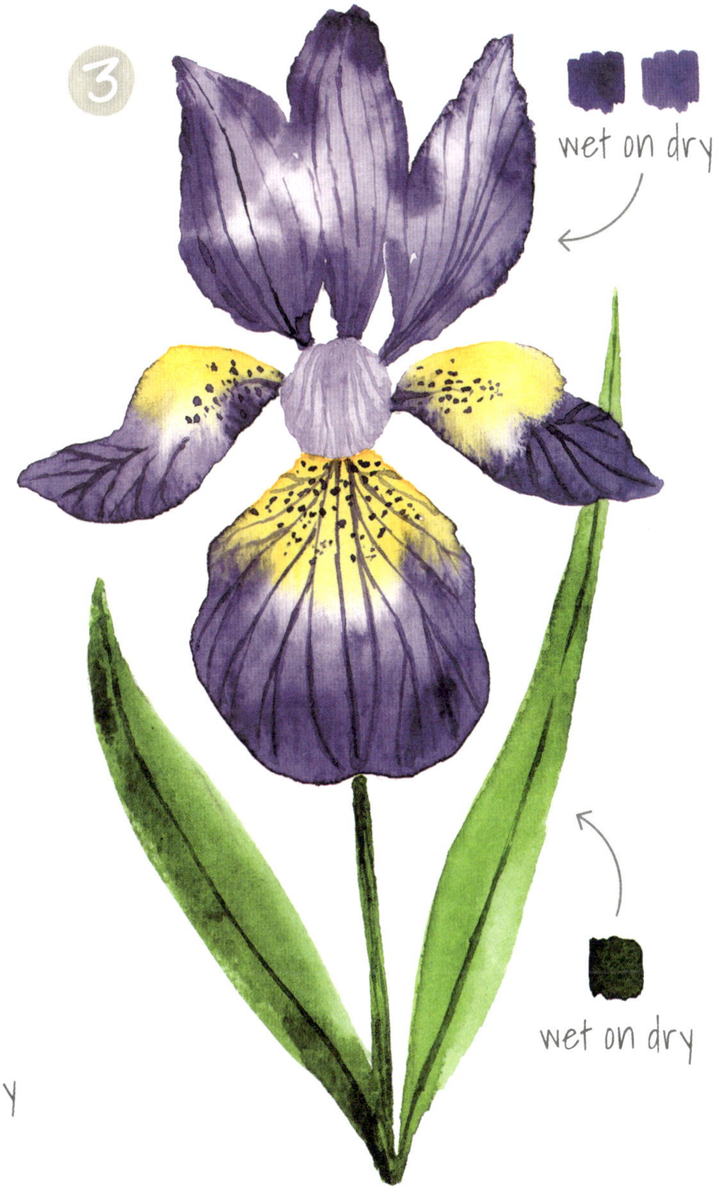

Lavender is well loved for its beautiful scent and healing properties. It is believed to have a calming effect. Paint lavender for a friend in need of peace and serenity.

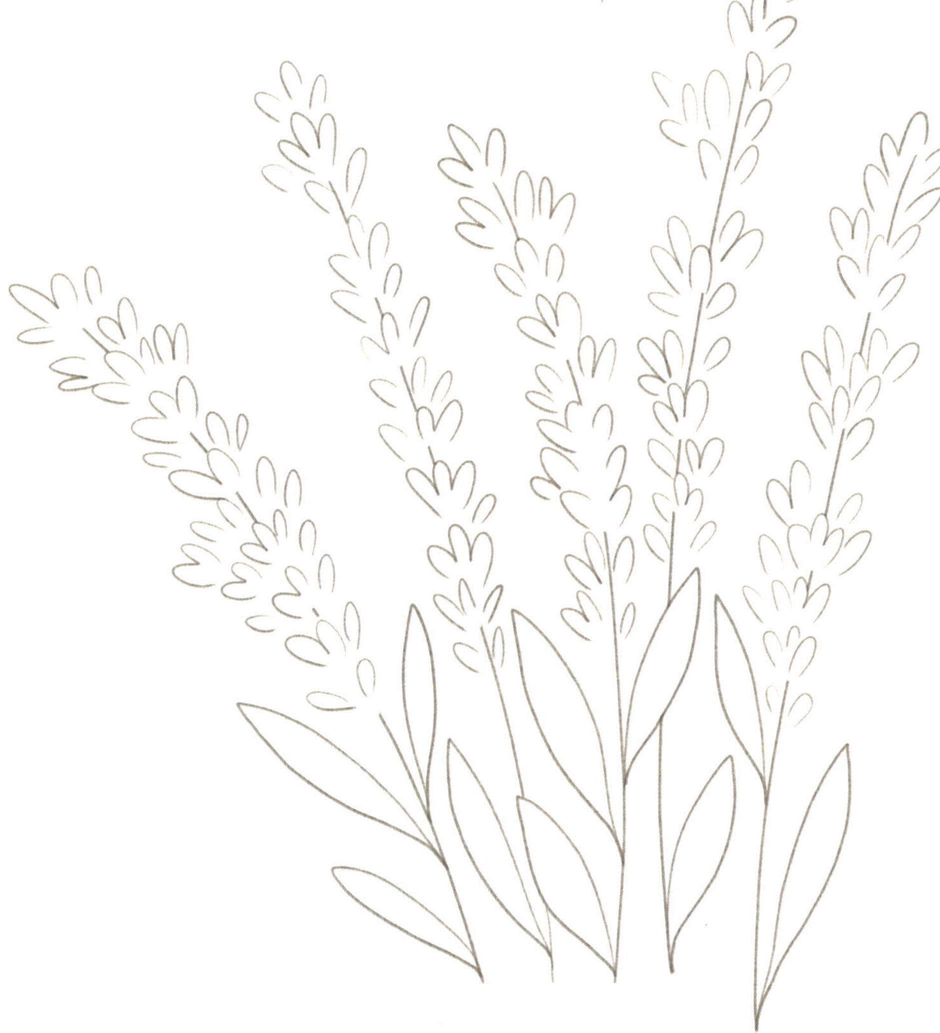

BRUSHES

- Medium/large brush (6, 8)

COLOR PALETTE

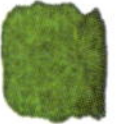  
  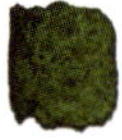

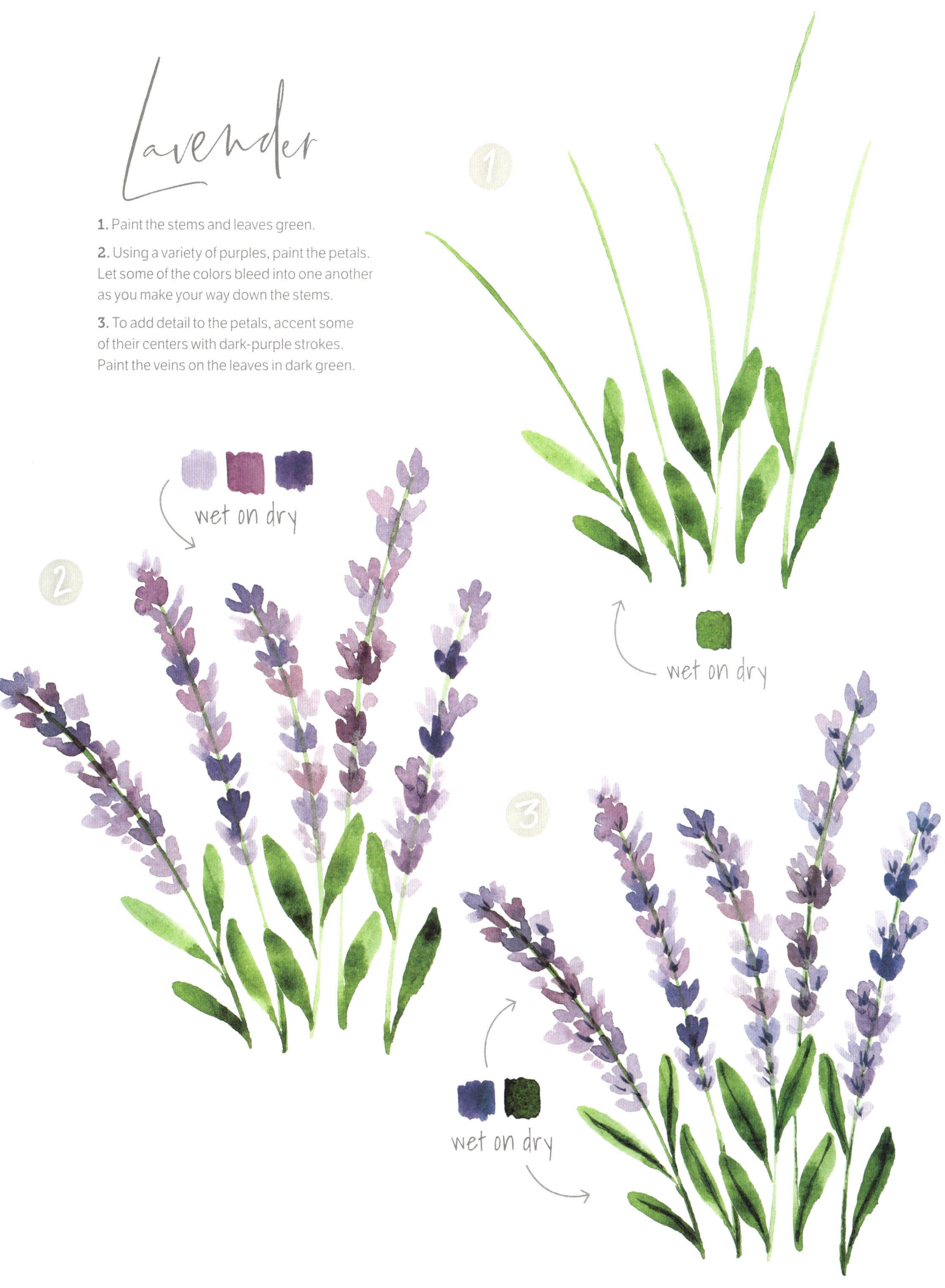

Lavender

1. Paint the stems and leaves green.

2. Using a variety of purples, paint the petals. Let some of the colors bleed into one another as you make your way down the stems.

3. To add detail to the petals, accent some of their centers with dark-purple strokes. Paint the veins on the leaves in dark green.

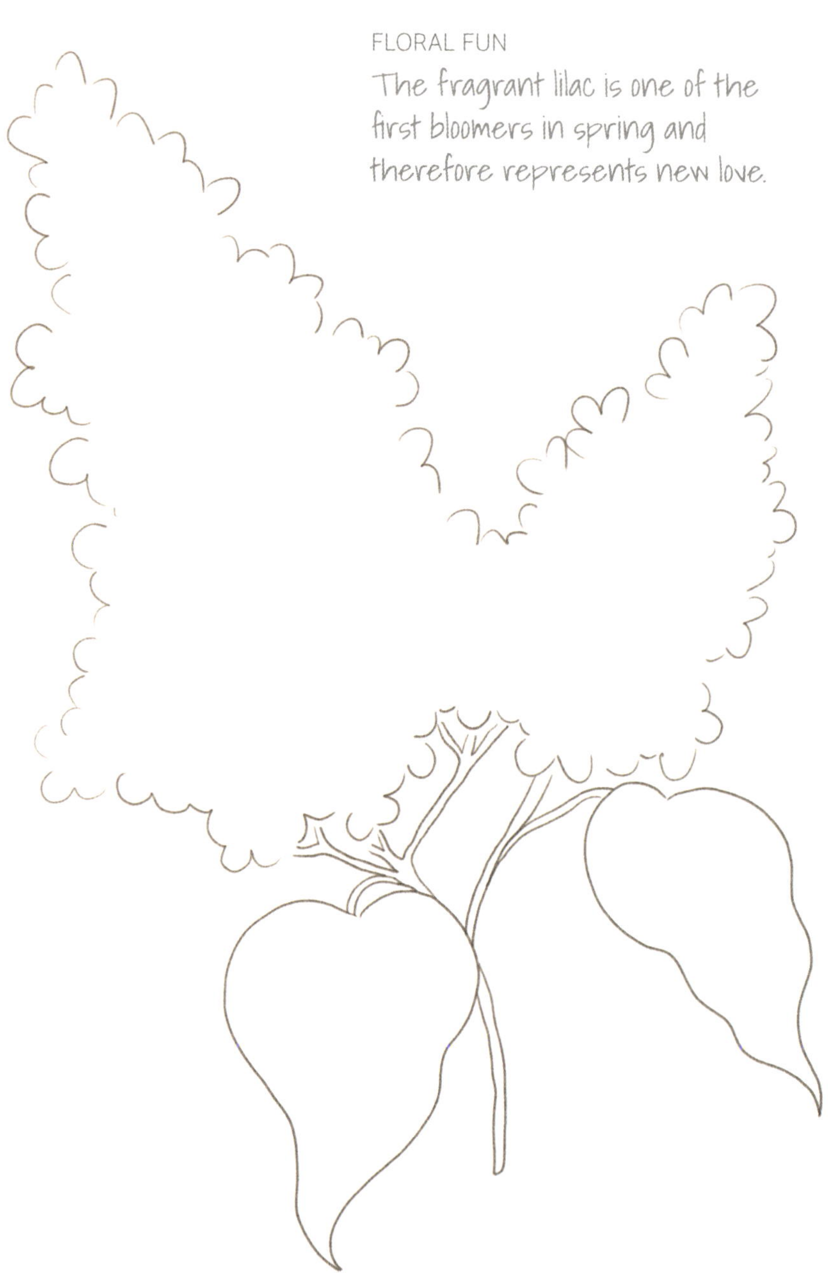

FLORAL FUN

The fragrant lilac is one of the first bloomers in spring and therefore represents new love.

BRUSHES

- Large brush (8)

COLOR PALETTE

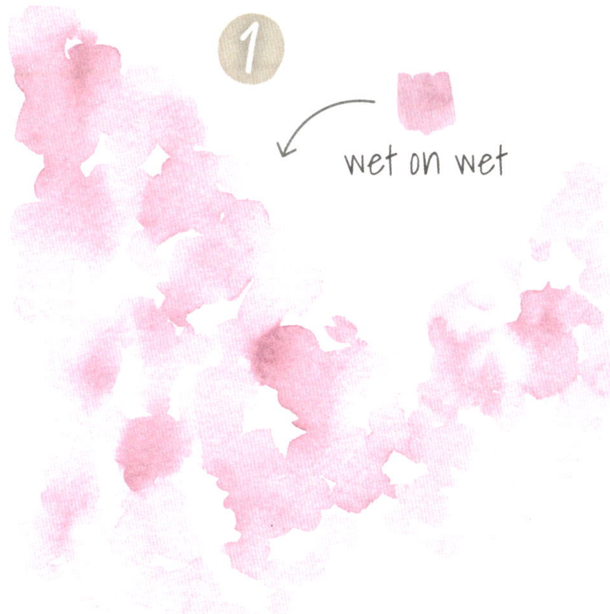

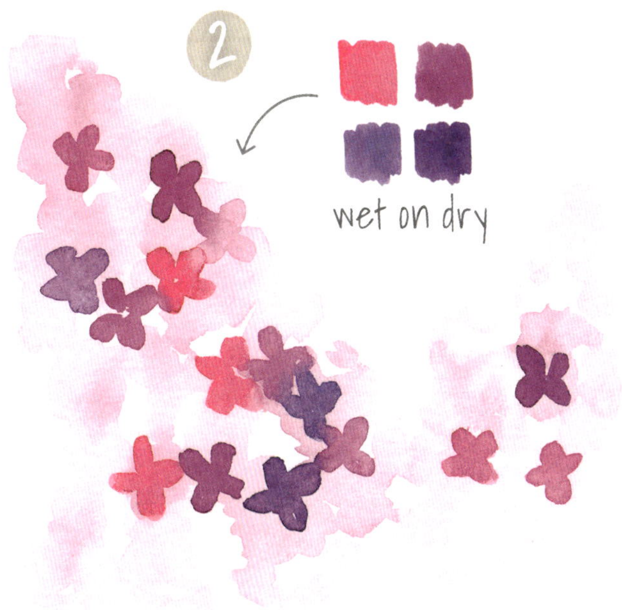

Lilac

1. Using a super-watery mix of pink, paint the first layer of the flowers.

2. Begin painting the petal clusters, using a variety of pinks and purples. Each cluster has four petals.

3. Continue adding petal clusters until you've filled the entire flower.

4. Paint the stems brown and the leaves green.

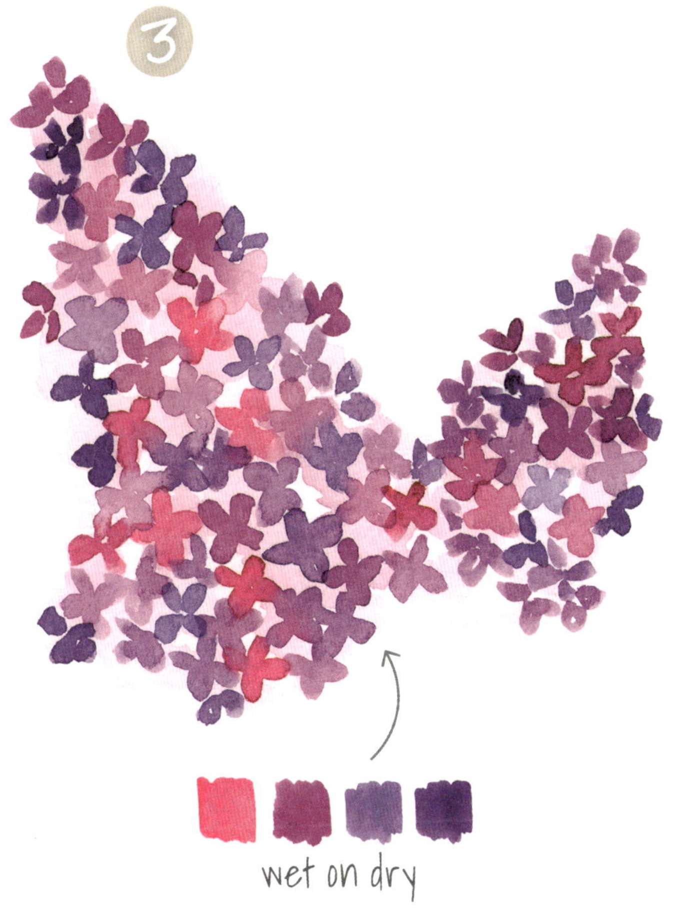

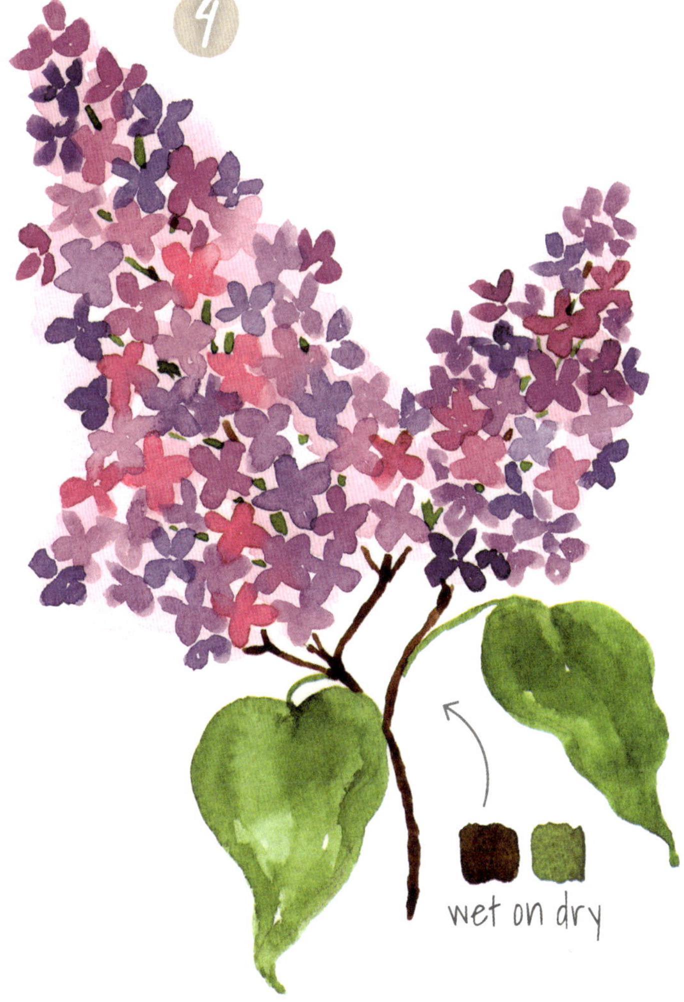

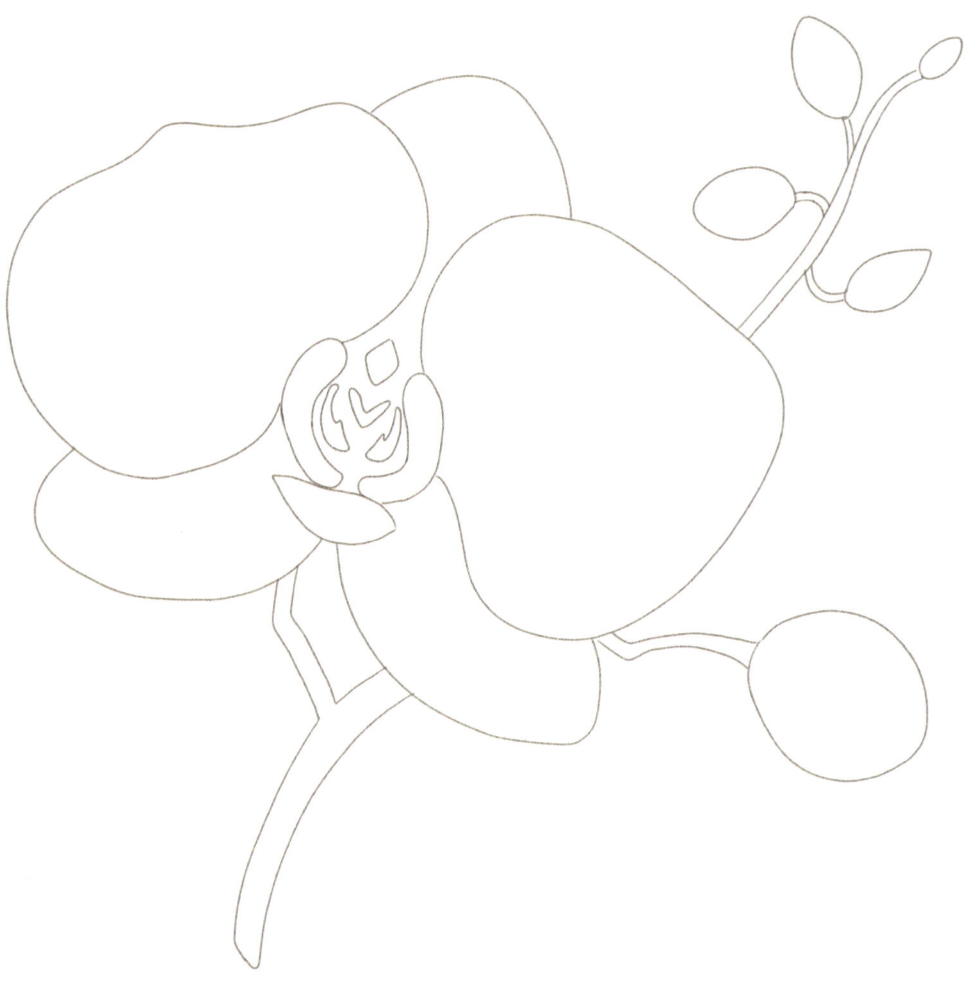

BRUSHES
• Medium/large brush (6, 10)

COLOR PALETTE

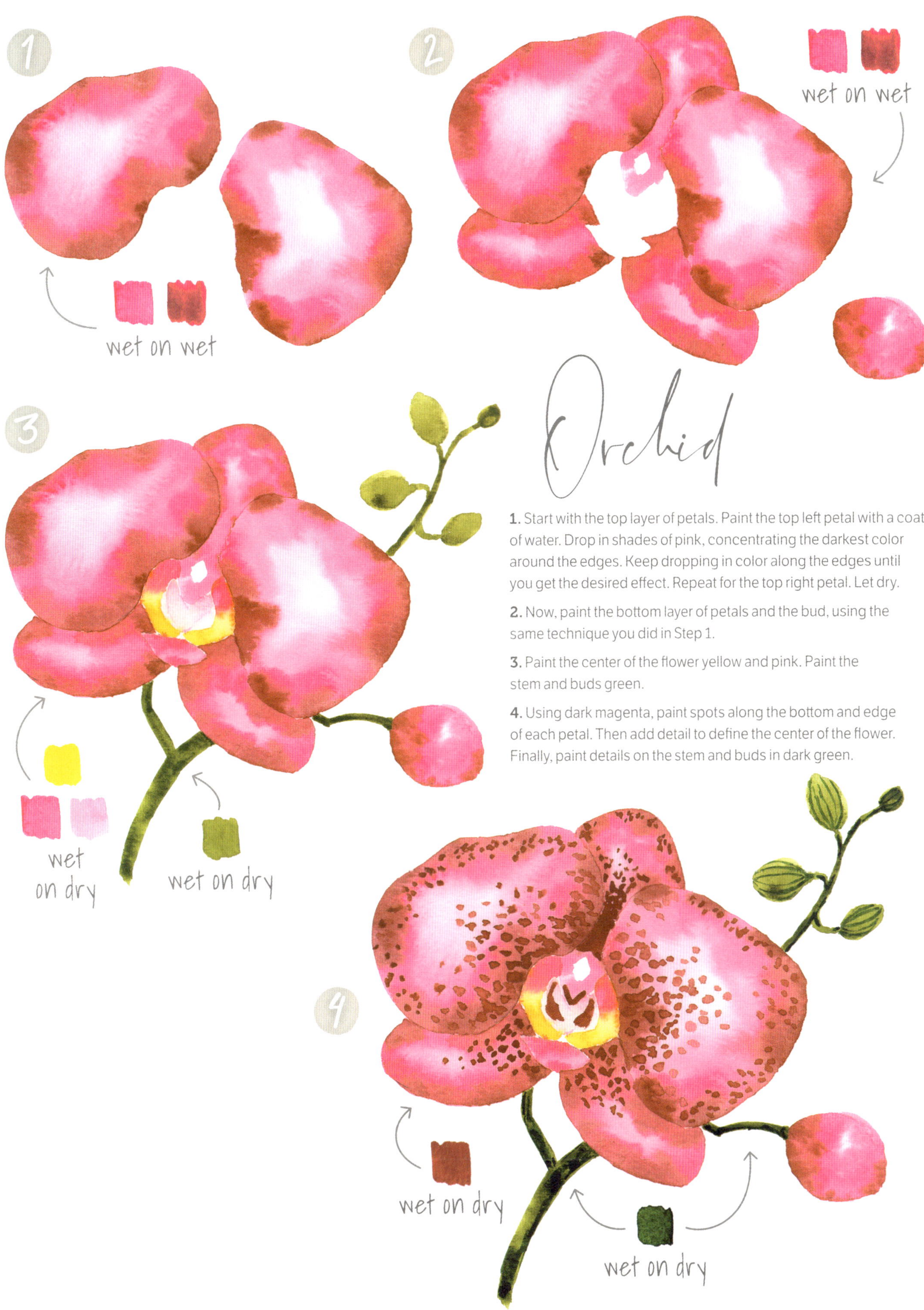

Orchid

1. Start with the top layer of petals. Paint the top left petal with a coat of water. Drop in shades of pink, concentrating the darkest color around the edges. Keep dropping in color along the edges until you get the desired effect. Repeat for the top right petal. Let dry.

2. Now, paint the bottom layer of petals and the bud, using the same technique you did in Step 1.

3. Paint the center of the flower yellow and pink. Paint the stem and buds green.

4. Using dark magenta, paint spots along the bottom and edge of each petal. Then add detail to define the center of the flower. Finally, paint details on the stem and buds in dark green.

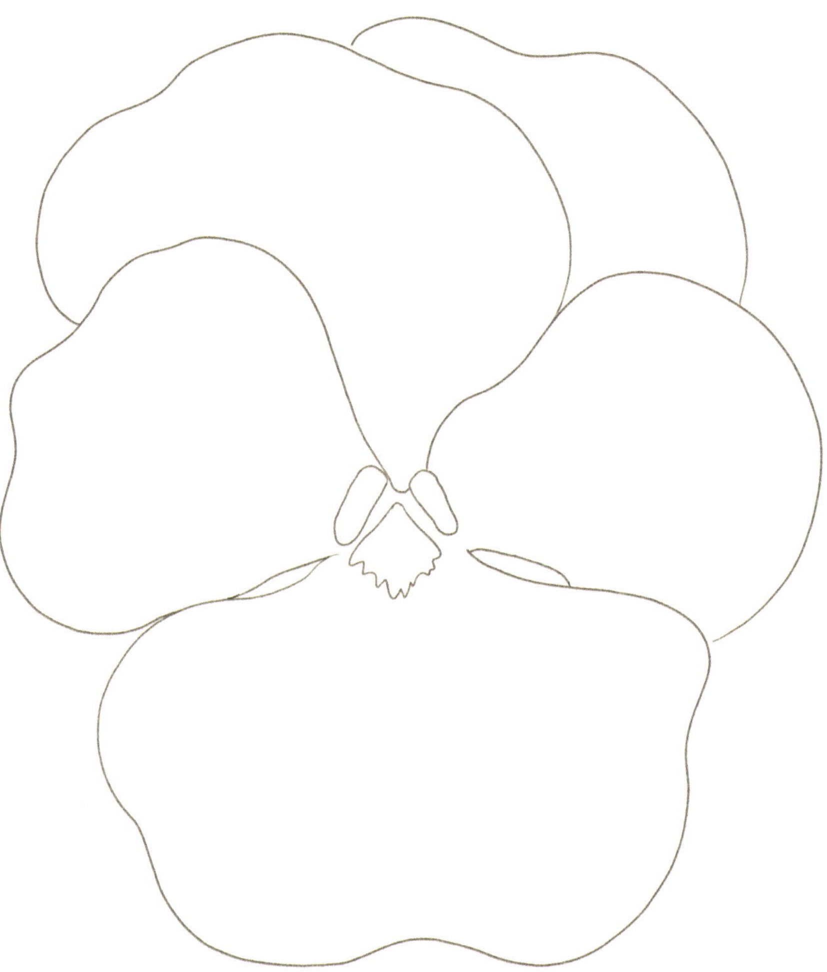

BRUSHES

• Medium/large brush (6, 10)

COLOR PALETTE

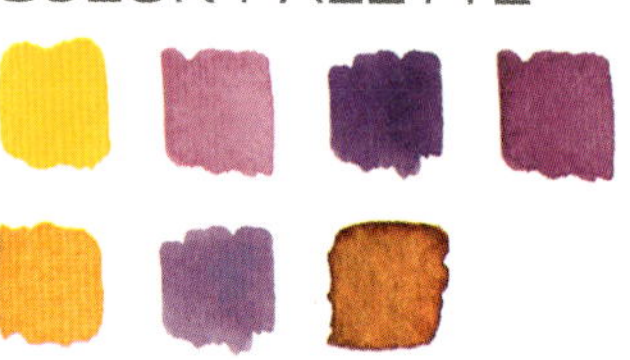

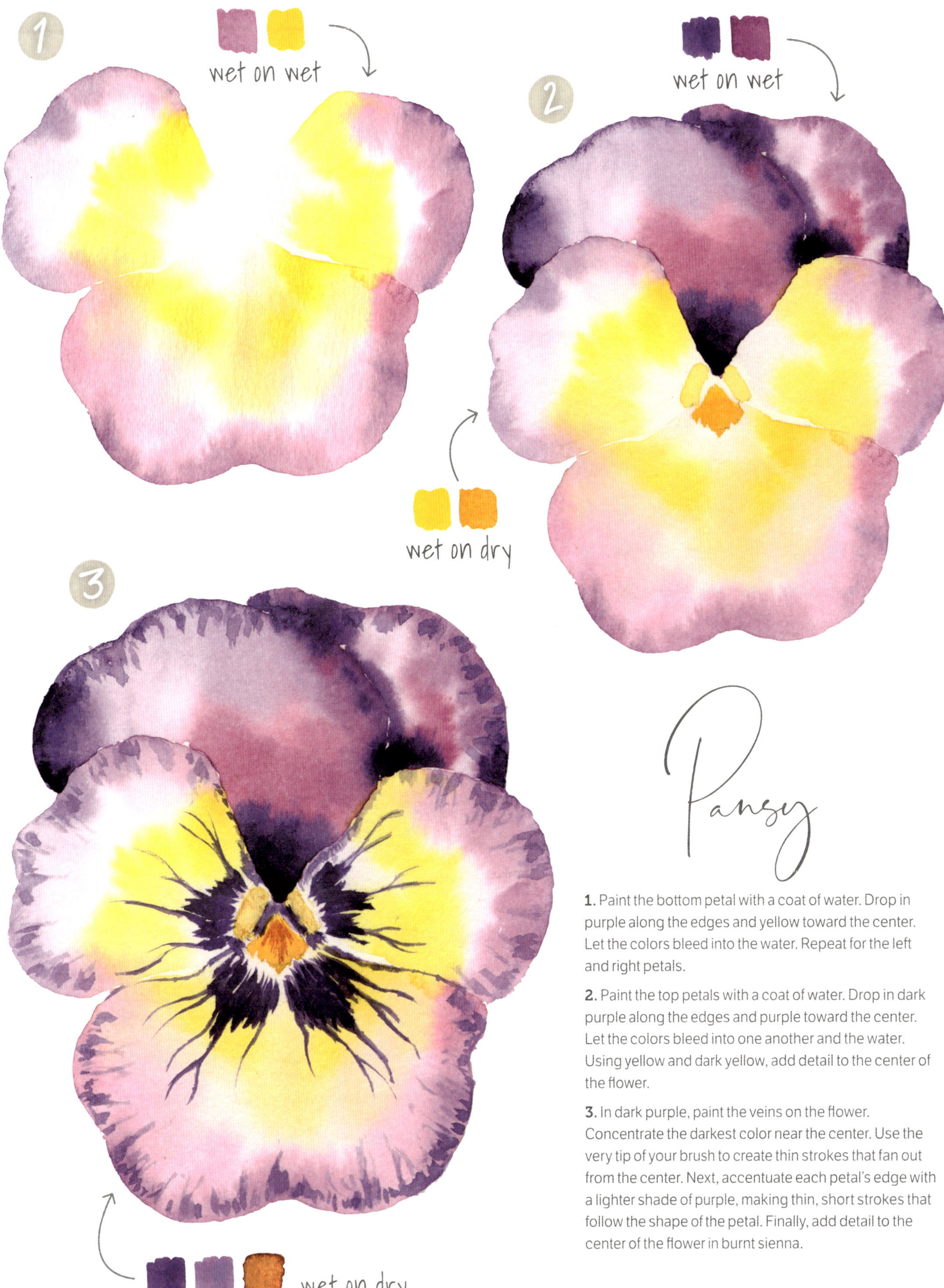

1. Paint the bottom petal with a coat of water. Drop in purple along the edges and yellow toward the center. Let the colors bleed into the water. Repeat for the left and right petals.

2. Paint the top petals with a coat of water. Drop in dark purple along the edges and purple toward the center. Let the colors bleed into one another and the water. Using yellow and dark yellow, add detail to the center of the flower.

3. In dark purple, paint the veins on the flower. Concentrate the darkest color near the center. Use the very tip of your brush to create thin strokes that fan out from the center. Next, accentuate each petal's edge with a lighter shade of purple, making thin, short strokes that follow the shape of the petal. Finally, add detail to the center of the flower in burnt sienna.

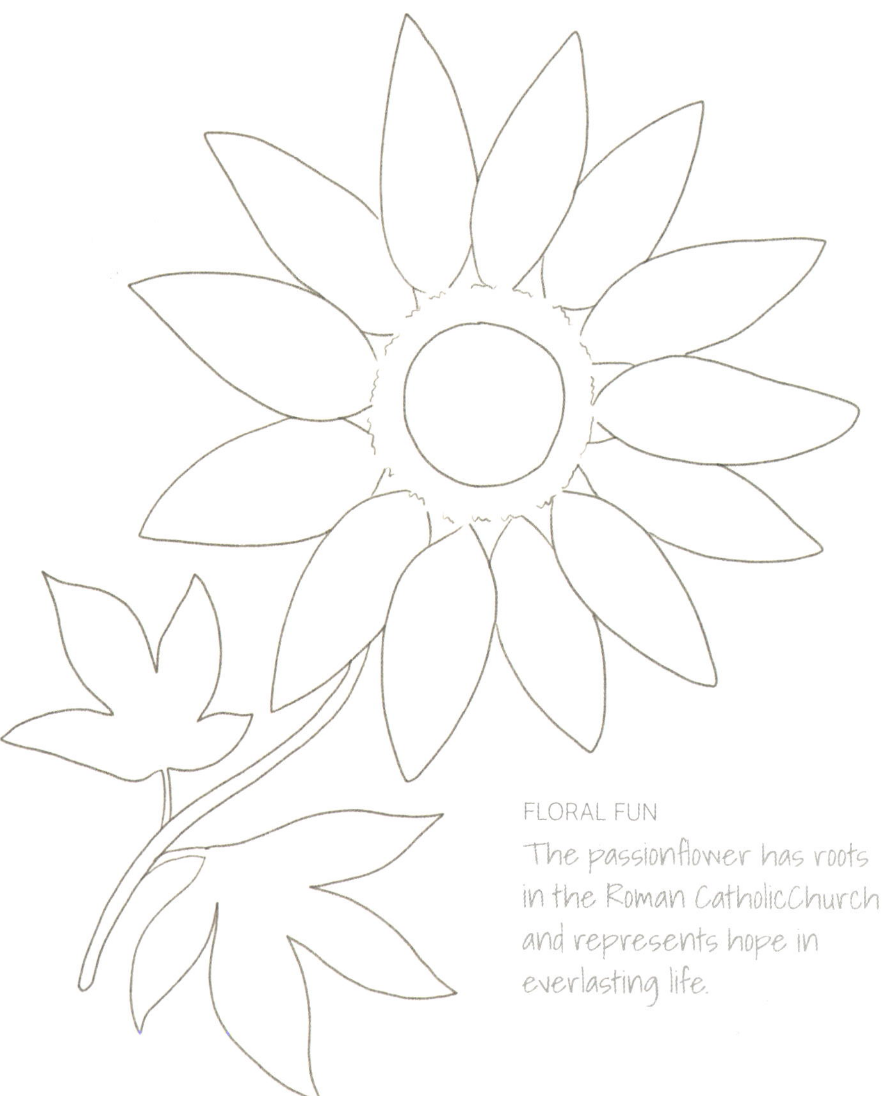

FLORAL FUN

The passionflower has roots in the Roman CatholicChurch and represents hope in everlasting life.

BRUSHES

• Medium/large brush (6, 8)

COLOR PALETTE

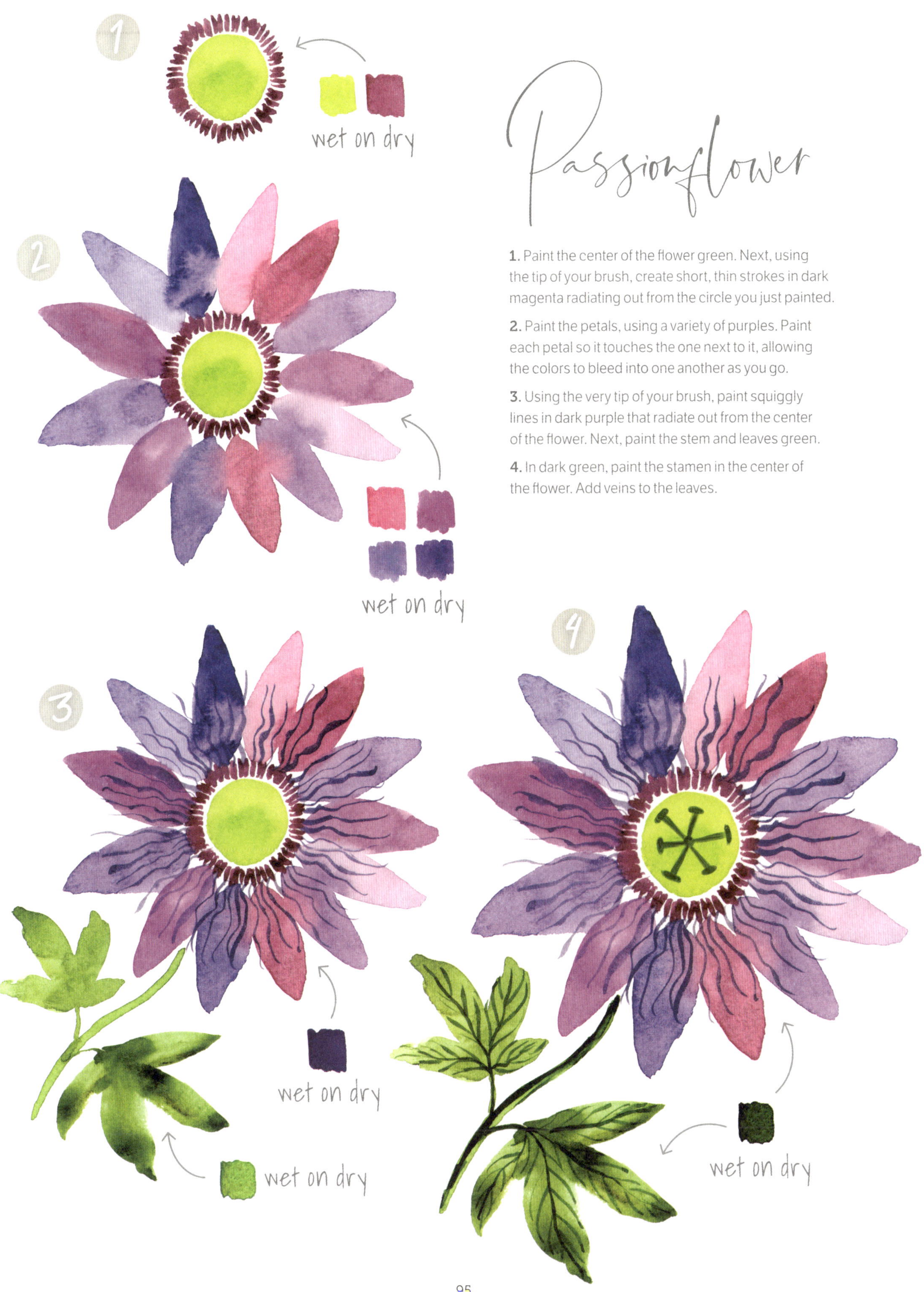

Passionflower

1. Paint the center of the flower green. Next, using the tip of your brush, create short, thin strokes in dark magenta radiating out from the circle you just painted.

2. Paint the petals, using a variety of purples. Paint each petal so it touches the one next to it, allowing the colors to bleed into one another as you go.

3. Using the very tip of your brush, paint squiggly lines in dark purple that radiate out from the center of the flower. Next, paint the stem and leaves green.

4. In dark green, paint the stamen in the center of the flower. Add veins to the leaves.

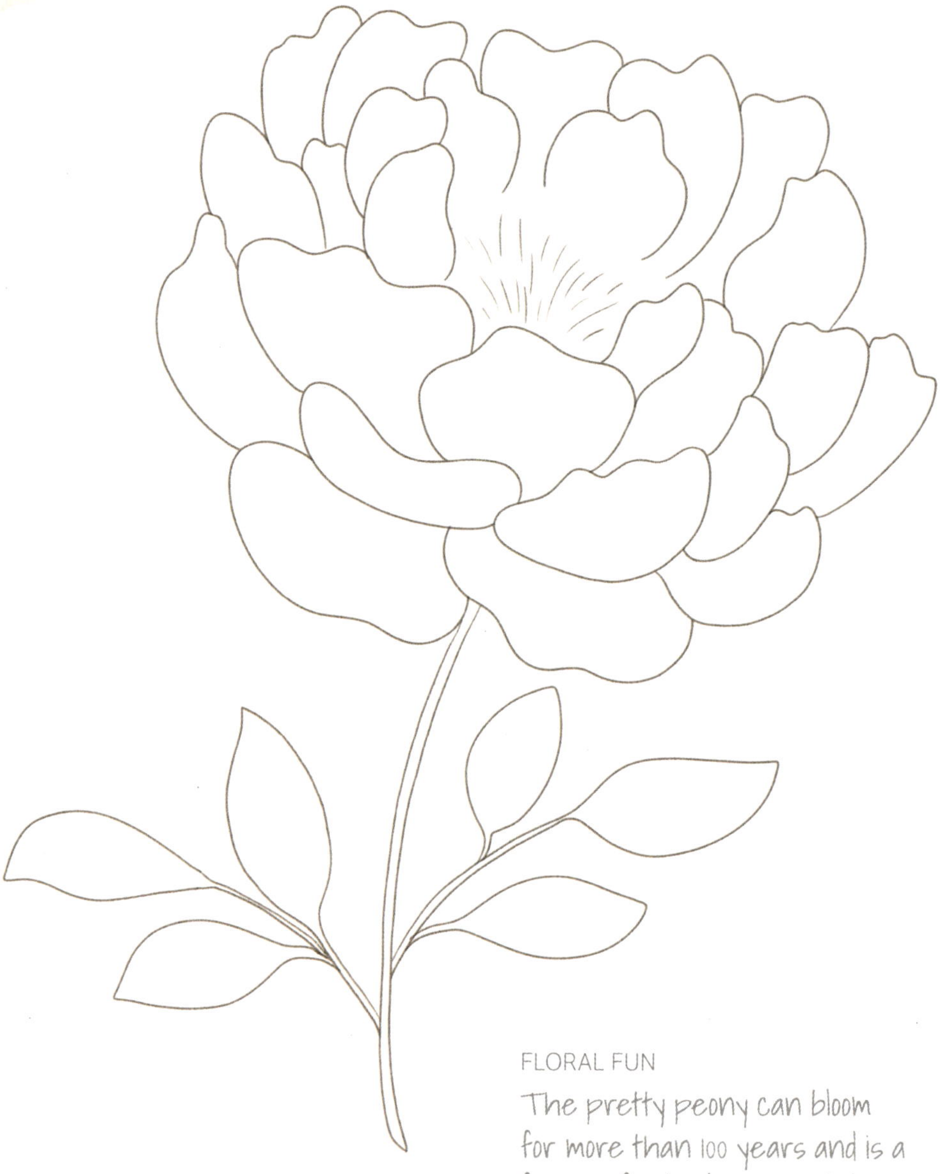

BRUSHES

- Medium/large brush (6, 10)

COLOR PALETTE

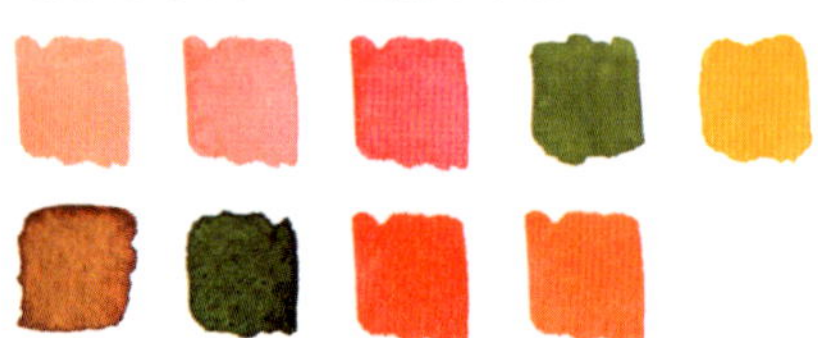

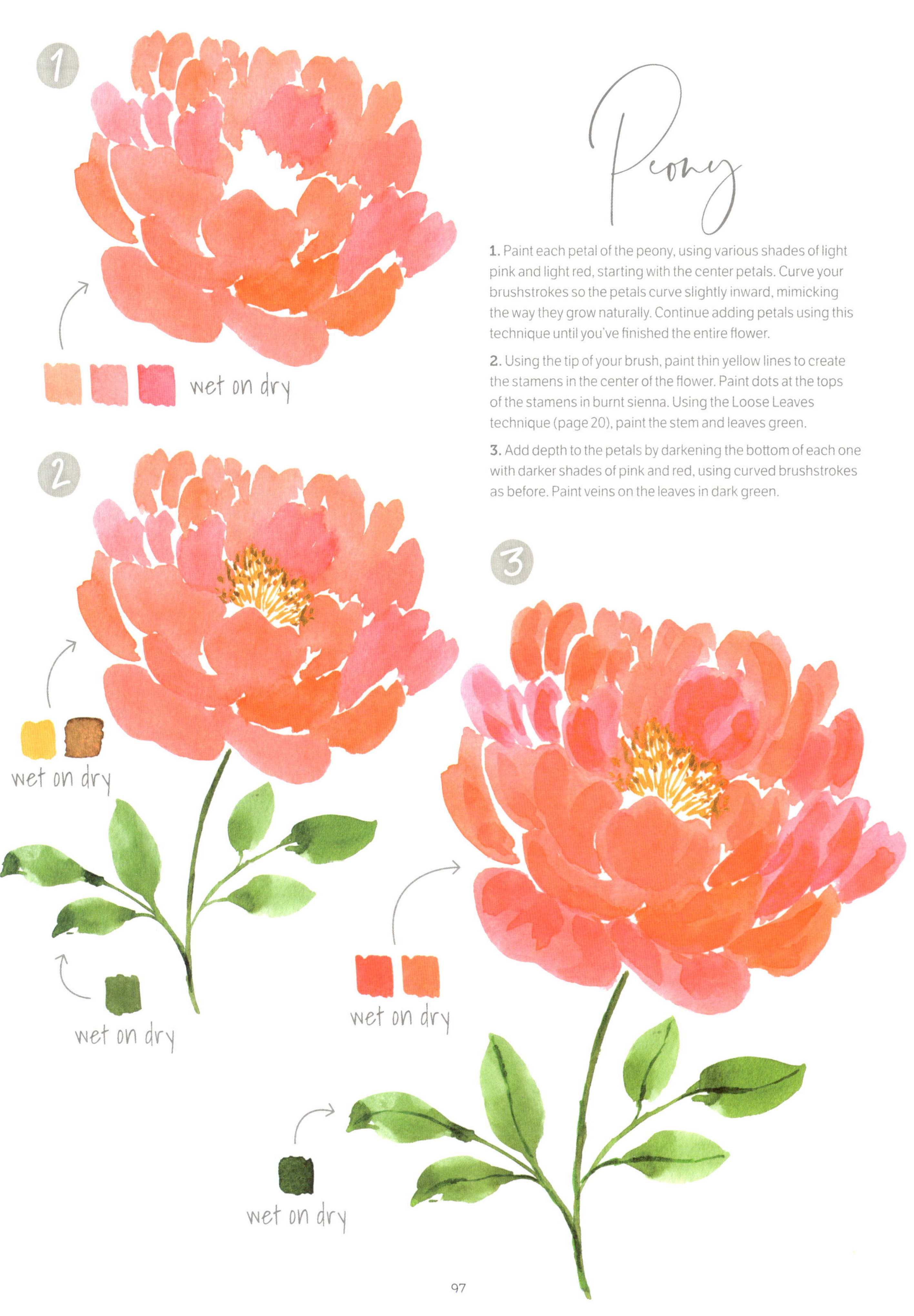

Peony

1. Paint each petal of the peony, using various shades of light pink and light red, starting with the center petals. Curve your brushstrokes so the petals curve slightly inward, mimicking the way they grow naturally. Continue adding petals using this technique until you've finished the entire flower.

2. Using the tip of your brush, paint thin yellow lines to create the stamens in the center of the flower. Paint dots at the tops of the stamens in burnt sienna. Using the Loose Leaves technique (page 20), paint the stem and leaves green.

3. Add depth to the petals by darkening the bottom of each one with darker shades of pink and red, using curved brushstrokes as before. Paint veins on the leaves in dark green.

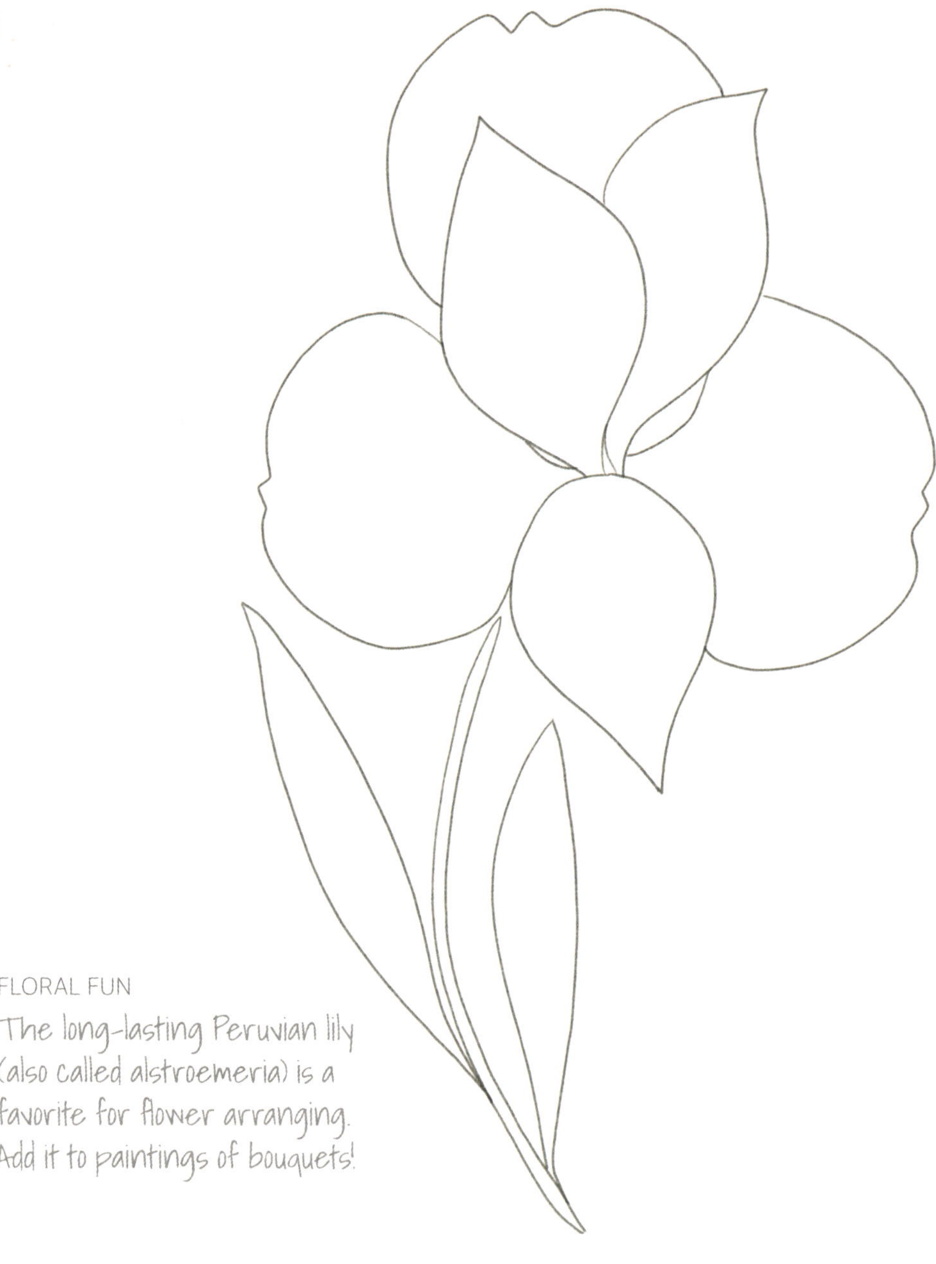

The long-lasting Peruvian lily (also called alstroemeria) is a favorite for flower arranging. Add it to paintings of bouquets!

BRUSHES
- Medium/large brush (6, 8)

COLOR PALETTE

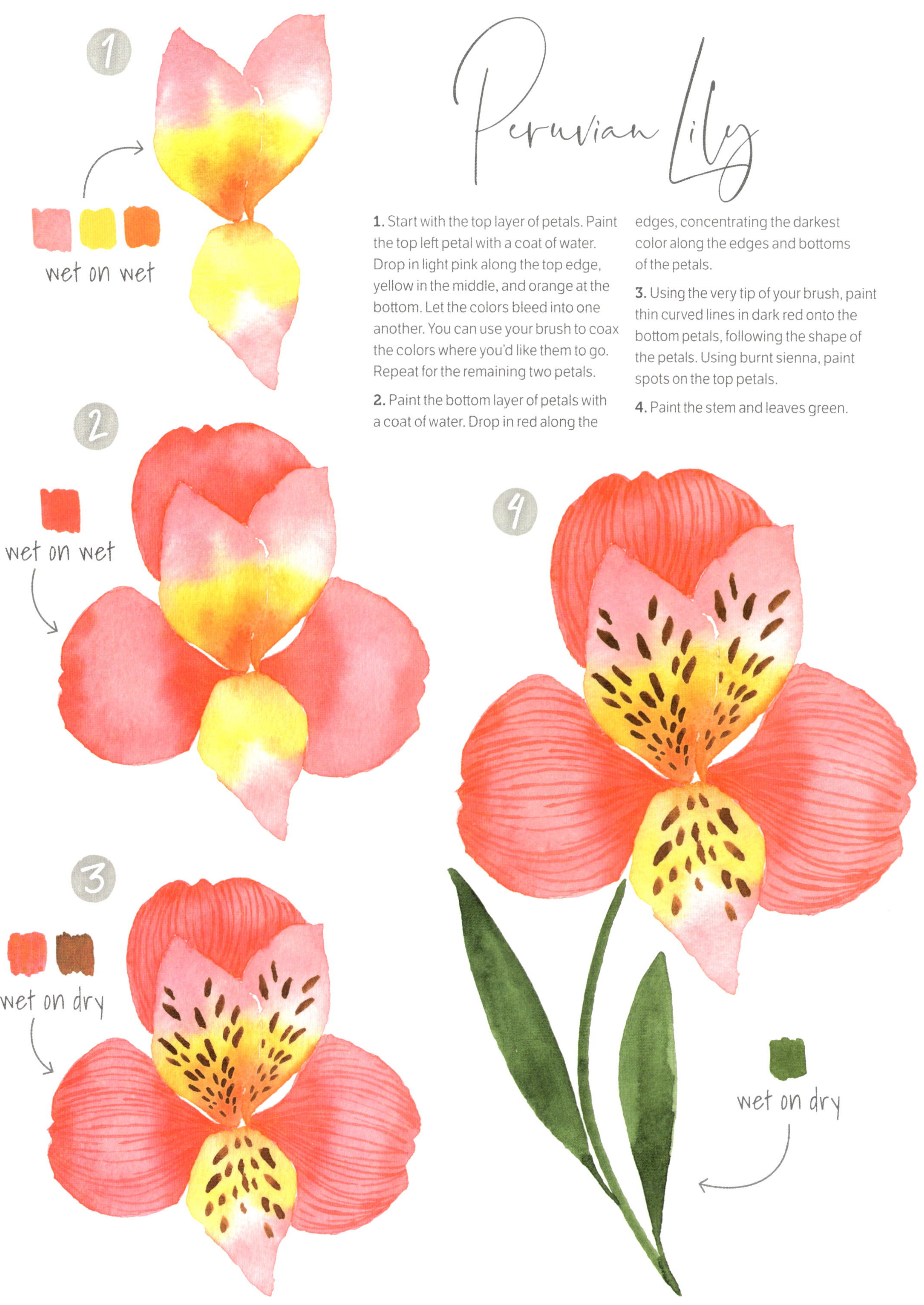

Peruvian Lily

1. Start with the top layer of petals. Paint the top left petal with a coat of water. Drop in light pink along the top edge, yellow in the middle, and orange at the bottom. Let the colors bleed into one another. You can use your brush to coax the colors where you'd like them to go. Repeat for the remaining two petals.

2. Paint the bottom layer of petals with a coat of water. Drop in red along the edges, concentrating the darkest color along the edges and bottoms of the petals.

3. Using the very tip of your brush, paint thin curved lines in dark red onto the bottom petals, following the shape of the petals. Using burnt sienna, paint spots on the top petals.

4. Paint the stem and leaves green.

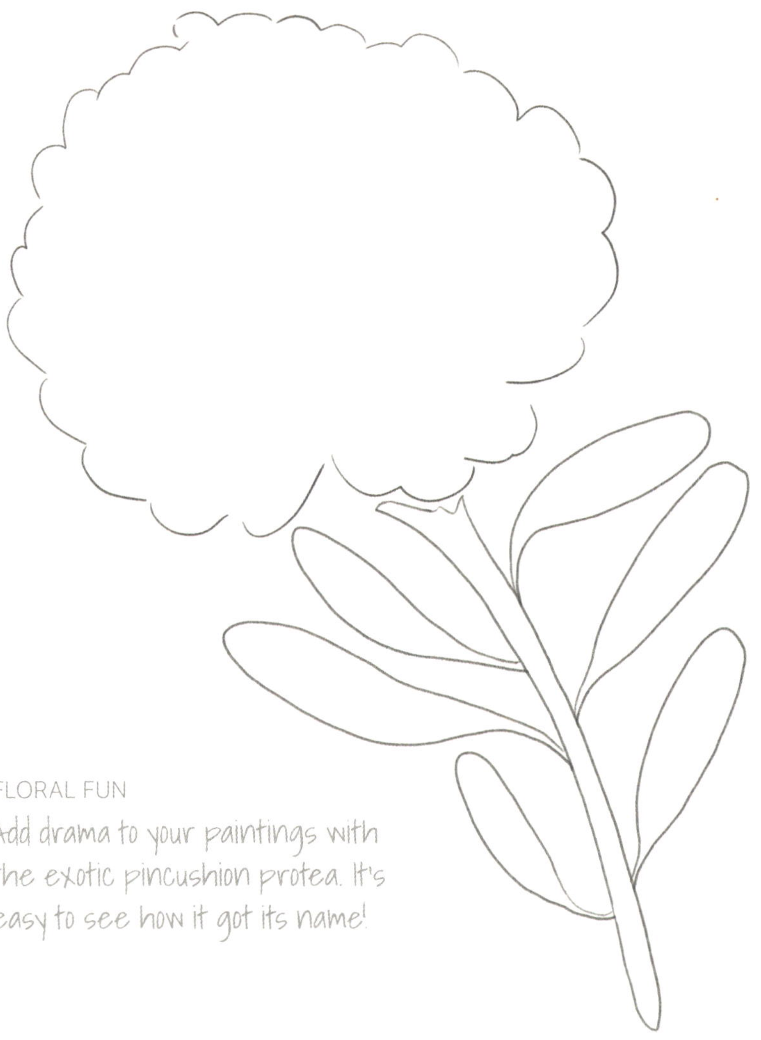

BRUSHES

- Medium/large brush (6, 8)

COLOR PALETTE

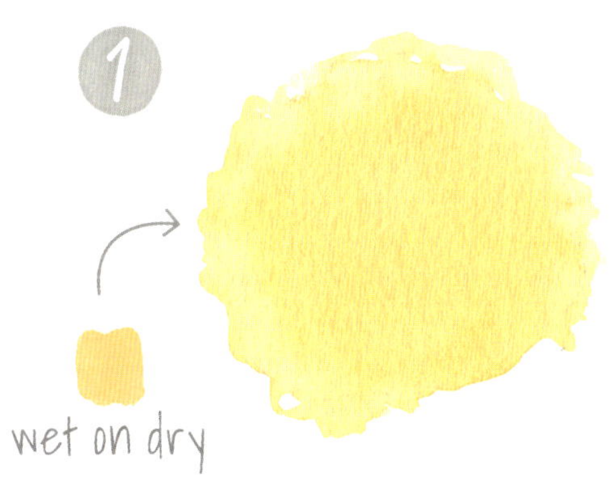

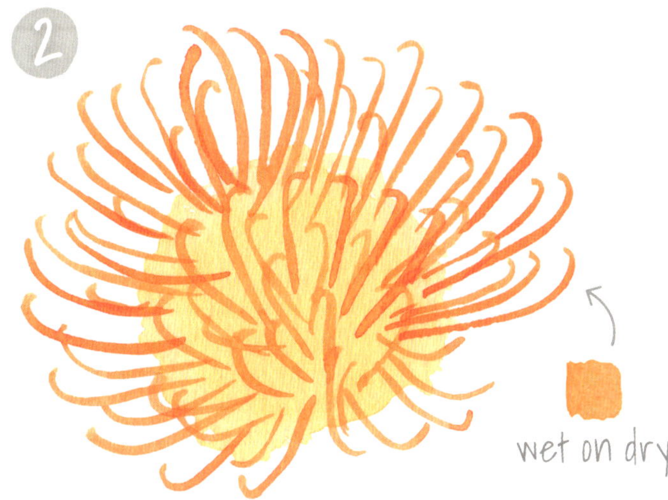

Pincushion Protea

1. Paint a roughly circular shape in light yellow for the center of the flower. The edges should be uneven and not perfectly smooth.

2. Using the tip of your brush, paint thin lines radiating out from the flower's center in orange. Notice how the lines curve and the ends form a hook shape. Try to mimic that shape with your brushstrokes.

3. Add more curved strokes in dark orange. Then, paint the stem brown and the leaves green.

4. Add detail to the flower by painting a red dot at the end of each curved line. Then paint the leaf veins in dark green.

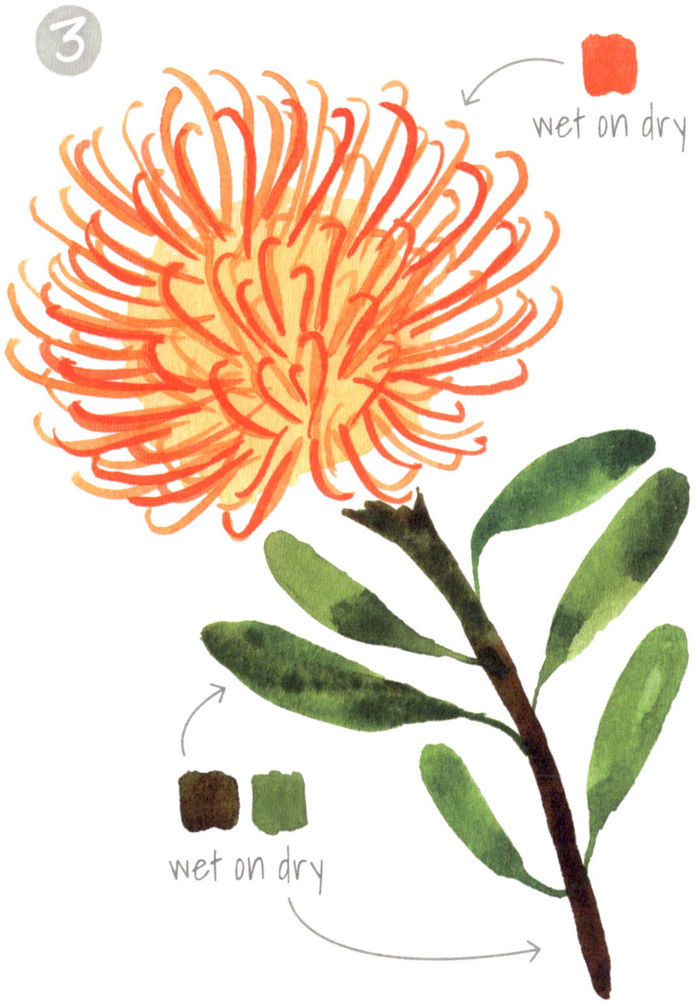

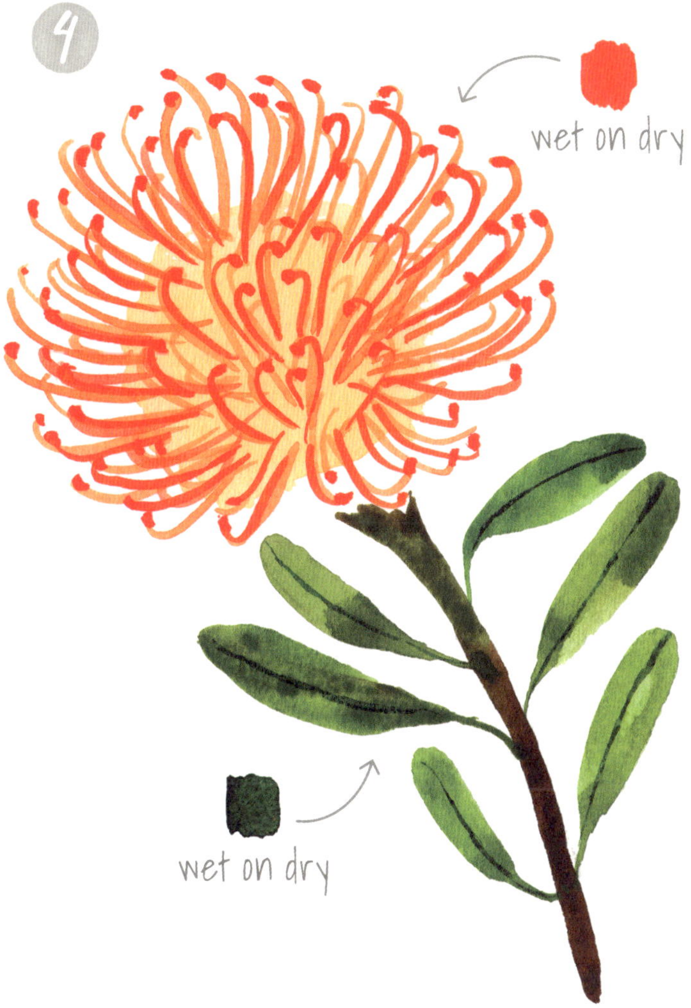

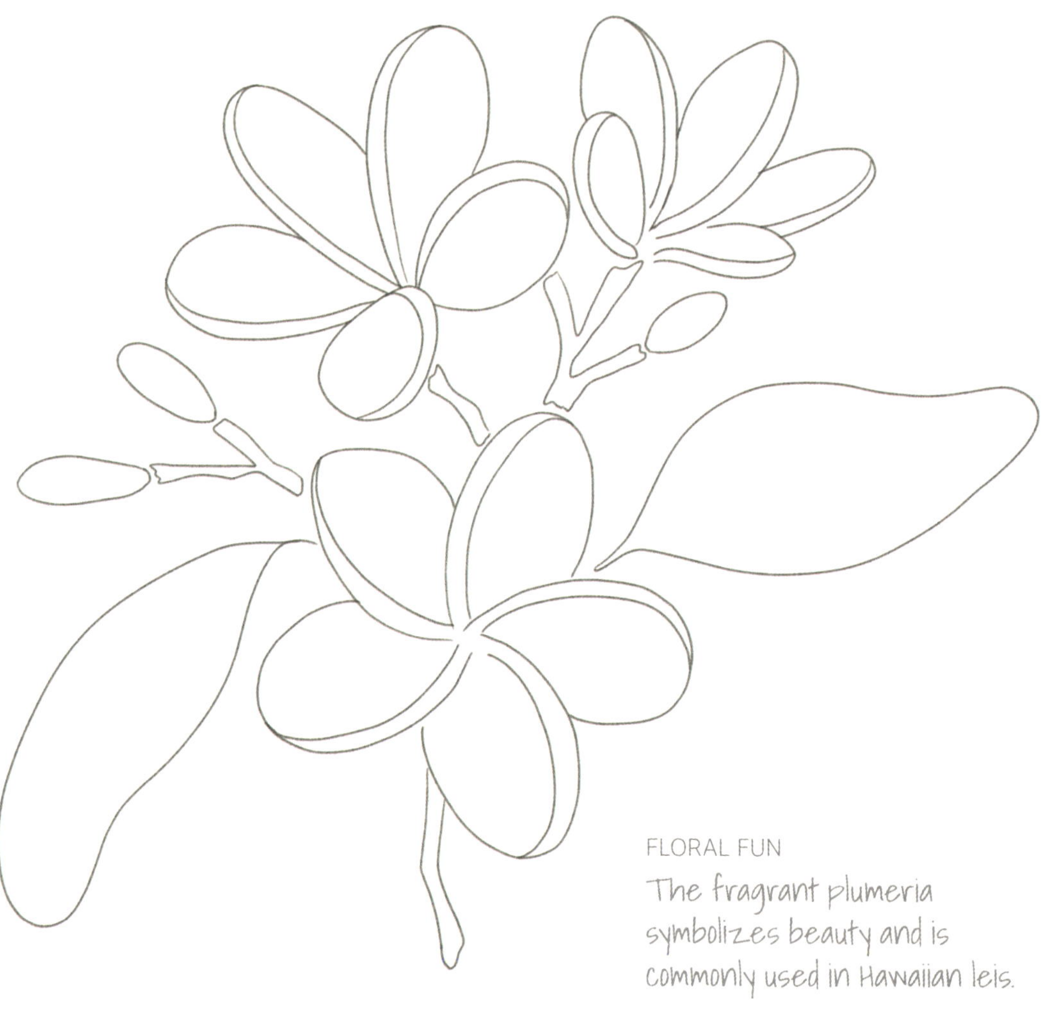

FLORAL FUN

The fragrant plumeria symbolizes beauty and is commonly used in Hawaiian leis.

BRUSHES

• Medium/large brush (6, 8)

COLOR PALETTE

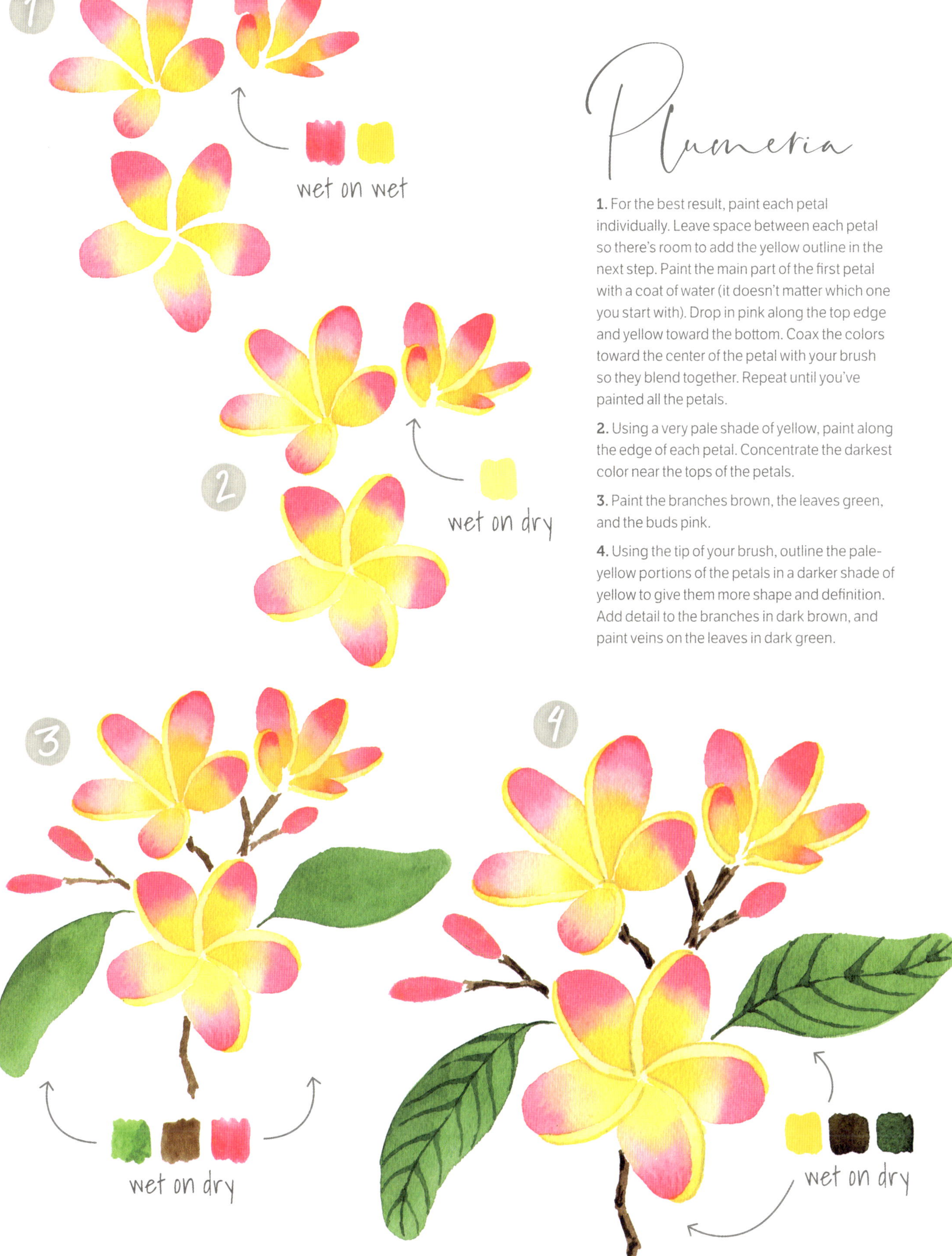

Plumeria

1. For the best result, paint each petal individually. Leave space between each petal so there's room to add the yellow outline in the next step. Paint the main part of the first petal with a coat of water (it doesn't matter which one you start with). Drop in pink along the top edge and yellow toward the bottom. Coax the colors toward the center of the petal with your brush so they blend together. Repeat until you've painted all the petals.

2. Using a very pale shade of yellow, paint along the edge of each petal. Concentrate the darkest color near the tops of the petals.

3. Paint the branches brown, the leaves green, and the buds pink.

4. Using the tip of your brush, outline the pale-yellow portions of the petals in a darker shade of yellow to give them more shape and definition. Add detail to the branches in dark brown, and paint veins on the leaves in dark green.

The poinsettia got its permanent place in Christmas traditions because of its red and green colors and star-shaped leaves. They represent good cheer and celebration.

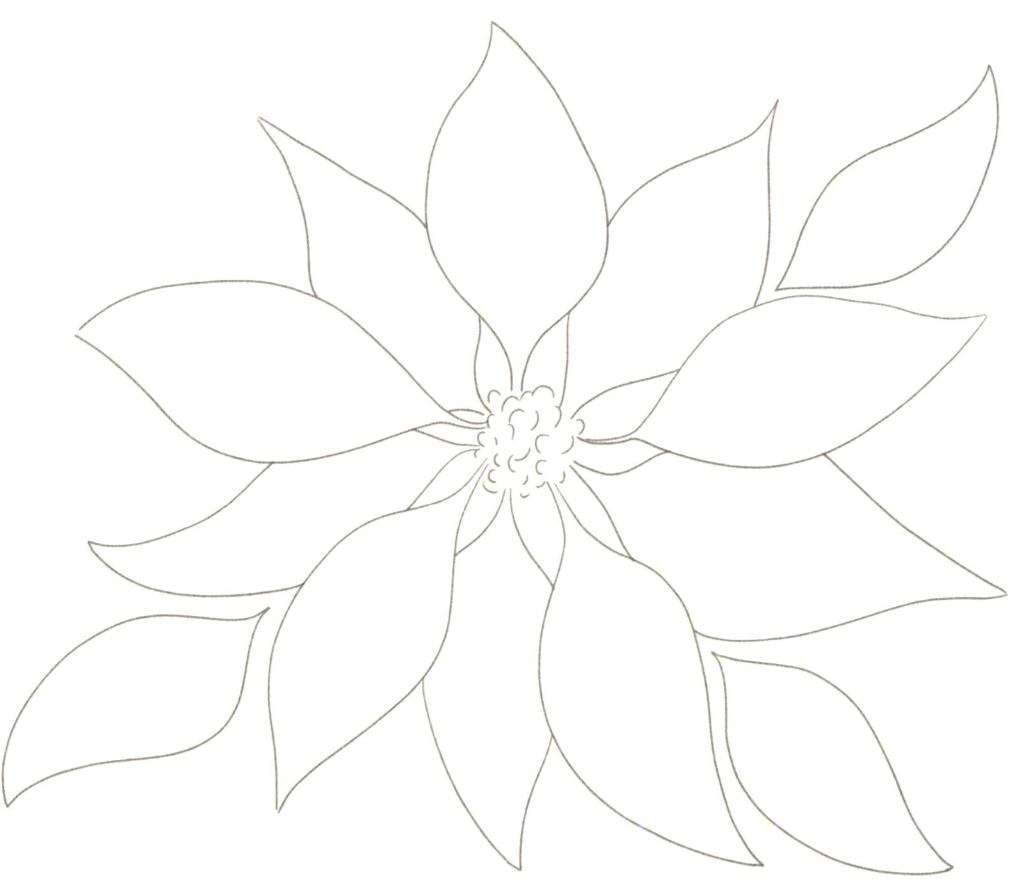

BRUSHES

• Medium/large brush (6, 8)

COLOR PALETTE

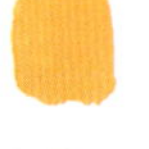   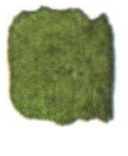
 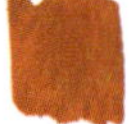 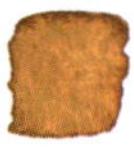

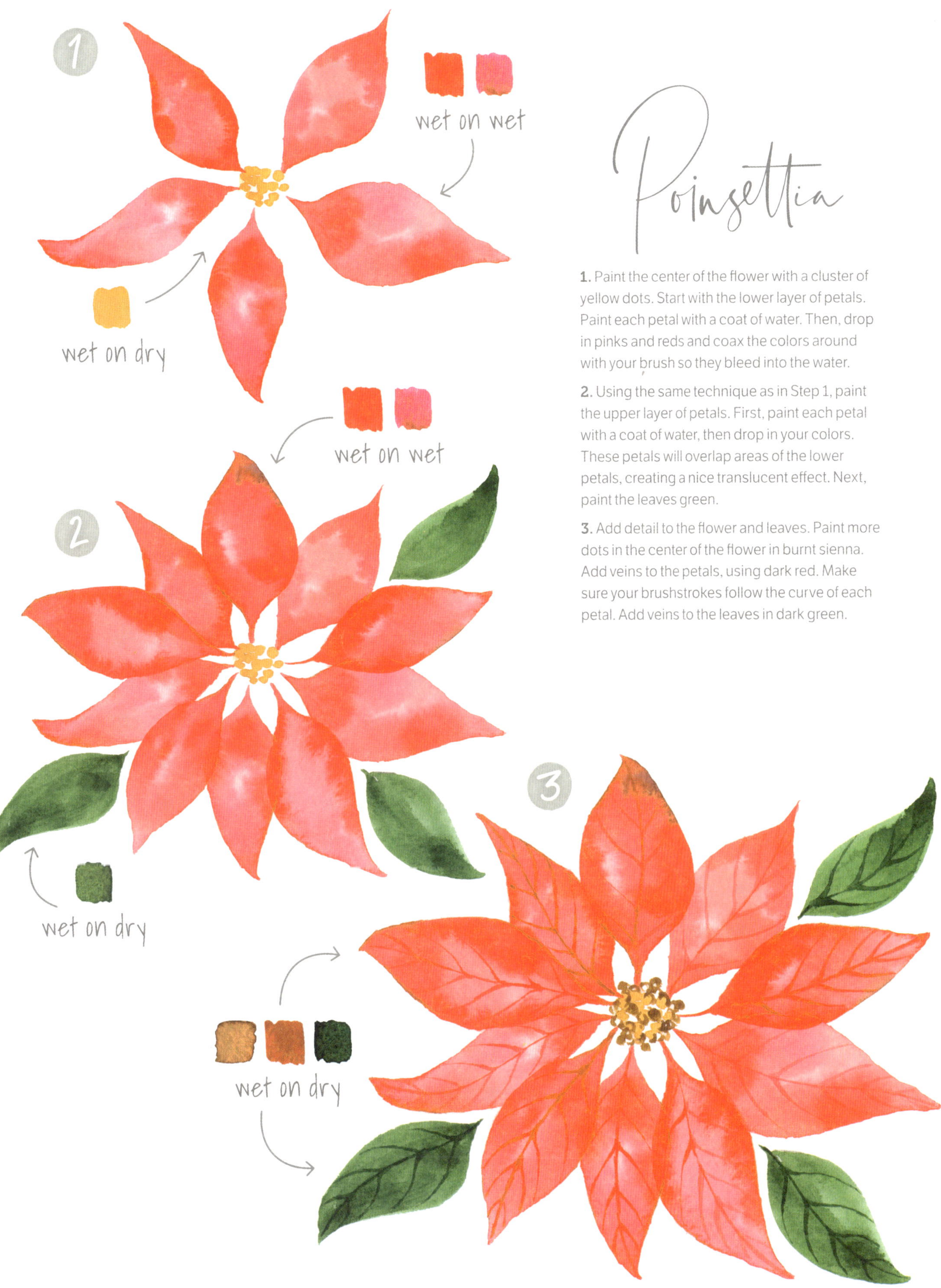

Poinsettia

1. Paint the center of the flower with a cluster of yellow dots. Start with the lower layer of petals. Paint each petal with a coat of water. Then, drop in pinks and reds and coax the colors around with your brush so they bleed into the water.

2. Using the same technique as in Step 1, paint the upper layer of petals. First, paint each petal with a coat of water, then drop in your colors. These petals will overlap areas of the lower petals, creating a nice translucent effect. Next, paint the leaves green.

3. Add detail to the flower and leaves. Paint more dots in the center of the flower in burnt sienna. Add veins to the petals, using dark red. Make sure your brushstrokes follow the curve of each petal. Add veins to the leaves in dark green.

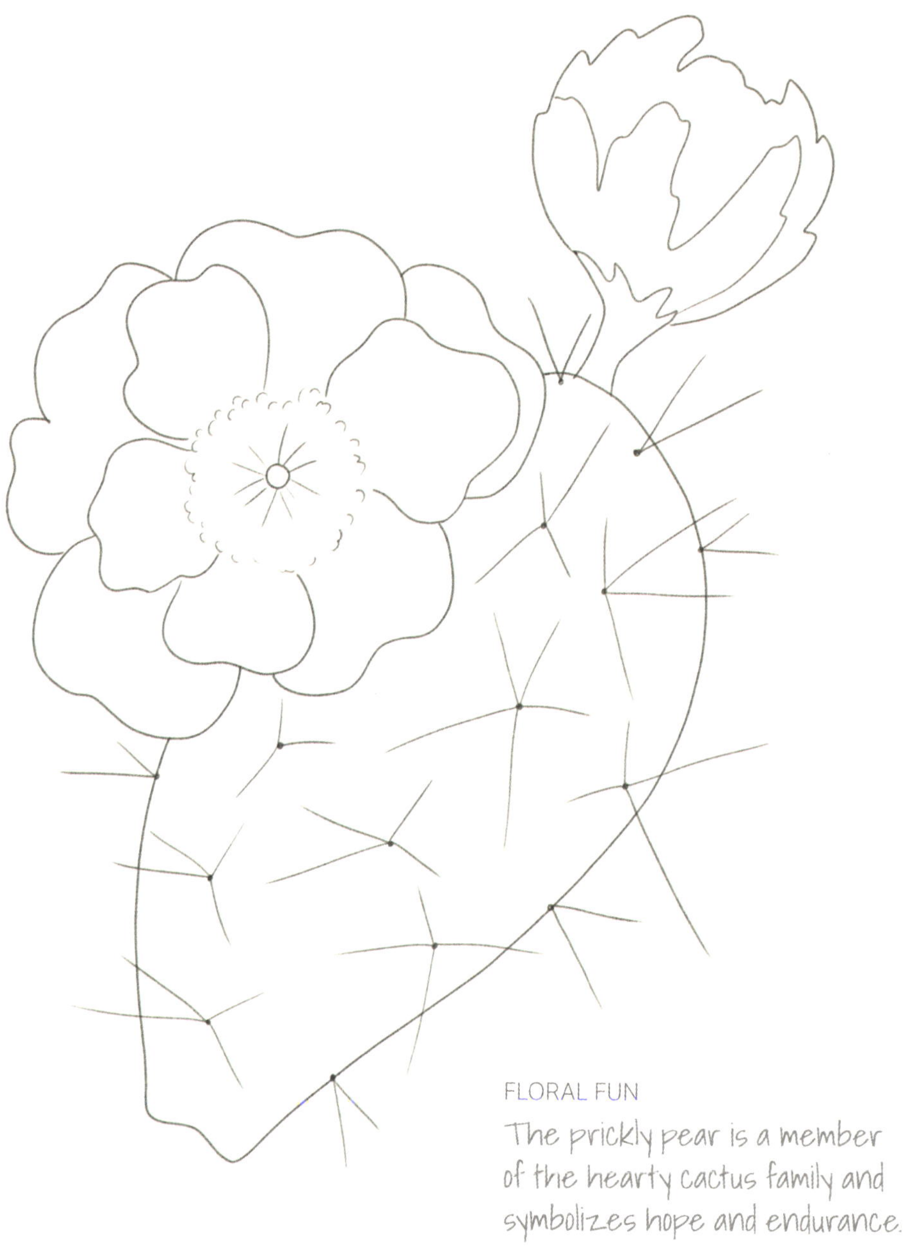

FLORAL FUN

The prickly pear is a member of the hearty cactus family and symbolizes hope and endurance.

BRUSHES

• Medium/large brush (6, 10)

COLOR PALETTE

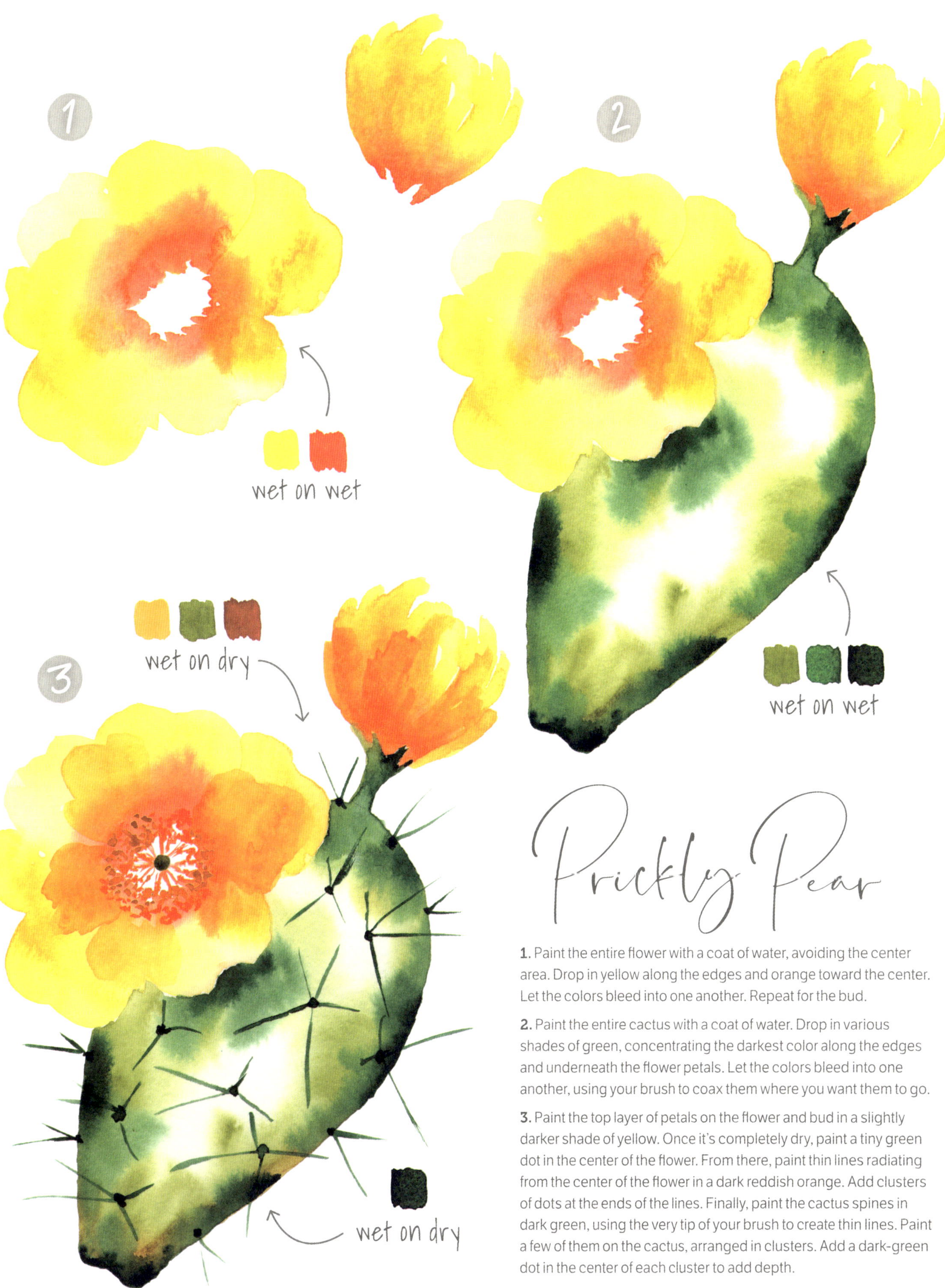

Prickly Pear

1. Paint the entire flower with a coat of water, avoiding the center area. Drop in yellow along the edges and orange toward the center. Let the colors bleed into one another. Repeat for the bud.

2. Paint the entire cactus with a coat of water. Drop in various shades of green, concentrating the darkest color along the edges and underneath the flower petals. Let the colors bleed into one another, using your brush to coax them where you want them to go.

3. Paint the top layer of petals on the flower and bud in a slightly darker shade of yellow. Once it's completely dry, paint a tiny green dot in the center of the flower. From there, paint thin lines radiating from the center of the flower in a dark reddish orange. Add clusters of dots at the ends of the lines. Finally, paint the cactus spines in dark green, using the very tip of your brush to create thin lines. Paint a few of them on the cactus, arranged in clusters. Add a dark-green dot in the center of each cluster to add depth.

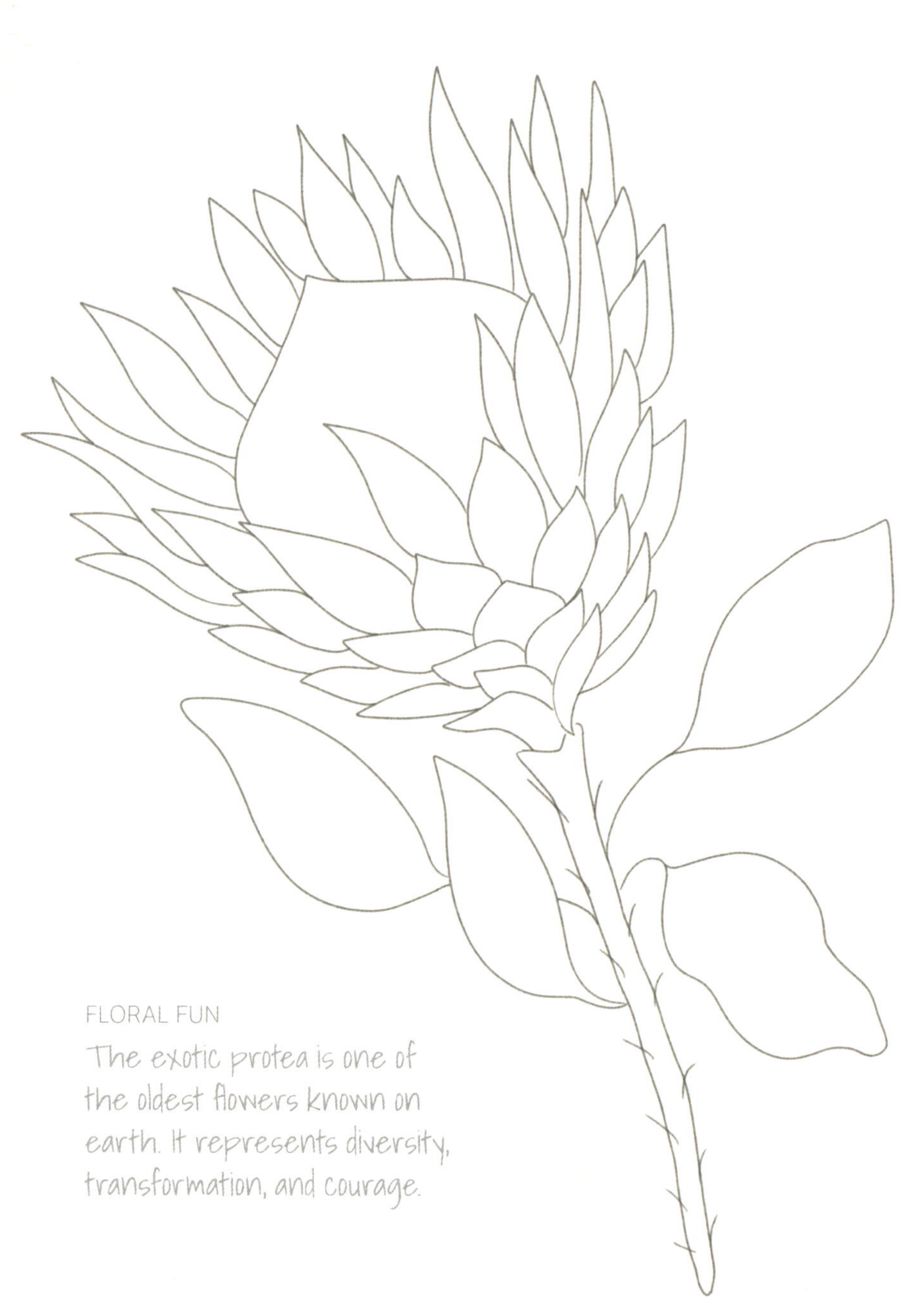

FLORAL FUN

The exotic protea is one of the oldest flowers known on earth. It represents diversity, transformation, and courage.

BRUSHES
• Large brush (8)

COLOR PALETTE

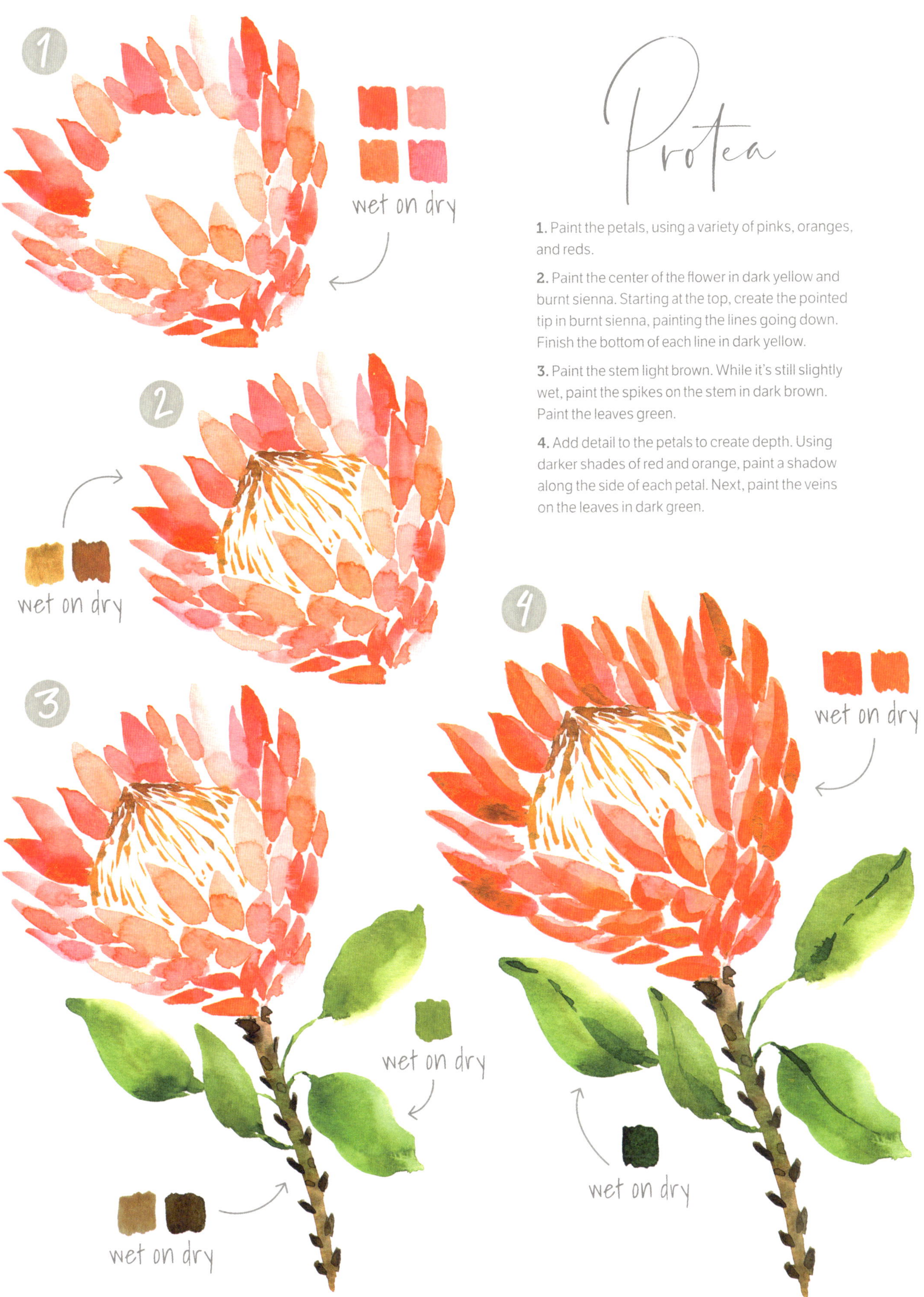

Protea

1. Paint the petals, using a variety of pinks, oranges, and reds.

2. Paint the center of the flower in dark yellow and burnt sienna. Starting at the top, create the pointed tip in burnt sienna, painting the lines going down. Finish the bottom of each line in dark yellow.

3. Paint the stem light brown. While it's still slightly wet, paint the spikes on the stem in dark brown. Paint the leaves green.

4. Add detail to the petals to create depth. Using darker shades of red and orange, paint a shadow along the side of each petal. Next, paint the veins on the leaves in dark green.

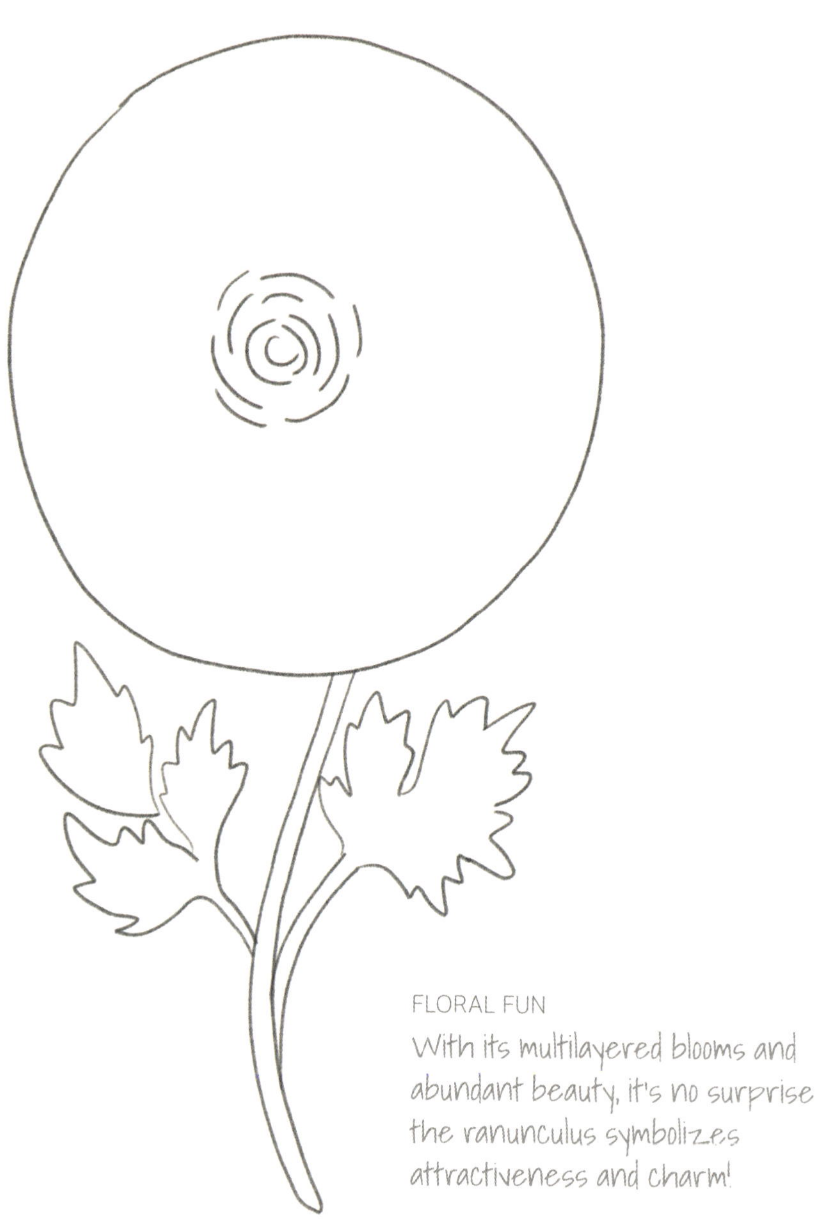

FLORAL FUN

With its multilayered blooms and abundant beauty, it's no surprise the ranunculus symbolizes attractiveness and charm!

BRUSHES

• Large brush (10)

COLOR PALETTE

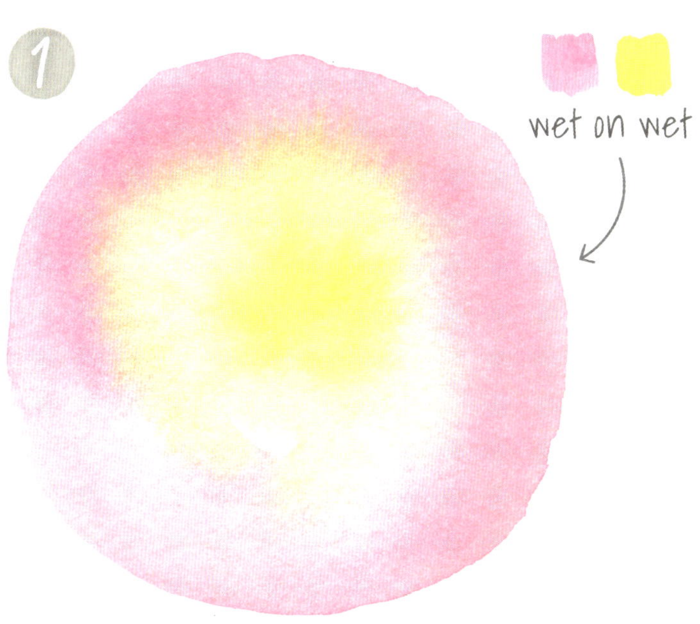

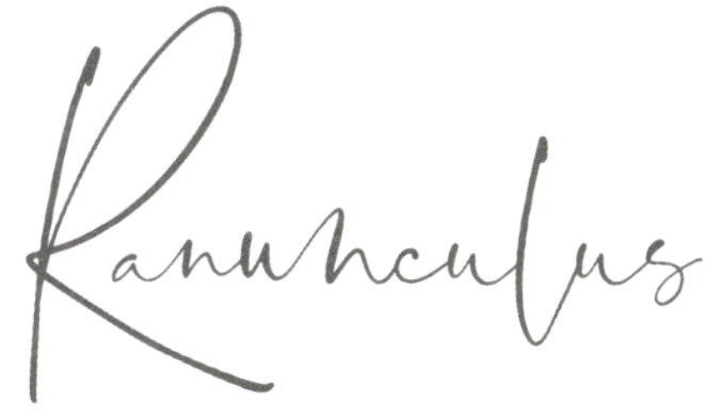

Ranunculus

1. Paint the entire flower with a coat of water. Drop in pink around the edges and yellow in the center, allowing the colors to bleed into the water. Let dry.

2. Once dry, paint the center of the flower in dark yellow and green. Use rounded brushstrokes to create a circular shape with each color.

3. Using the Loose Petals technique (page 21), add petals around the center of the flower in pink. Vary the size of your brushstrokes to create variety in the petals. Make sure your brushstrokes curve along the circular shape of the flower.

4. Continue using the Loose Petals technique (page 21) to add another layer of petals in pink and red to create depth. Add detail to the flower center in dark green and dark yellow. Paint the stem and leaves green.

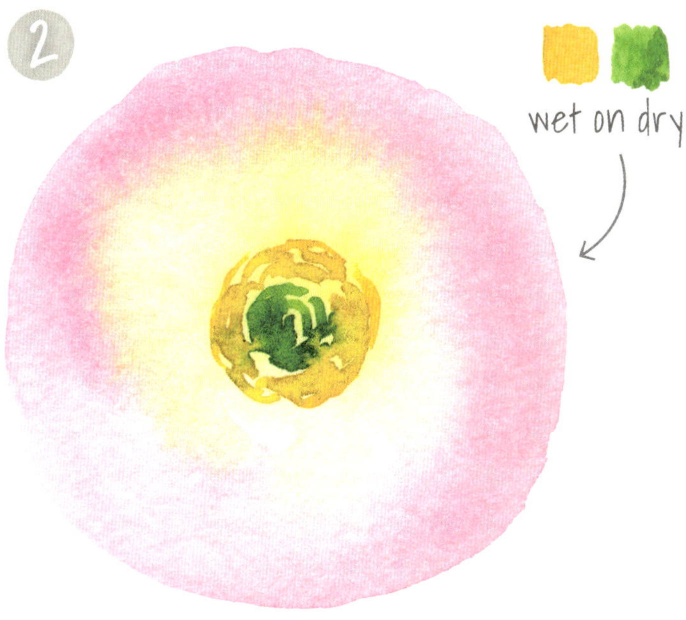

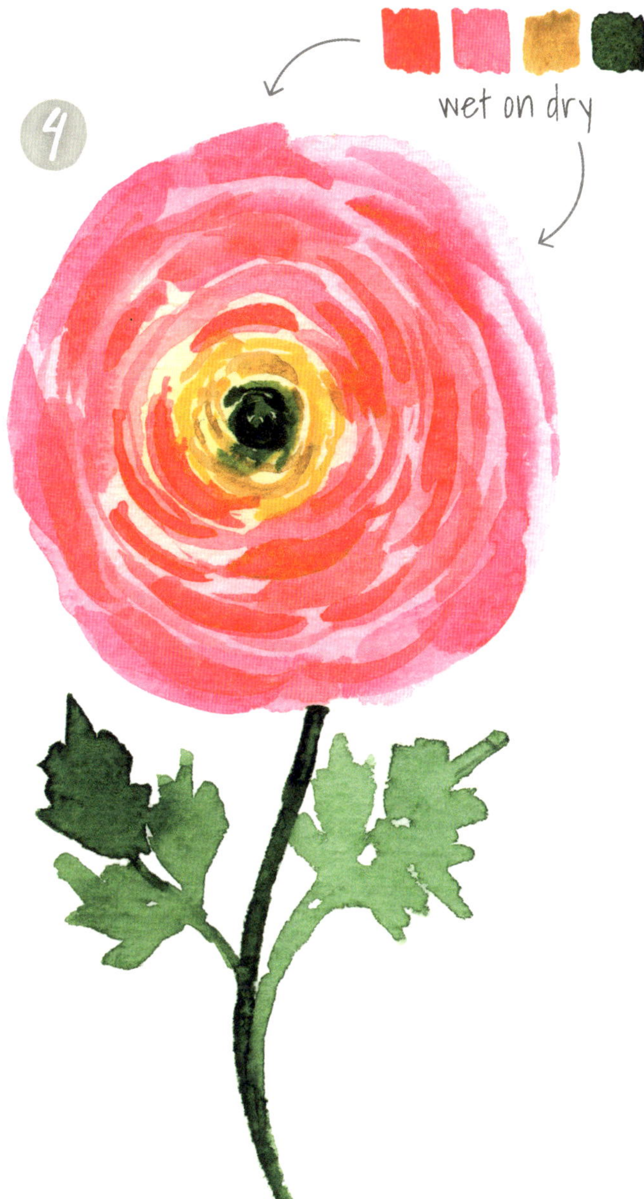

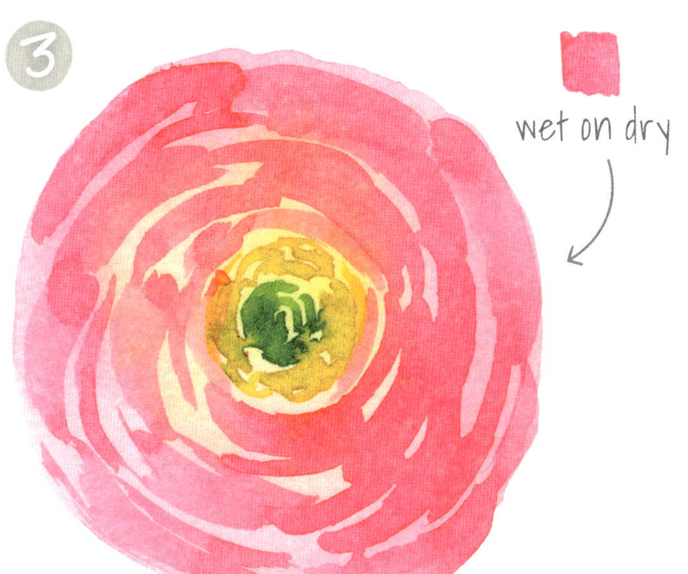

Widely regarded as a symbol of love, the rose represents all things romance. It is said that when giving a rose, the deeper the color, the deeper the adoration.

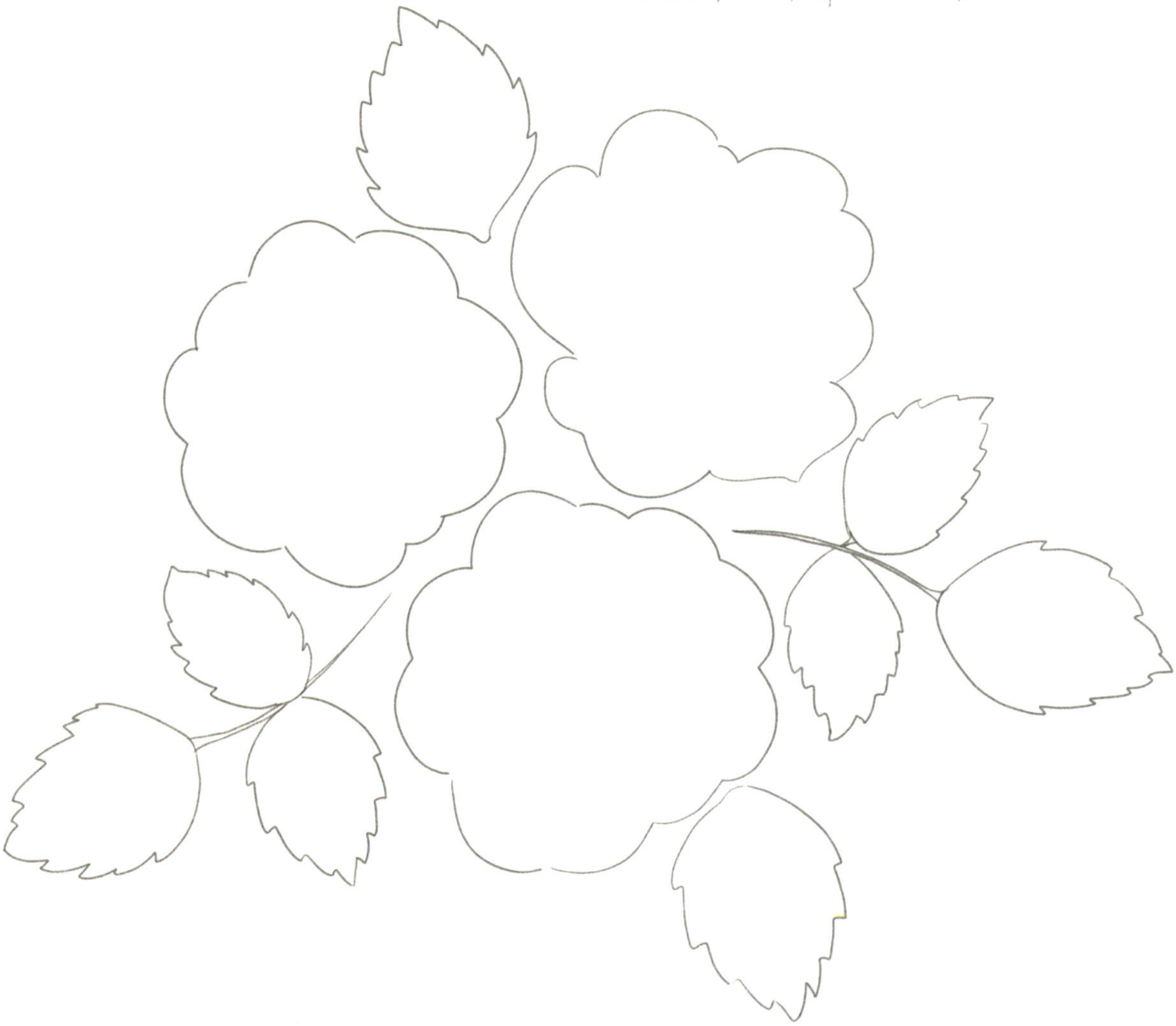

BRUSHES

• Large brush (8)

COLOR PALETTE

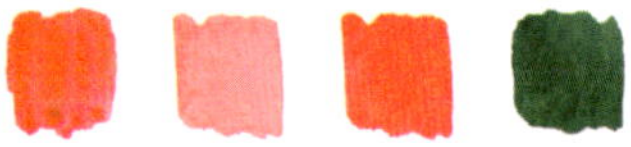

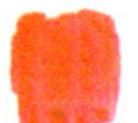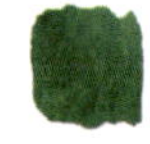

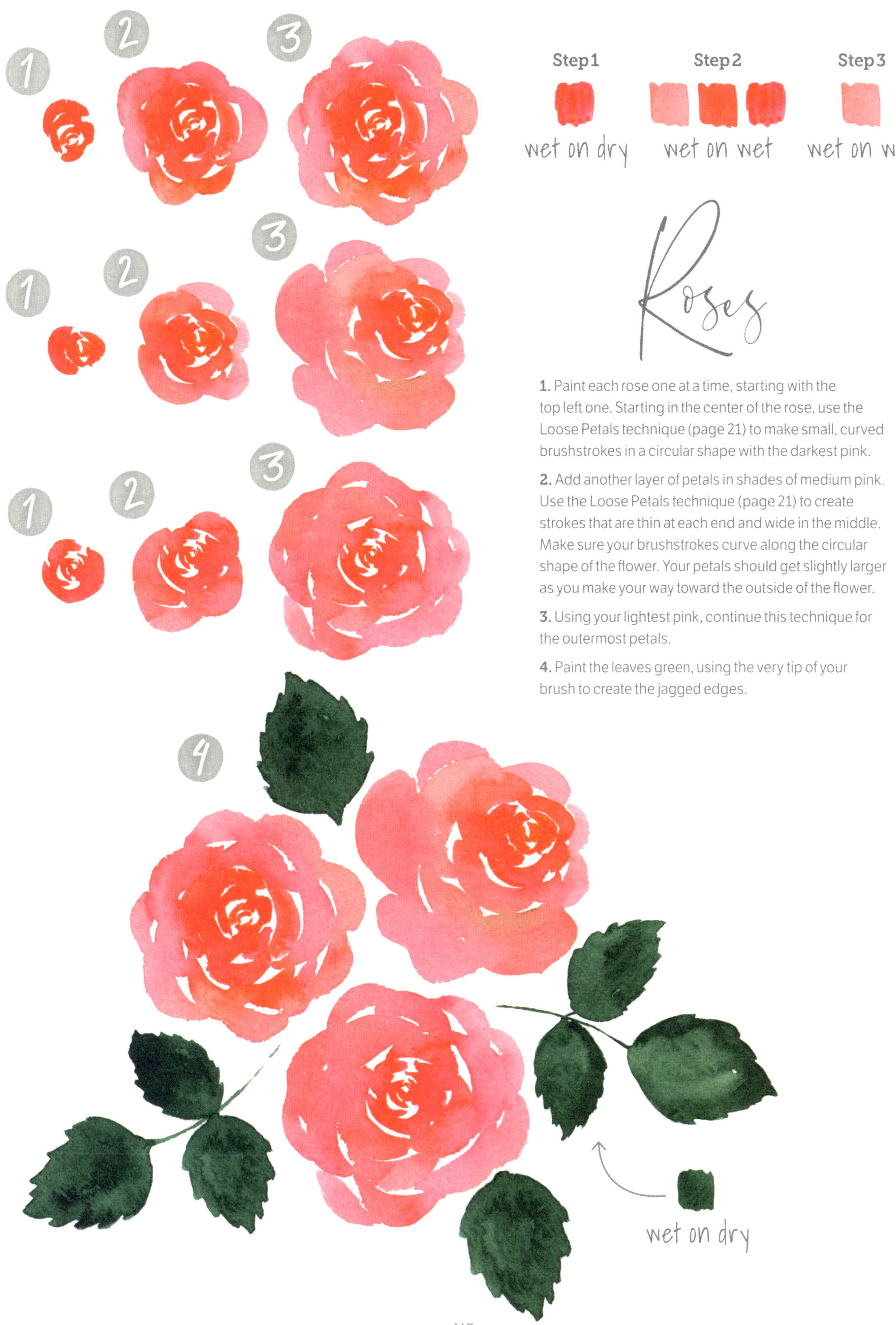

Roses

1. Paint each rose one at a time, starting with the top left one. Starting in the center of the rose, use the Loose Petals technique (page 21) to make small, curved brushstrokes in a circular shape with the darkest pink.

2. Add another layer of petals in shades of medium pink. Use the Loose Petals technique (page 21) to create strokes that are thin at each end and wide in the middle. Make sure your brushstrokes curve along the circular shape of the flower. Your petals should get slightly larger as you make your way toward the outside of the flower.

3. Using your lightest pink, continue this technique for the outermost petals.

4. Paint the leaves green, using the very tip of your brush to create the jagged edges.

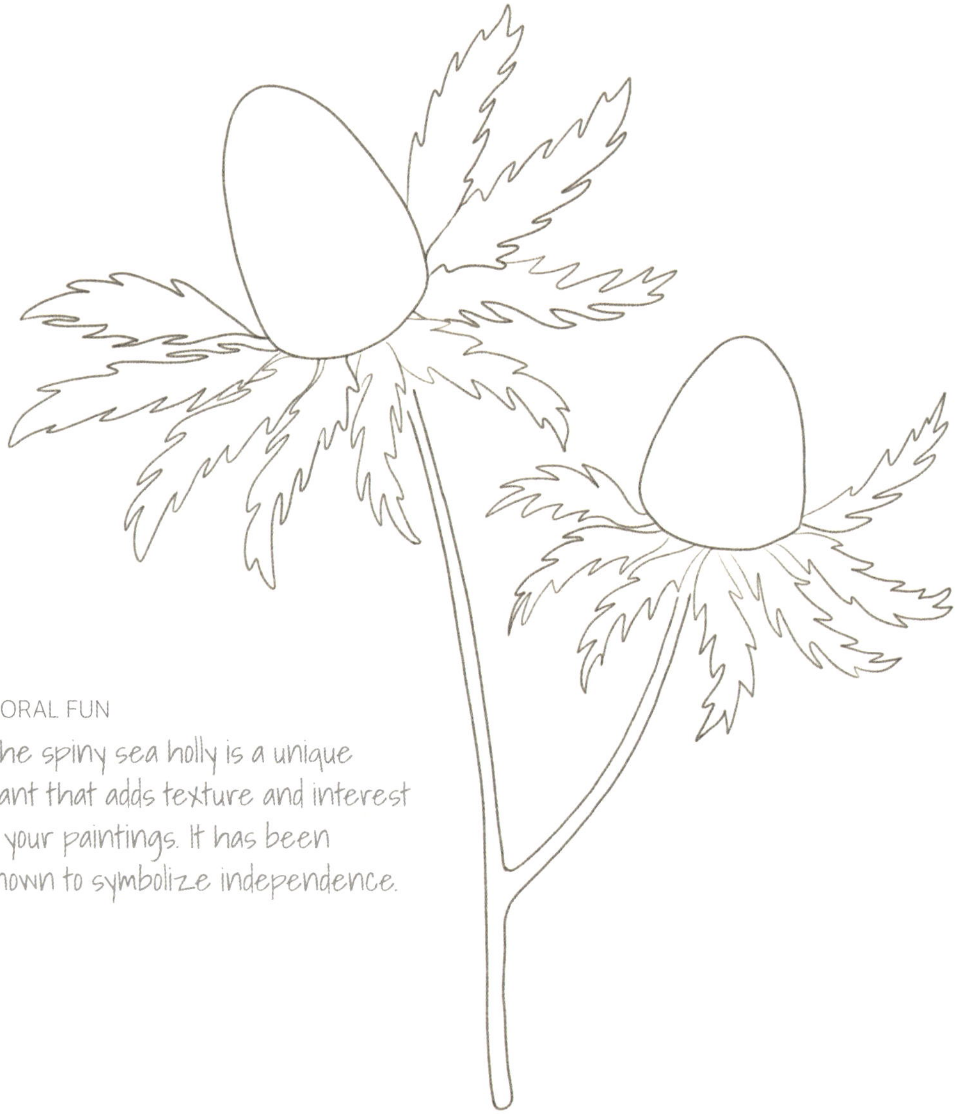

BRUSHES

• Medium/large brush (6, 8)

COLOR PALETTE

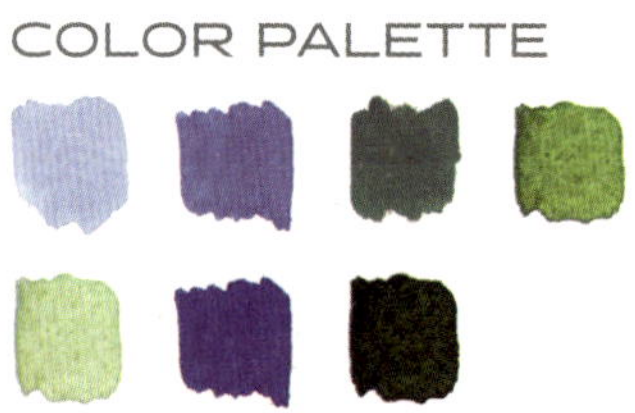

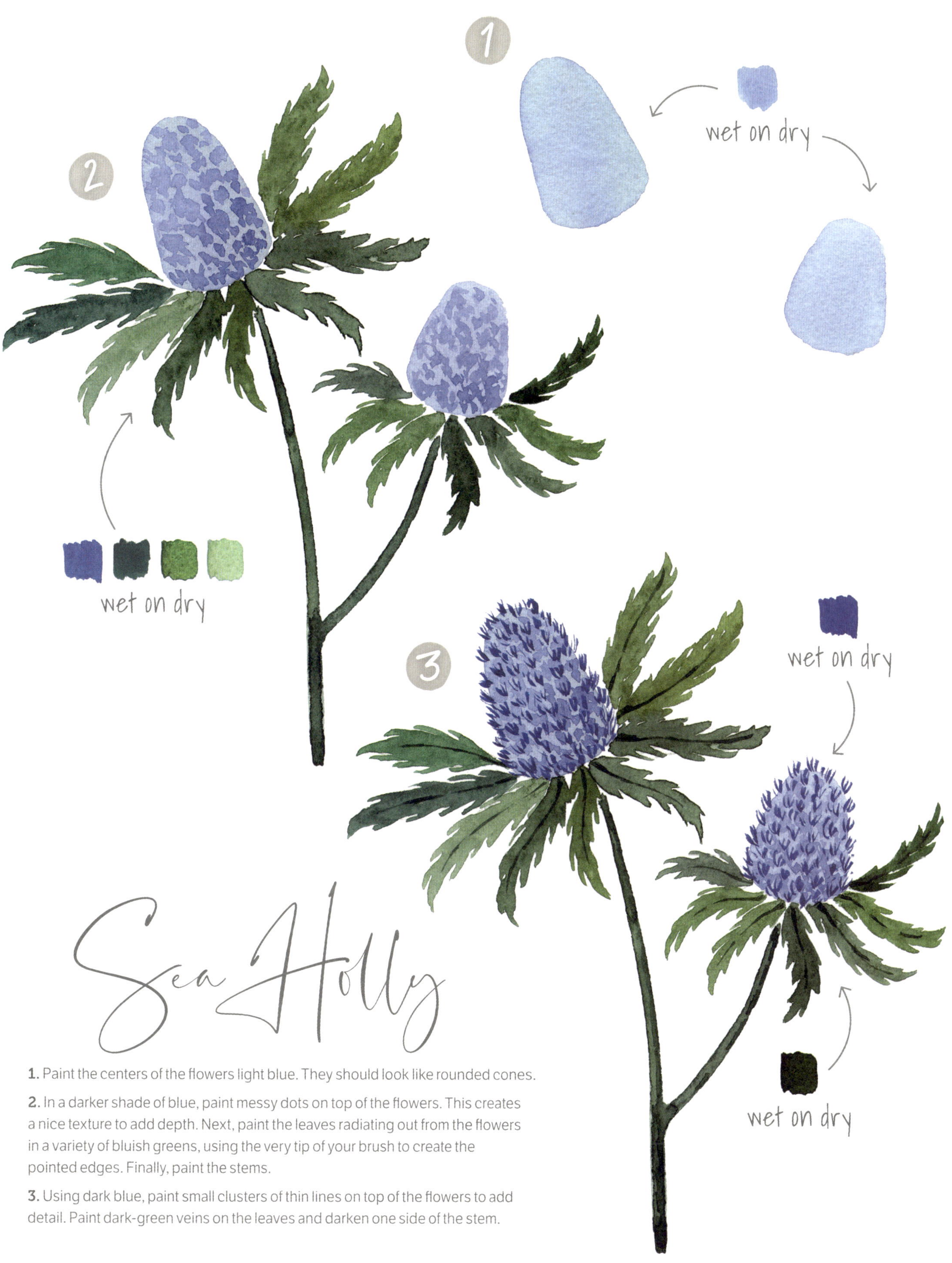

Sea Holly

1. Paint the centers of the flowers light blue. They should look like rounded cones.

2. In a darker shade of blue, paint messy dots on top of the flowers. This creates a nice texture to add depth. Next, paint the leaves radiating out from the flowers in a variety of bluish greens, using the very tip of your brush to create the pointed edges. Finally, paint the stems.

3. Using dark blue, paint small clusters of thin lines on top of the flowers to add detail. Paint dark-green veins on the leaves and darken one side of the stem.

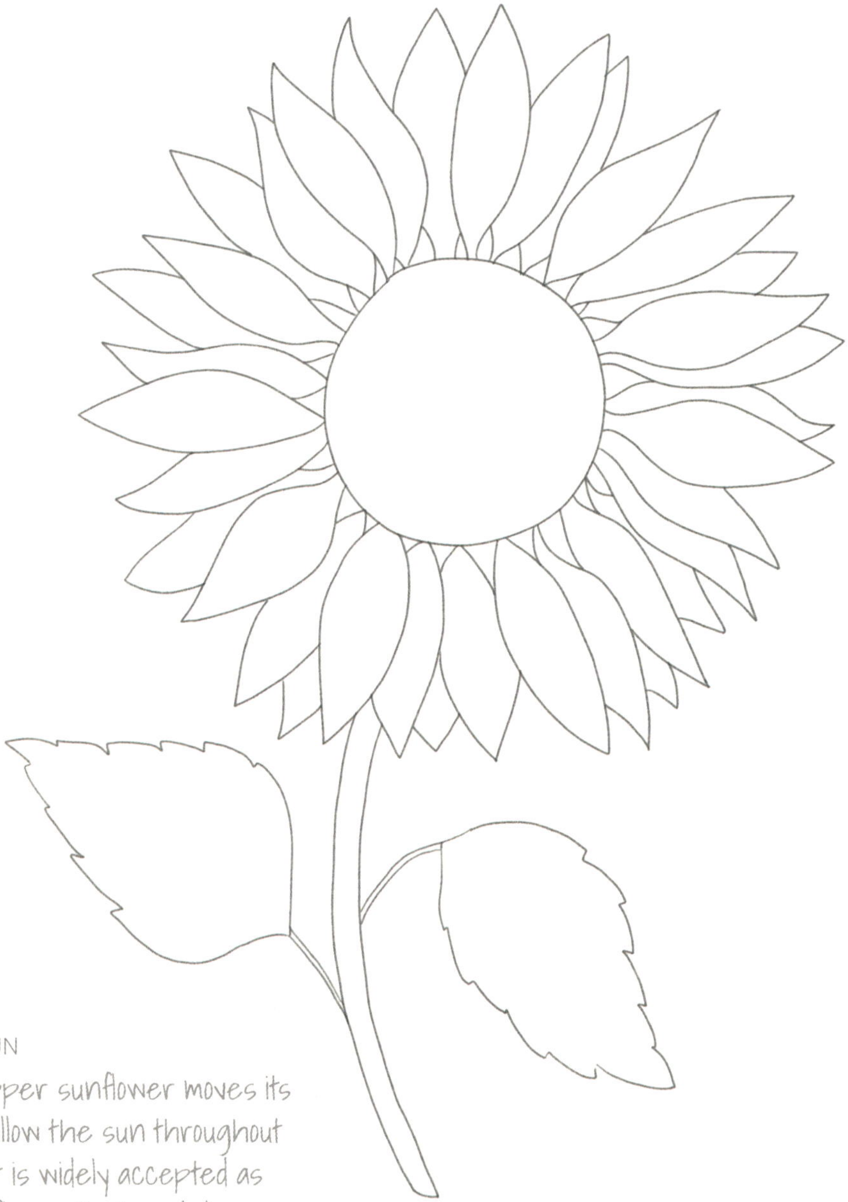

FLORAL FUN

The chipper sunflower moves its head to follow the sun throughout the day. It is widely accepted as a happy flower that symbolizes cheerfulness.

BRUSHES

• Medium/large brush (6, 8)

COLOR PALETTE

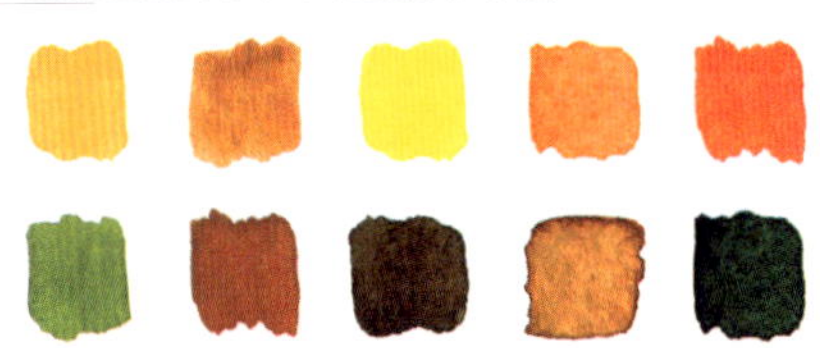

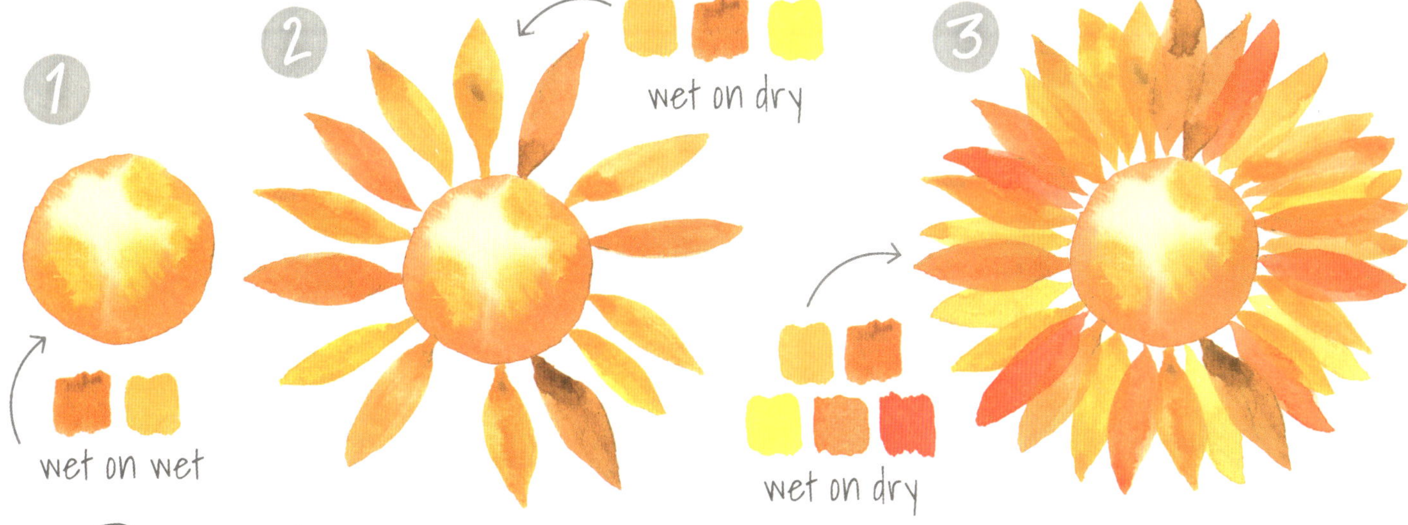

Sunflower

1. Paint the center of the flower with a coat of water. Drop in dark yellow along the edges and light yellow toward the center. Let the colors bleed into the water. Let dry.

2. Once dry, paint each petal individually. Using a variety of yellows and oranges, paint the first layer of petals. Try to space these petals far enough apart so they don't touch or bleed together. Let dry.

3. Once dry, paint the remaining petals. These will overlap your first layer of petals, creating a nice translucent effect.

4. Paint the leaves and stem green.

5. In dark brown, paint tiny dots along the edge and in the middle of the flower's center. In burnt sienna, paint tiny dots next to the dark-brown ones. Using dark orange and burnt sienna, add detail to the petals by painting thin lines curving out from the flower's center. In dark green, add veins to the leaves and darken one side of the stem.

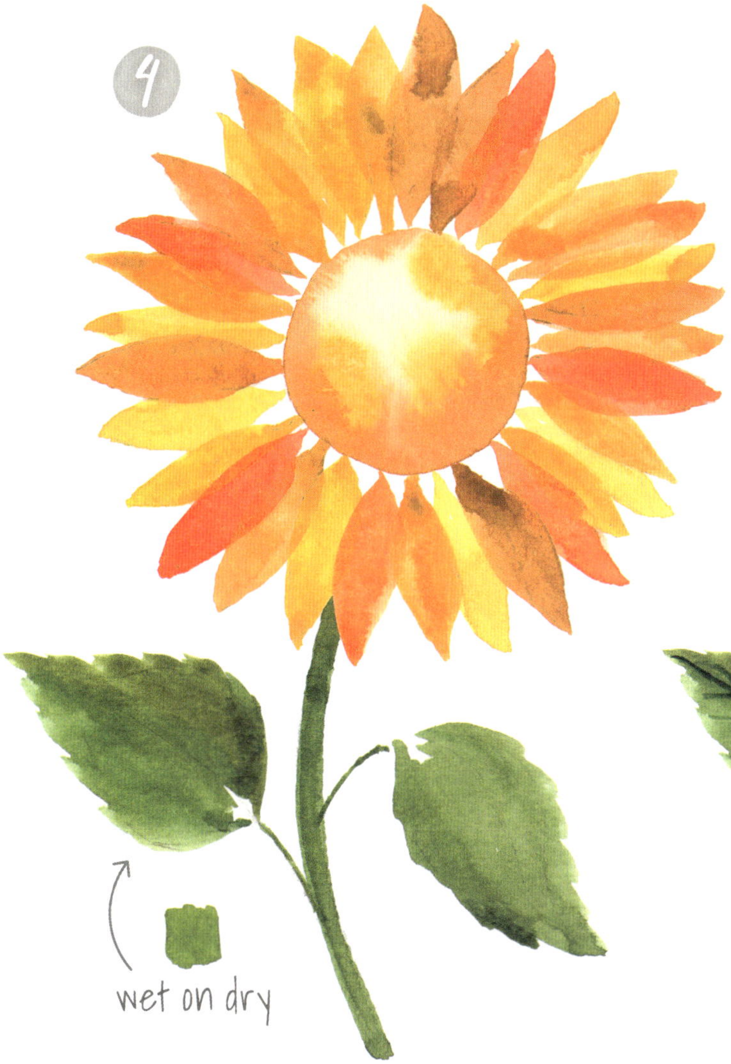

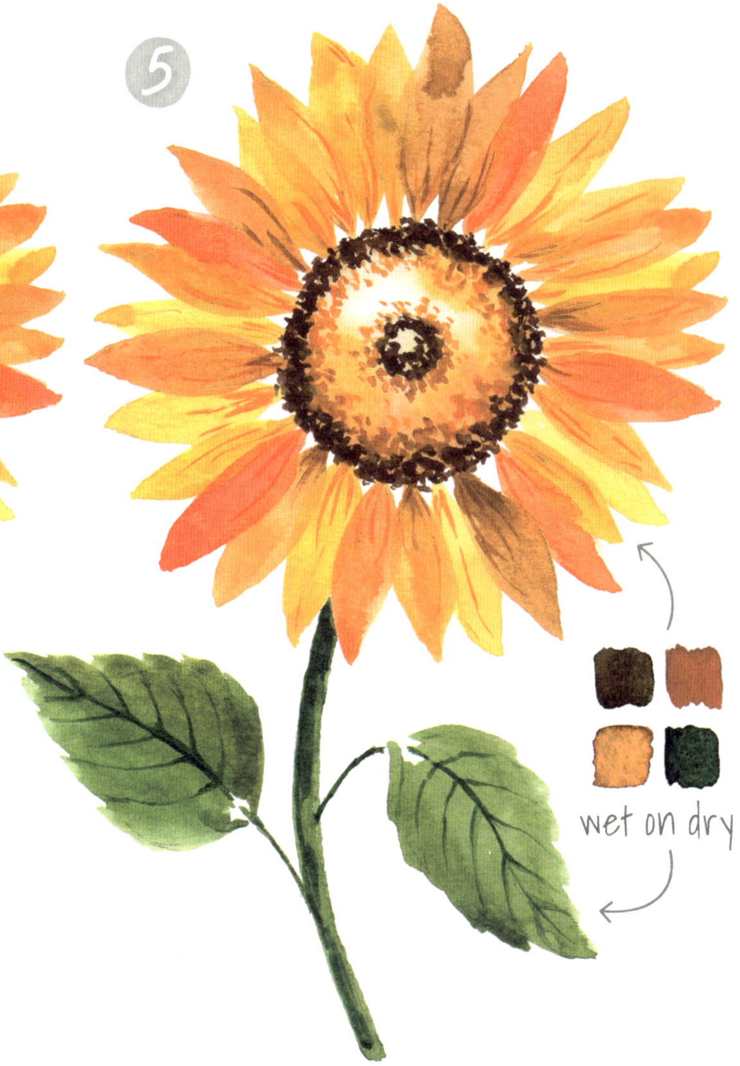

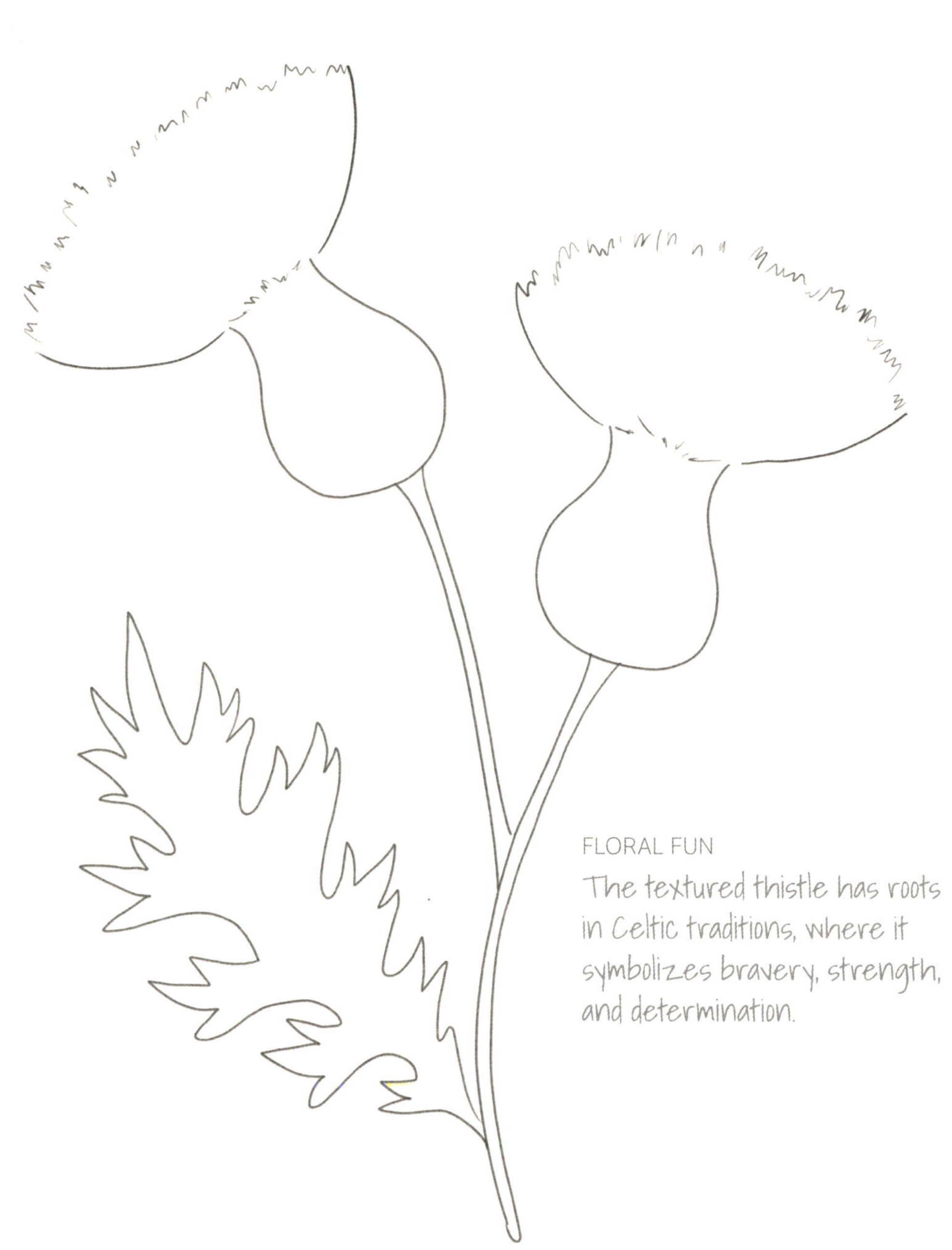

FLORAL FUN

The textured thistle has roots in Celtic traditions, where it symbolizes bravery, strength, and determination.

BRUSHES
• Large brush (8)

COLOR PALETTE

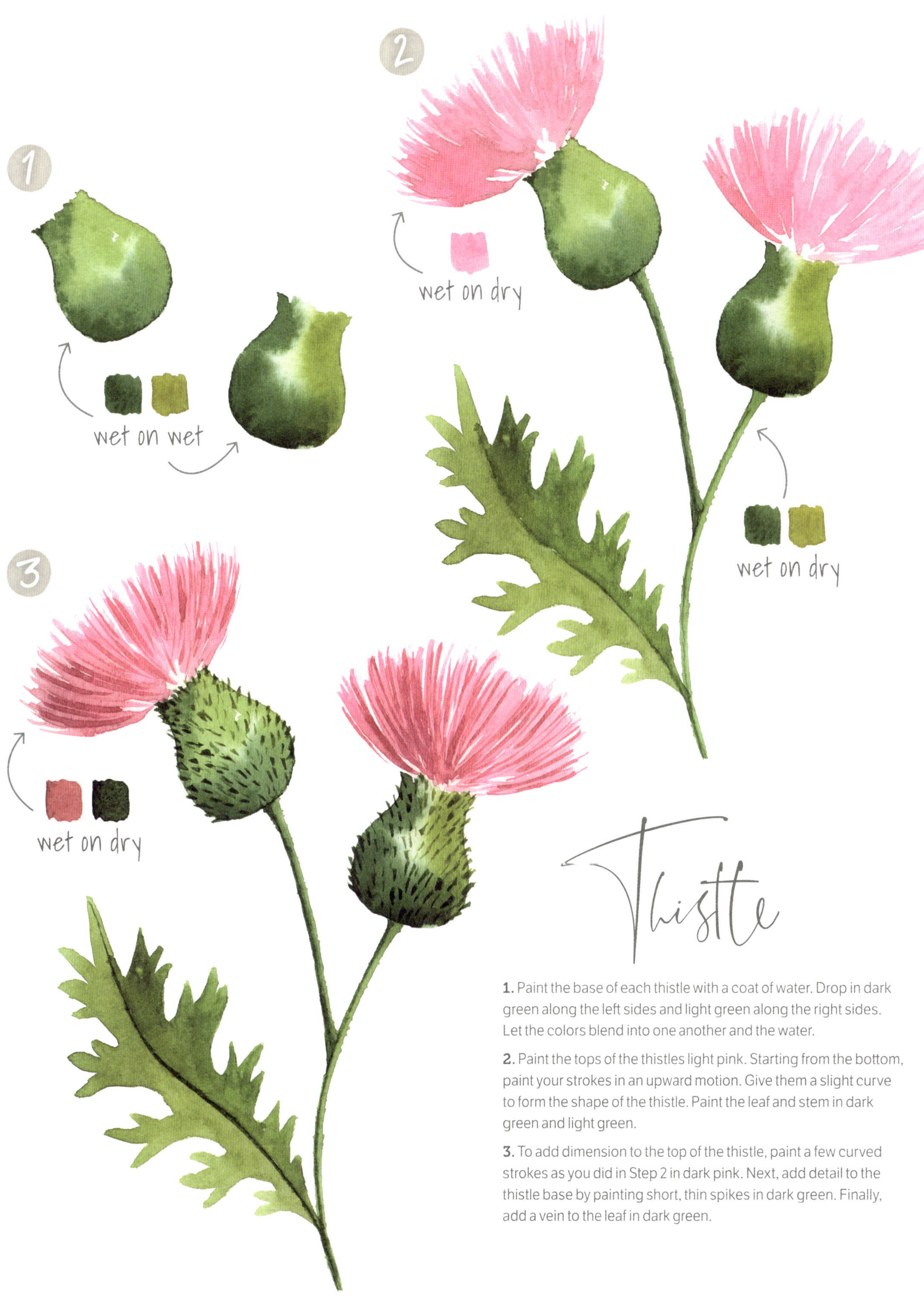

1. Paint the base of each thistle with a coat of water. Drop in dark green along the left sides and light green along the right sides. Let the colors blend into one another and the water.

2. Paint the tops of the thistles light pink. Starting from the bottom, paint your strokes in an upward motion. Give them a slight curve to form the shape of the thistle. Paint the leaf and stem in dark green and light green.

3. To add dimension to the top of the thistle, paint a few curved strokes as you did in Step 2 in dark pink. Next, add detail to the thistle base by painting short, thin spikes in dark green. Finally, add a vein to the leaf in dark green.

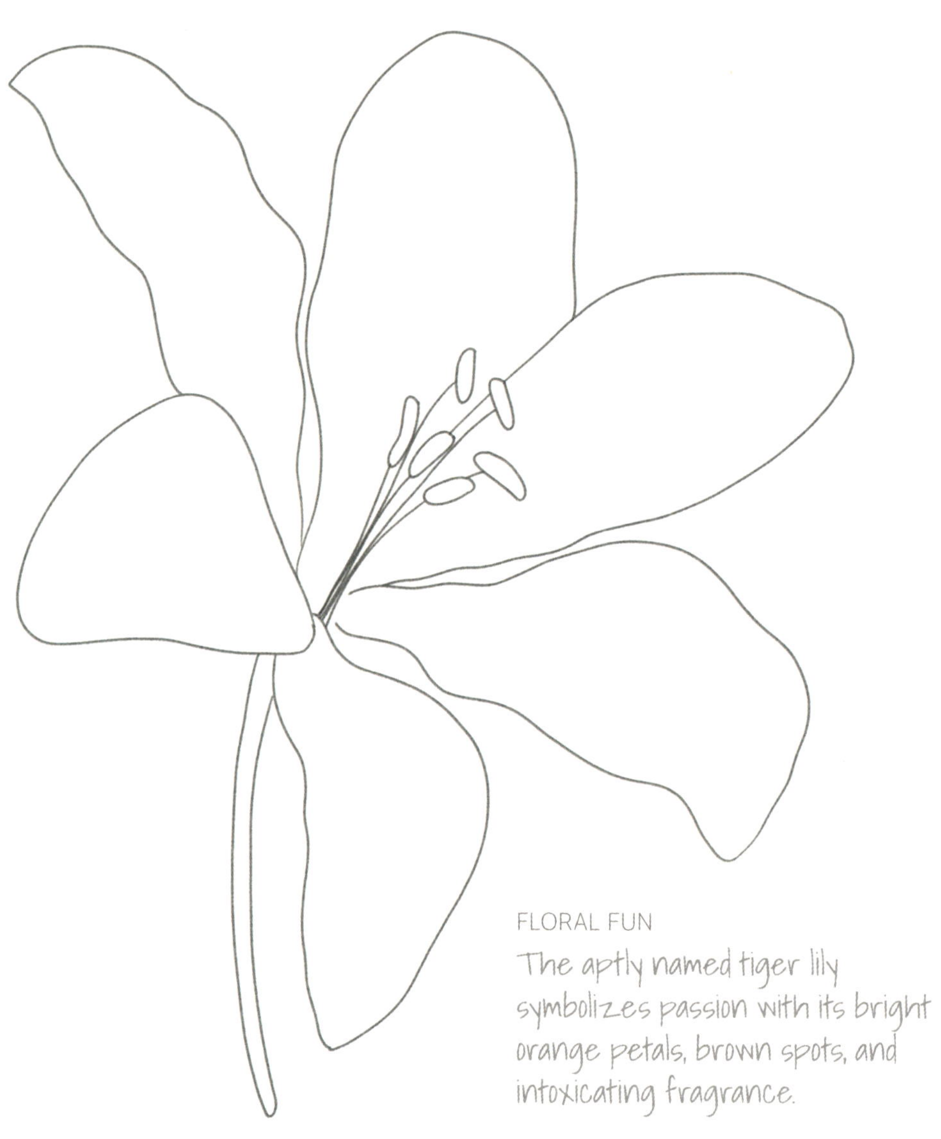

BRUSHES

- Medium/large brush (6, 10)

COLOR PALETTE

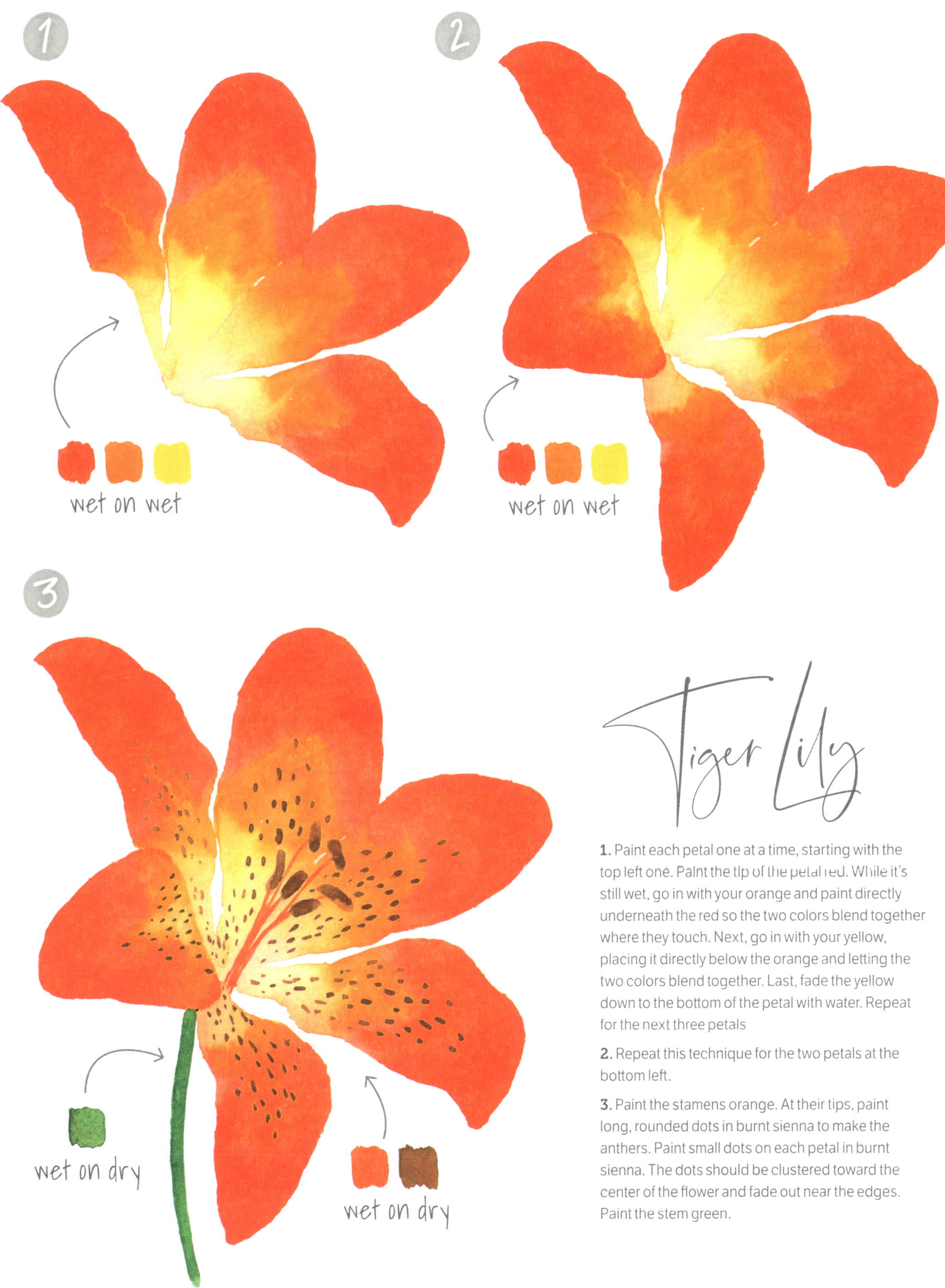

Tiger Lily

1. Paint each petal one at a time, starting with the top left one. Paint the tip of the petal red. While it's still wet, go in with your orange and paint directly underneath the red so the two colors blend together where they touch. Next, go in with your yellow, placing it directly below the orange and letting the two colors blend together. Last, fade the yellow down to the bottom of the petal with water. Repeat for the next three petals

2. Repeat this technique for the two petals at the bottom left.

3. Paint the stamens orange. At their tips, paint long, rounded dots in burnt sienna to make the anthers. Paint small dots on each petal in burnt sienna. The dots should be clustered toward the center of the flower and fade out near the edges. Paint the stem green.

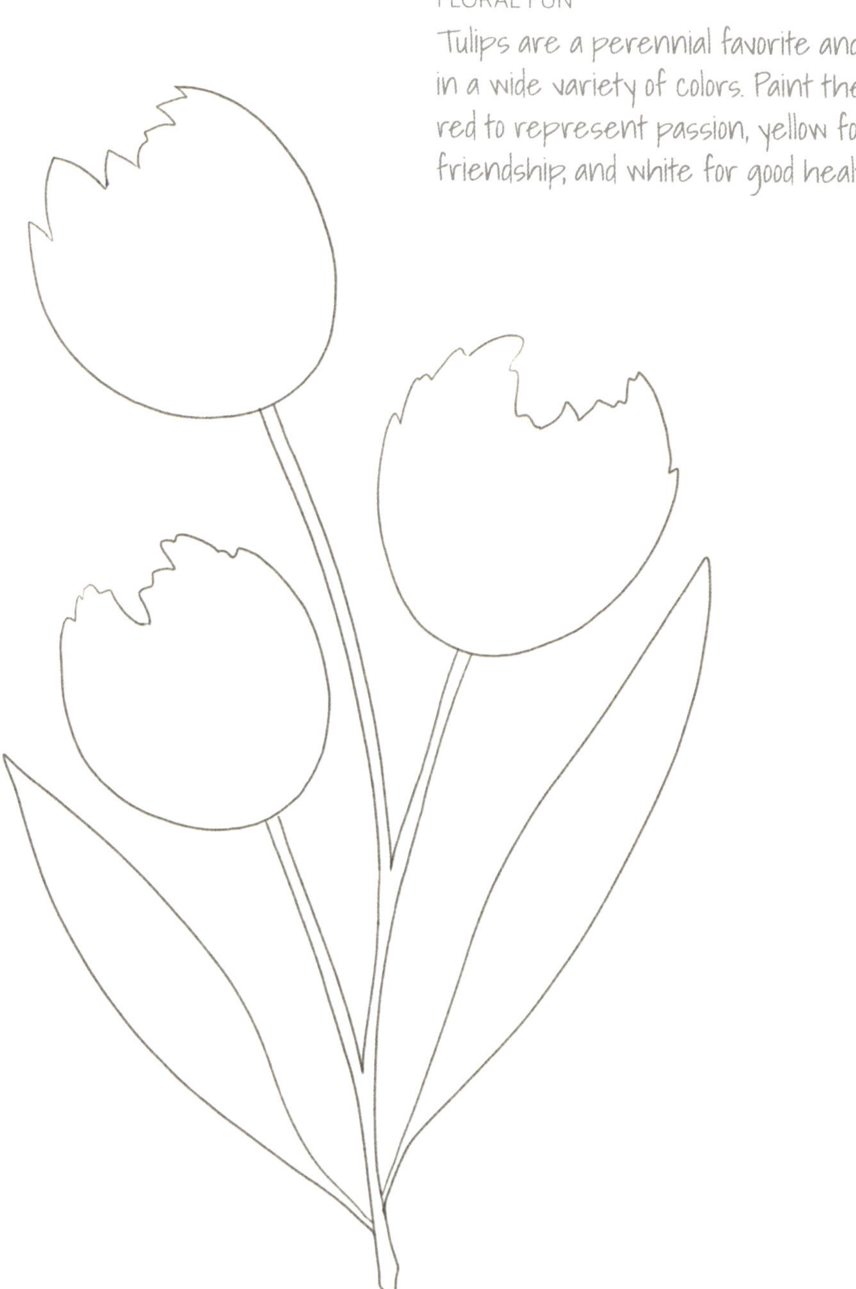

BRUSHES

• Large brush (8)

COLOR PALETTE

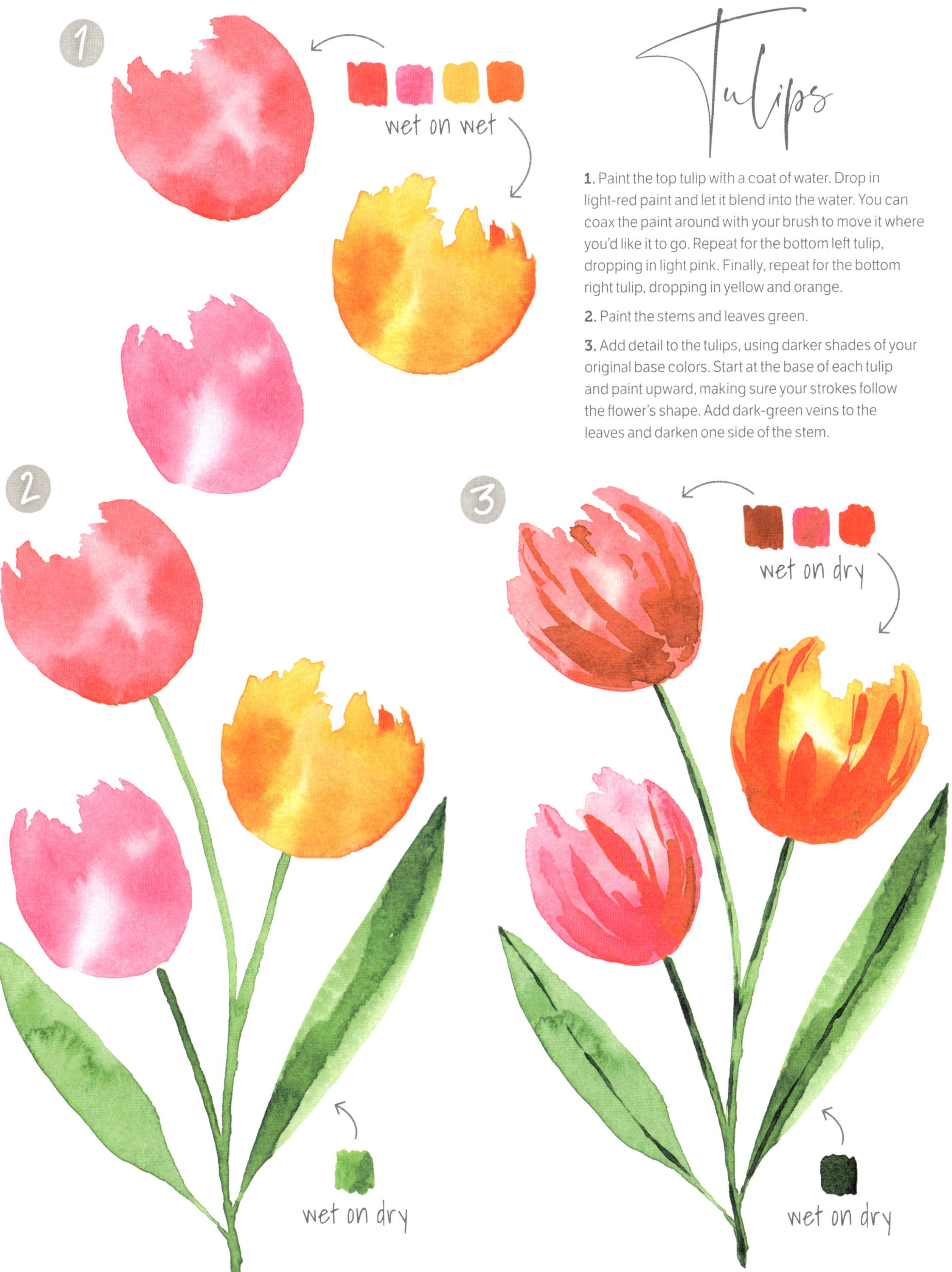

Tulips

1. Paint the top tulip with a coat of water. Drop in light-red paint and let it blend into the water. You can coax the paint around with your brush to move it where you'd like it to go. Repeat for the bottom left tulip, dropping in light pink. Finally, repeat for the bottom right tulip, dropping in yellow and orange.

2. Paint the stems and leaves green.

3. Add detail to the tulips, using darker shades of your original base colors. Start at the base of each tulip and paint upward, making sure your strokes follow the flower's shape. Add dark-green veins to the leaves and darken one side of the stem.

The water lily is also known as the lotus and represents enlightenment, growth, and prosperity.

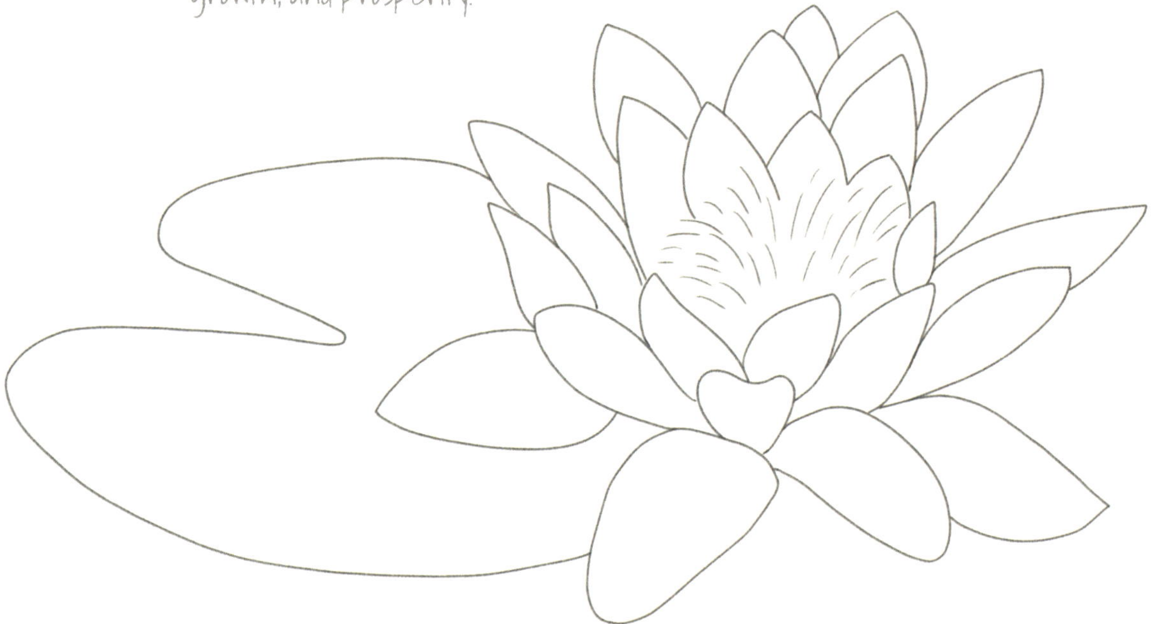

BRUSHES

- Large brush (8)

COLOR PALETTE

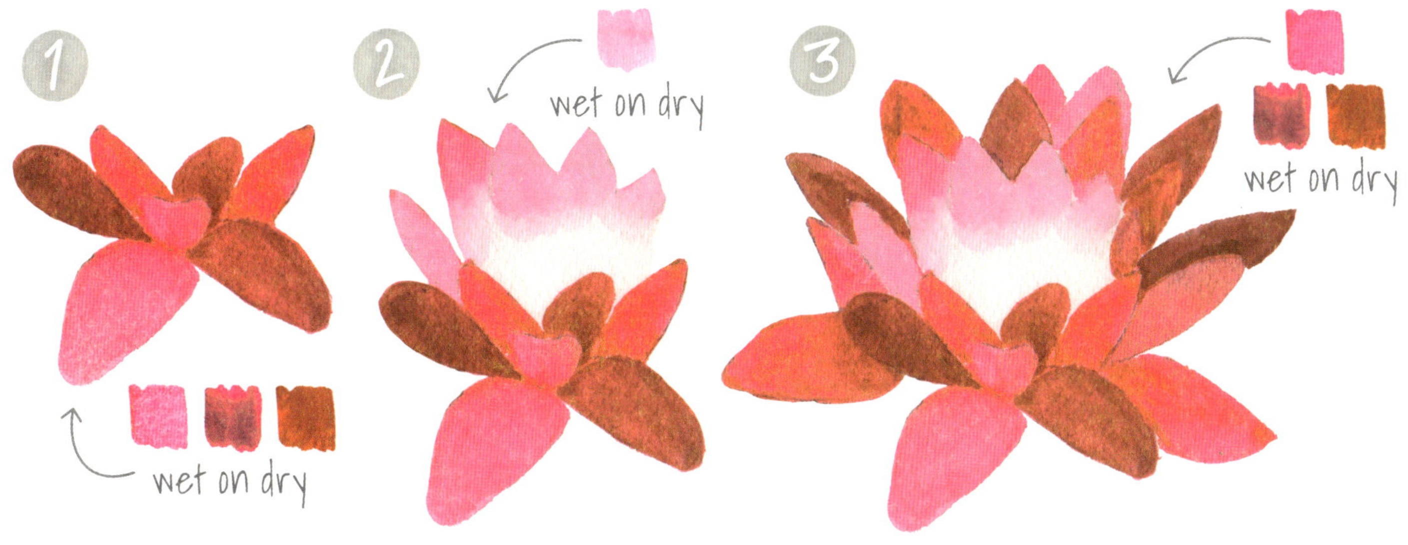

Water Lily

1. Using a variety of pinks and reds, paint each petal individually, starting with the base layer. Vary the shade of each petal to create variety.

2. Paint the center petals in light pink. Start by painting the tip of each petal pink. Then, use water to drag the color down with your brush, creating a soft gradient into the white of the paper.

3. Add the remaining layer of petals.

4. Paint the entire lily pad with a coat of water. Drop in greens and yellows along the edges, letting the colors bleed together and with the water.

5. Using light green, paint thin lines on the lily pad, radiating out from a single point. Next, using short, curved brushstrokes, paint the center of the lily in yellow and burnt sienna.

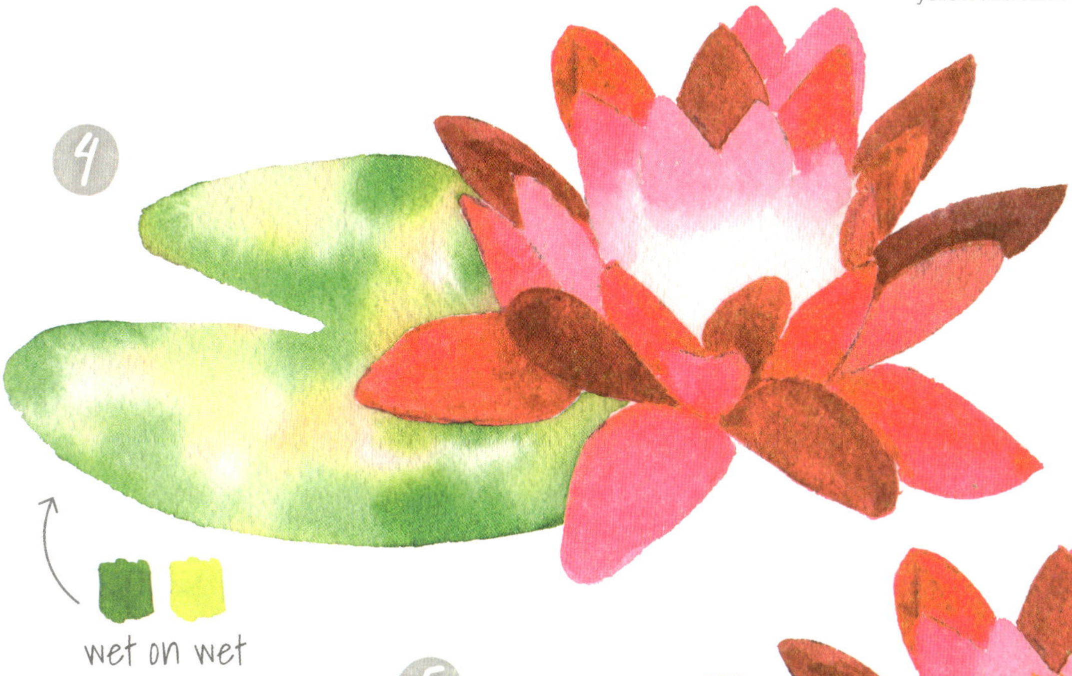

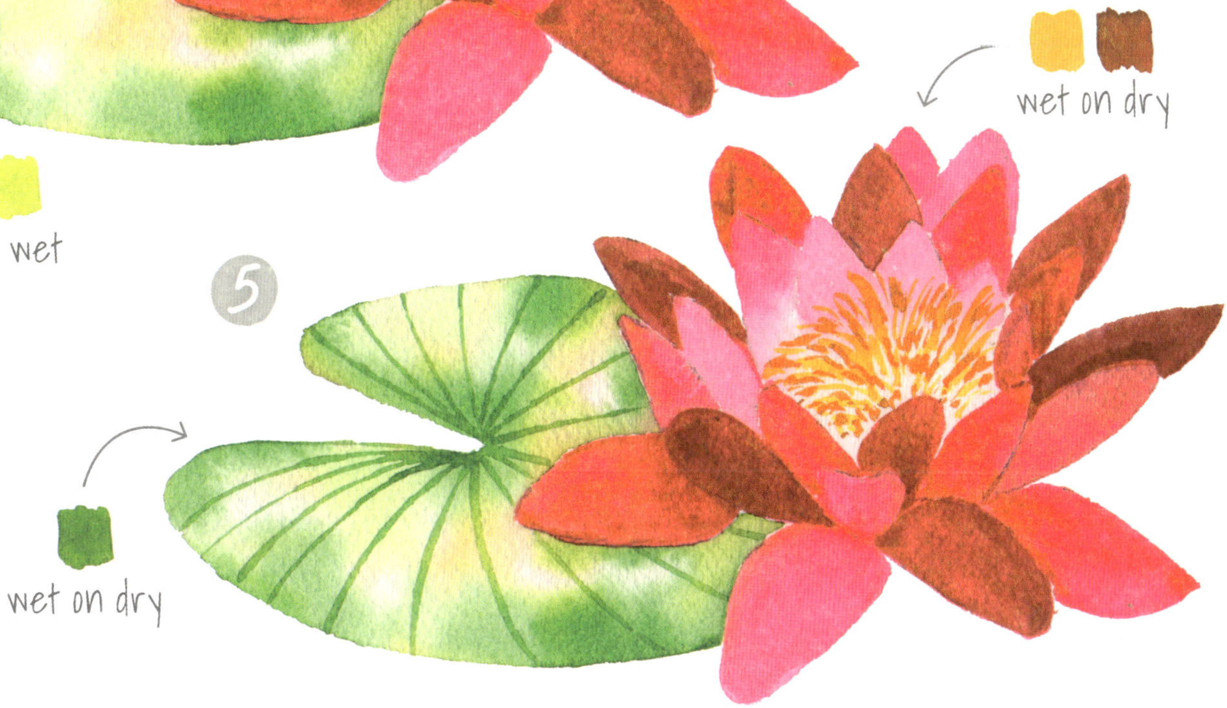

Spread good cheer this holiday season with this hand-painted wreath composed of holly and evergreen.

BRUSHES

- Large brush (8)

COLOR PALETTE

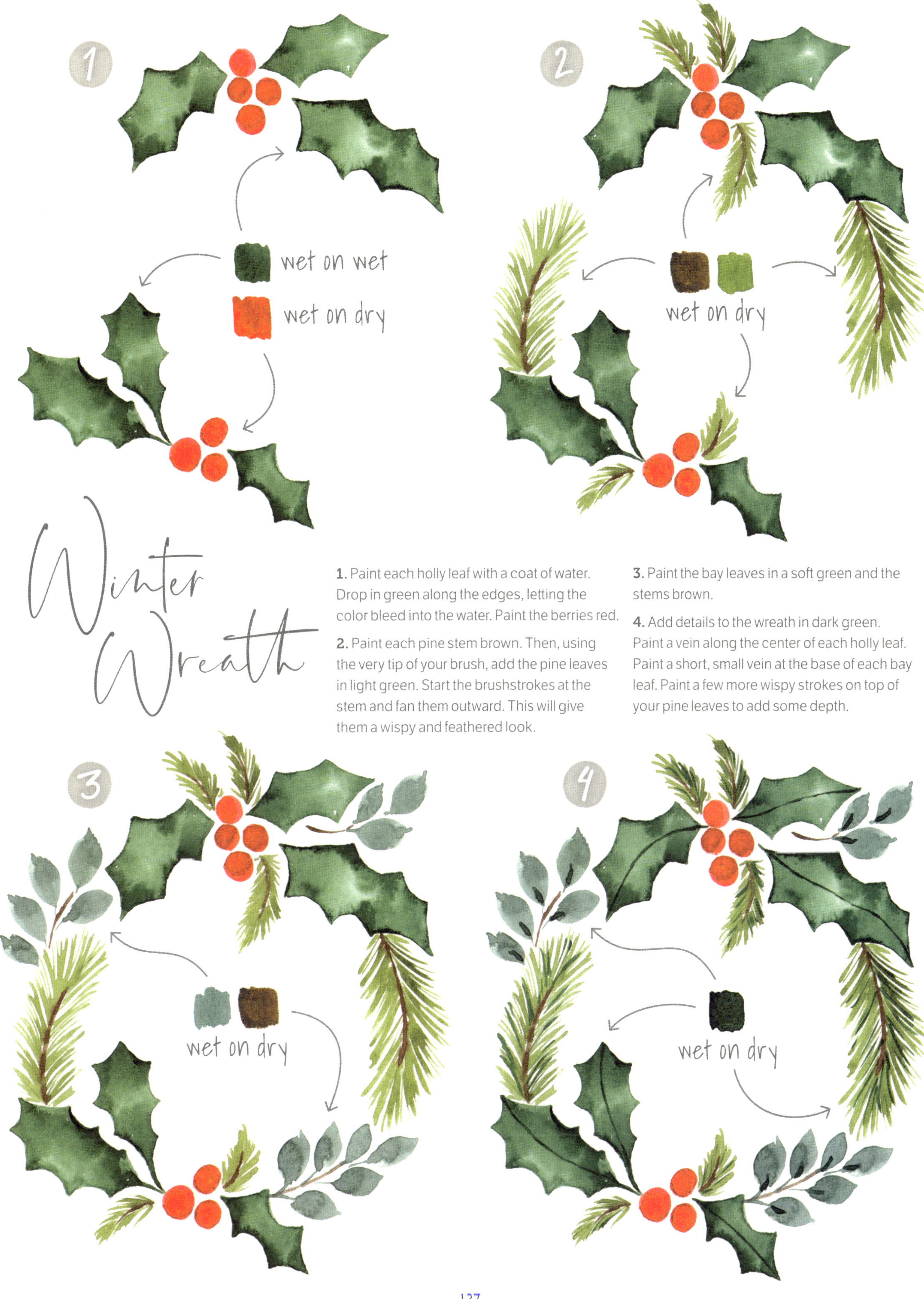

Winter Wreath

1. Paint each holly leaf with a coat of water. Drop in green along the edges, letting the color bleed into the water. Paint the berries red.

2. Paint each pine stem brown. Then, using the very tip of your brush, add the pine leaves in light green. Start the brushstrokes at the stem and fan them outward. This will give them a wispy and feathered look.

3. Paint the bay leaves in a soft green and the stems brown.

4. Add details to the wreath in dark green. Paint a vein along the center of each holly leaf. Paint a short, small vein at the base of each bay leaf. Paint a few more wispy strokes on top of your pine leaves to add some depth.

Business is personal at Better Day Books. We were founded on the belief that all people are creative and that making things by hand is inherently good for us. It's important to us that you know how much we appreciate your support. The book you are holding in your hands was crafted with the artistic passion of the author and brought to life by a team of wildly enthusiastic creatives who believed it could inspire you. If it did, please drop us a line and let us know about it. Connect with us on Instagram, post a photo of your art, and let us know what other creative pursuits you are interested in learning about. It all matters to us. You're kind of a big deal.

it's a good day to have a better day!™

BETTER DAY BOOKS™

HAPPY · CREATIVE · CURATED™

www.betterdaybooks.com

better_day_books